ANOREXIA NERVOSA AND BULIMIA

A Handbook for Counselors and Therapists

ANOREXIA NERVOSA AND BULIMIA

A Handbook for Counselors and Therapists

Patricia A. Neuman, Ed.S.
Moorhead State University

and

Patricia A. Halvorson, Ph.D.
North Dakota State University

 VAN NOSTRAND REINHOLD COMPANY
NEW YORK   CINCINNATI   TORONTO   LONDON   MELBOURNE

Published by Van Nostrand Reinhold Company Inc.
135 West 50th Street
New York, New York 10020

Van Nostrand Reinhold Company Limited
Molly Millars Lane
Wokingham, Berkshire RG11 2PY, England

Van Nostrand Reinhold
480 Latrobe Street
Melbourne, Victoria 3000, Australia

Macmillan of Canada
Division of Gage Publishing Limited
164 Commander Boulevard
Agincourt, Ontario M1S 3C7, Canada

15   14   13   12   11   10   9   8   7   6   5   4   3   2

Library of Congress Cataloging in Publication Data

Neuman, Patricia A.
    Anorexia nervosa and bulimia.

    Includes index.
    1. Anorexia nervosa. 2. Bulimarexia. I. Halvorson,
Patricia A. II. Title. [DNLM: 1. Anorexia nervosa—
Handbooks.   2. Appetite disorders—Handbooks.
3. Anorexia nervosa—Therapy—Handbooks. 4. Appetite
disorders—Therapy—Handbooks. WM 175 N492a
RC552.A5N48   1983   616.85'2   82-20005
ISBN 0-442-26849-1

*We lovingly dedicate
this book to our families
Paul and Rhett
and
Harry, Kaaren, and Siri*

Foreword

Anorexia Nervosa and Bulimia is written especially for counselors and therapists who are facing an ever increasing number of young adults deeply troubled by disturbed eating habits. This book, developed out of the counseling experience of the authors, offers practical suggestions that will serve in the evaluation and treatment of clients who have symptoms of anorexia nervosa and bulimia. General readers concerned about their own eating habits or the eating habits of their friends or family members will also find much useful information here.

While the problems created by eating disorders are becoming more evident, the causes and solutions to these disorders remain elusive. Magazine articles and television programs on anorexia nervosa and bulimia may generate hundreds or even thousands of requests for information by phone or mail. Centers specializing in the treatment of eating disorders are at times overwhelmed by the number of people who make requests for treatment. While many questions remain to be answered regarding the causes and treatment of these disorders, counselors and therapists are being called upon in increasing numbers to offer immediate help.

Patricia Halvorson and Patricia Neuman, in their roles as counselors of college students, have been working for a number of years with young people suffering from anorexia nervosa and bulimia. They have had to deal with a lack of information and treatment programs for these disorders. Therefore they decided to undertake writing this book. They sought the aid of Russell Gardner, M.D., Chairman of the Department of Psychiatry at the University of Northa Dakota Medical School. He responded by helping them contact other professionals in the field who were working with eating-disordered clients. With his assistance they promoted educational programs for therapists in their region where research concerning anorexia nervosa and bulimia was presented and where information was exchanged. They initiated their own support and treatment groups for bulimia and anorexia nervosa.

In this book, the authors have organized their experience into practical suggestions and guidelines. They have also surveyed much of the available medical literature in this field and offer this material as well, which is integrated into the text. This synthesis of personal experience and knowledge of the literature works well. The reader of this work will find much of value relative to the evaluation, diagnosis and treatment of eating disorders.

RICHARD PYLE, M.D.
JAMES MITCHELL, M.D.

Preface

When we first were confronted with anorexia nervosa and bulimia in the late 1970s, the professional literature concerning these disorders was sparse. The counseling profession's publications offered little; the medical, psychiatric, and dietetic literature was slightly more fruitful. However, this literature was not oriented toward non-medical personnel, and treatment outside of a hospital setting was generally not discussed. In the case of bulimia, treatment issues and techniques were largely nonexistent.

In struggling to develop treatment strategies and services for use on the college campus, we encountered hurdles that were not even minimally addressed in the journals or other literature — obstacles such as dealing with family issues when the client was separated from the family; developing a support network for ourselves so that back-up medical and psychiatric services and consultations would be available for our clients; establishing referral resources for those clients who either were moving or required more care than we were able to give; providing support and direction for residence hall personnel to deal with residence hall problems generated by the eating disorders; advising roommates whose food was being stolen or who "didn't know how to act" toward the afflicted roommate; and so forth.

We were, however, unusually fortunate in that we had a tremendous amount of support from our local psychiatric and mental health community. Psychiatric Grand Rounds were held on the topics of bulimia and anorexia nervosa; several psychiatrists made themselves readily available for medical consultation and referral. Dr. Russell Gardner, Chairman of the Department of Psychiatry at the University of Dakota School of Medicine, offered to conduct in-service programs on our campuses. Furthermore, specialists in the area of eating disorders from the University of Minnesota — Gretchen Goff, Director of the Bulimia Treatment Program; Dr. Richard Pyle, Director of the Outpatient Psychiatry Department; Dr. James Mitchell, Psychiatrist; Dr. Elke Eckert, Director of the Inpatient Anorexia Research Unit; Leah Labeck, R.N., Anorexia Research Unit — gave generously of their time and expertise to help us further our knowledge and establish our first support group for eating-disordered clients.

Being part of a university community offered us special advantages: a wide variety of professional journals, computers to carry out searches for relevant articles or books, and ready accessibility to campus medical personnel. Yet gathering the necessary information still proved a time-consuming and sometimes difficult task. Certainly many people in the counseling or other mental health professions do not have the above-mentioned luxuries, particularly in rural areas. How much more difficult this work would be under less favorable circumstances!

We found ourselves bemoaning the absence of a volume which would provide us, in one place, with all the basic information needed and which would not only describe the disorders but answer such questions as, How do we get those who need help to seek it out? What do we do when they *do* walk through our door requesting help? and What can be done of a preventative nature?

Clearly it would be easier to let the "experts" handle these disorders, but the experts are not available. First of all, few exist, and even they do not have all the answers. Secondly, there are usually waiting lists that clients must contend with — while some kind of help certainly ought to be provided in the interim. That leaves a large task for the rest of us. We have a responsibility to be informed, though we need not be experts.

This volume will provide the reader with an overview of both anorexia and bulimia, as well as related education, treatment, and prevention issues. The need for wading through research designs, statistics, and a profusion of medical terms is eliminated. This is a nuts-and-bolts approach for practitioners on the front line: in public schools, clinics, mental health centers, university campuses, and so forth. This is not meant to be a definitive work. It provides for the uninitiated a starting point from which further exploration can be conducted if desired, and it details a wide variety of additional resources.

Throughout the book we will use the feminine pronouns "she" and "her" to indicate the anorexic and bulimic individual. We do this for two reasons: expediency and the fact that most sufferers are female. We do not intend by this to convey to the reader that there are no male anorexics or bulimics, or that we consider them less important.

We wish to express our appreciation to the following individuals whose time and support helped us in writing this book: Russell Gardner, M.D.; Gretchen Goff, M.S.; Arnold Kadrmus, M.D.; Leah Labeck, R.N.; James Mitchell, M.D.; Barbara North, R.D.; Richard Pyle, M.D.; Katie Estee; Fay Steckroat; and our office colleagues. We want especially to thank Janet Pratt, M.S.Ed., and Nancy Bologna, Ph.D., for their written contributions to the book in the areas of secondary school counseling and family therapy. Most of all our thanks go to Meredith Meyer who faithfully helped us use the computer to type the book.

The content of this volume is derived from our own experiences; from the shared experiences of our colleagues, consultants, and clients; and from an integration of the writings of a variety of researchers and practitioners in the field.

Our venture into treating eating disorders developed into a greater odyssey than we had anticipated. It is our hope in sharing the fruits of that odyssey with other front-line professionals that they might be encouraged and fortified with the basic, essential knowledge of eating disorders to embark upon their own journey so that victims of anorexia and bulimia might find a greater availability of help and understanding.

A Personal Note to Our Clients

Although we cannot name all of you in our text, we are so very appreciative of you. It is because of our knowing you that made this book a reality. Your courage, your hard work, your questions, your discoveries, your sharing, your caring, and your trusting are what have made our information and knowledge possible.

So often when you asked a question, we would have to answer, "I don't know yet," but you did not lose faith. You tried out new ideas — some worked, some did not - but always *you* kept working. We have included in this book situations, examples, and case studies, but we have always changed and combined them so that none of you can be identified. This also has made our task more difficult: we would like openly to acknowledge each one of you because you are all the heroines of this book, yet in order to protect your identities, no credit can be openly given.

However, know in your hearts that we give this credit to you the only way we can: anonymously.

PATRICIA A. NEUMAN
PATRICIA A. HALVORSON

Contents

ANOREXIA NERVOSA
AND BULIMIA
A Handbook for Counselors and Therapists

1
Anorexia Nervosa

Time is passing *so slowly* within my crystal cube —
Sometimes I look out,
Blow a soft breath upon the glass walls and rub away the fog
To see what life's about.

And much to my surprise I've found
The world is racing by,
A blur of images and colors and smiles.
Inside my cube's the lie.

For time is not passing slowly
In truth it's racing on,
Won't someone please let me out of this crystal cube?
Hell! who am I attempting to con?

Because all this time I've held the key that locked the door
To inprison me.
Inside my lovely crystal cube
Where time is passing *so slowly.* *

*By Kit, a recovering anorexic

Our nation is infatuated with slimness. Diet centers, slimnastic classes, weight reduction support groups, and figure salons are prospering as never before. Calories, exercise programs, and the latest diet plans are common topics of conversation. Dieting accounts for the fastest growing industry in the United States. It is estimated that over 20 million Americans are seriously dieting at any given moment, spending more than 10 billion dollars a year in the process.

If our nation is infatuated with slimness, the media is obsessed with it. The slinky models who beguilingly smile at us from the covers of magazines, billboards, and television symbolize "the good life" and convey a message that equates happiness and success with a thin body. The insidious effect of this type of influence can be noted in a comment made on television by a well-known singer just before her performance: "When I weigh 125 pounds, my life is in the pits. When I weigh 109 pounds, my life is great."

Certainly not everyone responds in such a dramatic fashion to this "thin is in" message being developed and set forth by the media. While the population in general is at least somewhat influenced into believing that thinness is desirable, for most people this does not present a major problem. However, for two groups of people the desire for thinness becomes so overwhelming and out of control that it is considered pathological. The obsession with thinness becomes a major hindrance to, and takes priority over, everything else — including good health and interpersonal relationships. These people suffer from either anorexia nervosa or bulimia.* In this chapter we will provide an overview of anorexia; bulimia will be discussed in the following chapter.

DEFINITION

The term anorexia nervosa conveys a sense of strangeness and an air of mystery. It has the sound of a throwback to ancient times, an illness prevalent in an era long since past. Yet it is an ailment that today is increasingly on the rise.

The American Anorexia Nervosa Association† defines anorexia as a "serious illness of deliberate self-starvation with profound psychiatric and physical components." It is a complex emotional disorder that launches its victims on a course of frenzied dieting in pursuit of excessive thinness. This thinness is often believed to be the magical solution to life's problems. As one recovered anorexic reported to us, "The thinner I got, the happier I thought I'd be." The myth dies hard indeed.

A definition of anorexia nervosa cannot be complete without taking a glimpse from the inside looking out. Let us look at the following excerpt from one student's diary. At the time these entries were made, she was slightly underweight and had not yet been diagnosed as anorexic. The following day this student approached the counseling center for help, on the recommendation of her roommate who was acquainted with one of the authors.

---

* It must be noted there are also some individuals afflicted with bulimia for whom the desire for thinness is not the primary concern.
†This organization is described in Chapter 9, "Additional Sources of Information and Support."

Day	Time and Place	Type of Food	Thoughts
Mon.	8:00 - 9:00 A.M. In class	1 pack of gum	I need the gum to get me going. I wonder how many cavities I have. This is better than eating breakfast. I watched Jim eat and thought, "Wow! Is he consuming mega-calories." I'm glad I'm not.
	5:05 P.M. Campus store	1 apple	I wonder if anyone saw me buy this. They are probably thinking, "Boy is she fat. That's all she should eat!" I'll have to exercise for a while.
Tues.	10:00 A.M.	2 packs of gum	I feel like a blimp today. I hope I won't eat a lot. I wish I wouldn't eat so much gum. I can't help myself. It seems like I don't have any willpower.
	3:30 P.M. Dorm room	1 apple, a few pieces of cauliflower, 1/2 piece of bread, 1/2 piece of cheese, 1 pack of gum	Drat, I blew it! Nothing more for me to eat. I'm mad at myself. I feel like I ate too much. I want to cry. I had a TV dinner in the oven but I took it out — too many calories.
	Evening		I did it again — I took 1/2 box of laxatives. Why did I do that? I know it won't help because I need a whole box for it to do any good.
Wed.	6 packs of gum, throughout the day and evening		I'm going to go out tonight so I'm not going to eat anything or my stomach will stick out.
Thurs.	1:00 P.M. Dorm room	3 packs of gum 1 cup of popcorn 1 cup of spinach 1 tomato	I don't know why I ate that. Stop eating, you pig!
Fri.	8:00 – 10:00 A.M. In class	2 packs of gum	
	6:30 P.M. Dorm room	½ pear ½ cup of spinach 1 slice of cheese 1 soda cracker	I'm not doing very well today but I have lost 4 pounds so I feel a little better. I can't wait to go to bed so I can sleep all night and eat more tomorrow — especially gum.

Sat.	Throughout the day	8 packs of gum	
	11:00 P.M. Came home from a party	3 pieces of pizza 1 cup of spinach 1 piece of bread 5 soda crackers 1 bag of pretzels 1 cup of popcorn 2 pieces of cheese	I'm so hungry — I am going to eat and eat and eat. I'm really mad. I'm not hungry, but I can't stop eating. I asked my roommate to tell me to quit. She did and I quit. My stomach is gonna burst. I hope I can go to the bathroom.
Sun.	Throughout the day Dorm room	4 packs of gum	I'm not going to eat very much today. I have to make up for last night! Boy am I hungry.
	6:30 P.M. Dorm room	1 pear	This is the best pear I've ever had.
	9:00 P.M. Dorm room		I feel really scared. I thought about food all day today. I wish there was no such thing as food. I hate myself sometimes.

HISTORY

While it is generally acknowledged that anorexia nervosa now afflicts a greater number of individuals than ever, the disorder has not been confined to recent times. There is evidence of the existence of an identical condition dating back to ancient times, long before the official diagnosis was formulated. Later, in the Middle Ages, goodness came to be equated with thinness. Fasting became associated with virtue and purity. The prevailing view was that angels were so good, so pure, that they must be awfully thin. People sat around and discussed how thin these angels really were, and debated over how many angels could dance on the head of a pin. Out of this milieu came the so-called miracle maidens.

Peter Dally and Joan Gomez, in tracing the history of anorexia in their book *Obesity and Anorexia Nervosa: A Question of Shape,* report

In the middle ages and later, there were miracle maidens who purported to live on air, were fed by the fairies when nobody was there, or toyed occasionally with such delicacies as the juice of a roasted raisin. People traveled for miles to see these living wonders.

Most were frauds....but a few may well have had anorexia nervosa, a disorder which at that time was not recognized.

Another probable case of the disorder occurred in 1599 when a young girl in France developed a minor illness. For three or more years after recovering from the illness, she could not be persuaded to eat. Yet in spite of the self-imposed starvation, she remained highly active, though emaciated and cold. Naturally, this created quite a stir, and she became known as the famous "French Fasting Girl of Confolens."

Another century was to pass before the first clear medical definition of the disorder was given by Richard Morton. This report marked the beginning of what Alexander Lucas of the Mayo Clinic calls the "descriptive era" in the study of anorexia nervosa. Lucas (1981), in his paper "Toward the Understanding of Anorexia Nervosa as a Disease Entity," has compiled probably the most complete history of anorexia nervosa available. In this paper he delineates five historical eras which are summarized below: the descriptive, pituitary, rediscovery, psychoanalytic, and modern eras.

Descriptive Era (1689)

In 1689 in England, a society which found a rounded Rubenesque profile far more fashionable than thinness, Dr. Richard Morton described a condition he called "nervous consumption": deliberate self-starvation due to "an ill and morbid state of the spirits." Lucas (1981) recounts for us the case of a 17-year-old girl who, as described by Morton,

> fell into a total suppression of her Monthly Courses from a multitude of Cares and Passions of her Mind....From which time her Appetite began to abate, and her Digestion to be bad; her flesh also began to be flaccid and loose, and her looks pale....She was wont by her studying at Night, and continual pouring upon Books, to expose herself both Day and Night to the injuries of the Air....I do not remember that I did ever in all my Practice see one that was conversant with the Living so much wasted with the greatest degree of a Consumption, (like a Skeleton only clad with skin) yet there was no Fever, but on the contrary a coldness of the whole Body....(p. 255)

This girl refused treatment and died.

Another case related by Dally and Gomez (1980) was that of a 16-year-old boy, the son of a minister, whose illness dragged on for two years and was thought to result from "studying too hard and the passion of his mind. He recovered his health after he was sent from his home to the country, allowed no books, and fed on a diet of asses' milk" (p.66).

In 1767, nearly a hundred years later, another boy, who was seen by Robert Whytt, was emaciated, depressed, and refused to eat. Approximately a year later he relinquished his self-induced fast and became overweight from compulsive eating.

This condition was thoroughly described and named in the 1870s by a pair of English and French physicians, Sir William Gull and Professor Lesegue, who, as it happened, worked independently. Gull used the term "anorexia hysterica," while Lesegue used "anorexie hysterique." It was Gull who eventually created the term "anorexia nervosa." Both of these physicians experienced some success in treating the disorder through rest, nourishment, separation from the family, and supportive therapy. By the end of the nineteenth century, anorexia nervosa was a rare but recognized disorder afflicting the middle and upper classes.

Lucas (1981) tells us that in the 1913 American translation of *The Psychoneuroses and Their Treatment by Psychotherapy* by Dejerine and Gauckler, the condition was presented as an easily diagnosed, specific disease which takes either a primary (true) or secondary form. He goes on to quote the authors:

> The diagnosis of mental anorexia is extremely simple. It merely requires thought....the history guides you, and every time that you find that the patient has gone upon a restricted diet, either voluntarily or from some emotional cause, and this has been followed by a loss of the psychic idea of appetite, you can safely assume the existence of mental anorexia, either pure and simple or associated with something. (p. 255)

Pituitary Era (1914)

At this time, the medical community widely held that all diseases originated from some pathology of the organs and cells. However, many cases of emaciation occurred which were unexplainable from this viewpoint until Simmond's description of pituitary cachexia (1914). Simmond discovered lesions on the pituitary gland of a severely emaciated woman who had shown signs of pituitary failure and died. This further supported the cellular pathology view of disease, and patients suffering from otherwise unexplained weight loss also came to be diagnosed as having Simmond's disease. Such patients were routinely treated with pituitary gland extracts, even when there were no signs of actual pituitary failure.

Rediscovery Era (1930)

While references occasionally continued to be made to anorexia, these were rare and most medical cases were attributed to Simmond's disease. Lucas tells us that it was not until 1930 that anorexia nervosa was essentially rediscovered by Berkman, who published the first large-scale report (117 patients) and outlined principles for treatment.

Other reports surfaced sporadically, questioning the diagnosis of Simmond's disease for all patients with severe emaciation and pointing out the differences between anorexia and pituitary insufficiency. Finally, in 1942, Escamilla and Lisser, through a world review of the medical literature on Simmond's disease, determined that most of the 595 reported cases were, in all probability, cases of anorexia nervosa rather than pituitary disease.

In the 1950s and 1960s, there was a trend toward overgeneralization in regard to anorexia, with no differentiation made between primary and secondary groups; the diagnostic criteria utilized were excessively broad. Lucas cites Bliss and Branch's study (1960) in which the sole criterion used for the diagnosis of anorexia was a 25-pound weight loss due to psychological causes.

Psychoanalytical Era (1940)

The psychoanalytical era began in 1940 and overlaps the previous era. The era commenced with a paper by Waller, Kaufman, and Deutch, in which they proposed that anorexia symptoms were the result of fantasies and fears of oral impregnation.

Another movement that developed under psychoanalytic influence was the psychosomatic movement. It was demonstrated through classical experiments by Walter Counnon that emotional states produce physiological changes. The mind and body were seen as impacting one another in the development of disease, including anorexia nervosa.

Modern Era

Hilde Bruch, one of the foremost authorities in the United States in the area of eating disorders, delivered a paper in 1961 entitled "Perceptual and Conceptual Disturbances in Anorexia Nervosa." Lucas asserts that this paper was the herald of the modern era, in which Bruch "set the stage for a new level of understanding" (p. 257).

Bruch differentiated between "primary anorexia nervosa" (the classic form as described by Morton and Gull) and "atypical anorexia nervosa" (self-starvation due to other psychiatric illnesses). The classic or true form, according to Bruch (cited in Lucas, 1981), is characterized by the following psychological disturbances:

1. A disturbance in body image of delusional proportions,
2. A disturbance in the accuracy of perception or cognitive interpretation of stimuli arising withhin the body with failure to recognize signs of nutritional need, and
3. A paralyzing sense of ineffectiveness pervading all thinking and activities. (p. 257)

So we can see that anorexia is not merely a current phenomenon. It has been with us for hundreds of years, persisting even in those milieus that did not deem slimness attractive. Thus it is not likely to pass quietly away as society gives up its emphasis on slimness. Then just what is the basis of this disorder? How prevalent is it and why does it seem to be an increasingly common occurrence? Who is vulnerable to developing this problem and how can we prevent it from occurring? These are questions we will address throughout this chapter.

DIAGNOSIS

Before the above issues are addressed, we must first answer the question, When is a person anorexic? How do we differentiate the zealous dieter who is not anorexic from the one who is?

Diagnostic Criteria

Descriptions of the diagnostic categories for all mental disorders can be found in the third edition of the *Diagnostic and Statistical Manual of Mental Disorders* (DSM-III) published by the American Psychiatric Association in 1980. The five diagnostic criteria for anorexia nervosa, according to the DSM-III (p. 69), are as follows:

1. Intense fear of becoming obese, which does not diminish as weight loss progresses. The intense fear of obesity that anorexics experience takes on the qualities of an obsession. Anorexics seem to have a greater fear of getting fat than of dying from the effects of their self-imposed starvation. The intensity of this fear can be glimpsed through the following situation. A young woman in her middle twenties had been plagued with anorexia for a number of years and consequently was hospitalized as a patient in a special treatment program. While in this program she became acquainted with several other severe anorexics who, in fact, did die from the consequences of not eating. She herself had at one time passed out and was in such a severe state of dehydration that she nearly expired. Certainly this woman was aware of the dangers involved in continuing to restrict her intake of food. Yet, despite this intellectual awareness, she continued her refusal to eat an adequate amount of food. She was also able to verbalize the illogic of the situation and stated that although she knew death was a distinct possibility, she did not believe it would happen to her and she had no fear of it. She was terrified, however, of gaining weight.

Another unusual twist occurs in relation to this fear of growing fat. The average person concerned about weight gain will feel a sense of relief as she loses weight. However, the anorexic is unlike other people in this respect: for her, the fear does not diminish. As one recovered anorexic student related, "The thinner I got, the fatter I thought I was." As her weight drops, the anorexic's fear becomes more entrenched. She becomes increasingly stubborn and rigid in her approach to food.

2. Disturbance of body image, e.g., claiming to "feel fat," even when emaciated. The disturbance of body image in anorexia is an unclear phenomenon. Most anorexics have distorted perceptions of themselves. Some insist that their emaciated bodies are grotesquely overfleshed. Others perceive their spindly legs and shrunken stomachs as attractive and "just right." Still others recognize their emaciated bodies for what they are. The presence of body image distortion is just one of the many aspects of anorexia nervosa that we do not understand fully. According to some researchers, however, the more distortion present, the worse is the prognosis (Slade, 1973).

3. Weight loss of at least 25 percent of original body weight or, if under 18 years of age, weight loss from original body weight plus projected weight gain expected from growth charts may be combined to make the 25 percent. The primary symptom of anorexia nervosa is severe weight loss. While this is one of the major criteria for making the diagnosis, we believe the 25 percent reduction to be misleading. The situation would be markedly different for an individual who is overweight than for an individual who is already thin prior to the weight loss. Moreover, most victims of anorexia have not been particularly overweight; therefore, a 25 percent reduction in weight is an excessive requirement for them. Are we to wait until the disorder is life threatening before we diagnose and treat it for what it is? Of course not. If the other criteria are present and an individual seems to be bent on a course of continuing weight loss, the situation should be considered serious.

It is often incorrectly assumed that anorexics were previously obese. While the disorder is often preceded by "normal" dieting, only one-third of anorexics have been overweight and most of these only mildly so. Two-thirds have never been overweight, although they may have been the targets of comments regarding their physical development. For example, the brother of one of our clients had dubbed her with the nickname "thunder thighs." Even though she was very slim, her tight-fitting jeans from the preceding year no longer fit her budding body without bulging at the seams. What she needed was not to lose weight, but to buy new clothes! While the anorexic may not personally have a history of weight problems, it is quite likely that another family member is either over- or under-weight.

4. Refusal to maintain body weight over a minimal normal weight for age and height. The loss of weight may be obtained by eating less, decreasing fat and carbohydrate intake, self-induced vomiting, exercise, use of laxatives and/or diuretics, or any combination of the above. Even under close observation, anorexics are typically ingenious at devising ways to carry out these methods. They will conceal their eating habits by lying about what, when, and where they eat. Usually they don't like to eat in front of others, and tend to withdraw to avoid food or confrontations about their eating habits and their appearance. After eating, especially if they are forced to eat, many anorexics will get rid of the calroies ingested by forcing themselves to regurgitate or by using laxatives. Bathrooms tend to be very popular after meals!

Despite being undernourished, victims of this disorder typically manifest an extraordinarily high energy level. Their obsession with burning up calories leads to incessant exercising. We continually hear from these women reports of rising at 4:00 A.M., for example, in order to get in the requisite number of sit-ups or miles of jogging before school begins, and then of exercising late into the night as well. One anorexic, whose roommate objected to late night activities, devised a series of exercises she could complete after going to bed. This hyperactivity can persist even after the disorder has become severe and muscle weakness and fatigue have set in.

Anorexia sometimes occurs after an individual has lost weight due to illness. Pleased by this loss of weight, the individual deliberately continues weight reduction. The previous illness, however, does not account for the anorexia.

Peculiar behavior related to food is exhibited by the anorexic. This may range from the mildly unusual to the bizarre. Generally there is a tremendous preoccupation with food, recipes, and even cooking. One of the authors had a neighbor whose high school age daughter was anorexic. This young woman prepared elaborate meals for the family. Emphasis was placed on "natural foods," and wood utensils were preferred as they were also more "natural." The table setting was inevitably impeccable, and dishes used for preparation of the food were washed before the meal was served. Freshly baked sweets would accompany the meal. However, very little was consumed by the cook herself — certainly not the dessert. Other authors report anorexics' hoarding and concealing of food, including food that is rotten or moldy, while fresh food is refused. Strange eating habits often occur; for example, food may be cut into tiny pieces then pushed around — arranged and rearranged on the plate.

5. *No known physical illness that would account for the weight loss.* There are illnesses other than anorexia in which a refusal to eat occurs. Depression often results in a lack of appetite and consequent weight loss. Individuals who fear being poisoned may refuse food. Bizarre eating patterns can occur with schizophrenia. The distinguishing feature of anorexia nervosa is the motivation behind the refusal of food: the intense fear of weight gain (and the accompanying desire for weight loss). This particular fear is not generally present in these other disorders; if it is, anorexia must also be investigated as an additional diagnosis.

Another established feature, and in fact a hallmark, of anorexia is amenorrhea (absence or suppression of menstruation) in females. Why this occurs is still a puzzle. Interestingly, in a high percentage of cases, this is the first sign of the disorder, appearing before any noticeable loss of weight (Bemis, 1978). Ultimately, at one point or another, it occurs in nearly all cases.

In addition to these criteria that have been specified for diagnosis, other features which accompany the disorder merit our attention. We present these psychological and physical aspects in order to give the reader a more in-depth portrayal of the typical victim of anorexia nervosa. Keep in mind that not all of the following characteristics pertain to every anorexic. Some individuals encountered will not appear to fit into the following picture very well; others will be classic and exhibit all of the characteristics delineated. Naturally, the client's own individual experience is of great importance.

Psychological Aspects of Anorexia Nervosa

Anorexia is often preceded by a stressful life situation. This may range from family conflict or major changes such as a change in schools, a family move, the loss of a boyfriend or girlfriend, or an illness, to less obvious difficulties such as a casual remark made by an athletic coach or dance instructor about "dropping a couple of pounds," or teasing by classmates or siblings. Change, in general, seems to be particularly stressful for anorexic individuals; even positive changes in their lives can seem to exacerbate their condition. An example of this can be observed in the case of a high school girl whose classmates had bestowed upon her the honor of becoming homecoming queen. This would seem to be a positive, affirming experience, but for her it became a cross. In her mind she now carried an obligation to her classmates — to be always friendly, smiling, and helpful; never to show irritation or sadness. Living up to her exaggerated homecoming queen image became overwhelming.

The childhood history of those who develop anorexia typically reveals a "model child." In fact, this is one of the most consistent personality findings associated with anorexia. Many anorexics describe themselves as "people pleasers." As children, they are often described by parents and teachers as introverted, conscientious, and well behaved. They tend to be perfectionist and compulsive, and thus, overachievers. A comment frequently made by parents is, "She's never given us any trouble before." It is imperative to note that while this personality trait is one of the most consistent findings, it is not always present, which demonstrates the importance of looking at each client as a unique human being.

Other psychological changes that often manifest themselves as the illness progresses are irritability, indecisiveness, stubbornness, a sense of helplessness, unsociability, and as mentioned previously, a dislike of change. There is a tendency for anorexics to be nonassertive in dealing with other people and to react in either a passive or a defiant manner. Depressive, obsessional, hysterical, and phobic features are also common with anorexia.

Some of these features are illustrated in the following case. One young, anorexic, college woman, being very depressed, had trouble sleeping and concentrating on her schoolwork. She was majoring in engineering and repeatedly expressed an intense dislike for the subject. Despite high grades and a recommendation from the department for a job as a tutor, she was absolutely certain that she would flunk her classes. She felt totally helpless and unable to deal with the situation, yet she felt compelled to keep the engineering major since someone had told her it was a good field to go into. All efforts encouraging her to explore other areas were strongly resisted, as was any change in her life. Each quarter she signed up for more engineering. At every counseling session she sobbed hysterically over various decisions that had to be made, certain that any of the alternatives would result in failure. Although she expressed a great deal of hostility about everyone and everything, she was terrified of getting anyone angry with her and she never appropriately asserted herself. This example may give the reader some sense of the entrapment experienced by the victim of anorexia.

The anorexic's perception of events can be extremely distorted, accompanied by reactions that approach panic. Some of the university students we see complain of doing horribly on exams, or being sure they've flunked, and work themselves into an incredible dither. Yet when grades arrive, their scores are among the highest in the class. Bright, articulate sufferers have described themselves as "dumb," "stupid," "idiot," and "no good bum." The words "I can't" tumble from their lips repeatedly. Then again, it is possible that some victims of the disorder may not display this at all. We need to keep in mind, however, that outward appearances do not necessarily portray the inner feelings. Anorexic individuals tend to be highly competent "people pleasers," and are used to smiling and appearing happy even when miserable.

One client had to give a practice teaching demonstration in an education class. Afterwards, she reported that the experience was a disaster. She had performed poorly, the class had not participated as they should have, and the instructor had been critical of her work. When asked the following week what grade she received for the presentation, she very sheepishly replied, "An A." Even when high grades are received, as in this instance, they are often discounted. The instructor may then be blamed for being "too easy" or for giving the grade away out of pity, etc. One student, living in a residence hall, perceived all the women living on her floor as rejecting her. This was in spite of the fact that everyone, in a remarkably concerted effort, went out of their way to include her in activities, to greet her, and to be truly concerned for her welfare. These are just two examples of how events can be distorted by anorexics.

Compulsive behavior is often present in conjunction with anorexia nervosa. Excessive orderliness, cleaning, studying, and exercise are common. Anything less than perfection is upsetting to the anorexic, and everything undertaken seems to be done in excess, including the dieting behavior.

Victims of anorexia often resist treatment and rarely seek help on their own initiative. Most diagnoses are made after the condition becomes so advanced that it forces them into a doctor's office or the hospital. They deny that anything is wrong with them and may see doctors or therapists as antagonists, "the enemy" who is only interested in forcing them to eat and gain weight (get fat). This denial of a problem may persist even in the face of abnormal medical findings which indicate physical instability.

Another feature accompanying anorexia is delayed psychosexual development. Boyfriends, for instance, may be desired but usually only in a fairy-tale sense — to live "happily ever after." There is little, if any, sexual interest expressed. This is a topic that can be difficult for anorexics to discuss, not out of embarrassment so much as because it is so foreign: they are totally out of touch with the sexual part of their being. To return to the example of the anorexic neighbor who loved to cook, she also was a talented seamstress and made her own clothes, for example, pinafores, which she wore with knee-highs and little white button-up blouses. Her clean, tidy, little girl look avoided any sexual connotation or allure.

A contagion factor has been evident in certain situations. English boarding schools have occasionally had to deal with an "outbreak" of anorexia nervosa. One student would develop the disorder, and it would then seem to take on a strange, infectious quality, afflicting others as well. When the primary victim was removed, however, the other cases were easily resolved. In a college setting, residence halls provide a similar opportunity for this contagion factor to manifest itself. We have had instances of roommates and friends of anorexics (and bulimics) developing the disorder. However, this is not typical, and in our experience when it does occur, it seems to be farily short-lived.

Physical Characteristics of Anorexia Nervosa

As might be expected, a host of physical complications accompany acute anorexia nervosa in addition to emaciation. Cessation of menstruation (amenorrhea) is one of the more perplexing physical phenomena. As stated before, amenorrhea occurs before the actual weight loss in a substantial number of cases and may be the first sign of anorexia. Yet loss of body fat also has an effect on menstruation. Body fat typically comprises 26 to 28 percent of a woman's weight. If that percentage drops significantly, as it sometimes does with women athletes, menstruation tends to stop. Thus amenorrhea can be, but is not necessarily, the result of starvation. (Emotional experiences such as shock, excitement, hysteria, and fright can interfere with the menstrual cycle. However, in these cases the interference is usually short-lived, even under continuing stressful conditions.) This is a complex area that is still being researched.

Constipation and abdominal distress are frequent. A variety of gastric complaints are heard from clients, especially complaints of being bloated or having ulcer-like symptoms. Long-term laxative abuse can produce permanent damage to the colon with malabsorption and loss of the ability to evacuate naturally.

The skin abnormalities that arise in anorexia are dryness; lanugo hair, which is a fine down that appears on the body; and yellowish skin, which usually indicates that a high level of carotene is present in the blood. Hair loss is another complication which may or may not appear. If it does, the loss is not permanent, and upon recovery the individual's hair will grow back.

The most potentially serious physical complications that occur regularly with anorexia nervosa are fluid and electrolyte abnormalities. These abnormalities can result in death. The most dangerous are dehydration and a deficiency in potassium. Potassium deficiency produces muscle weakness, abdominal distension, nervous irritability, apathy, drowsiness, mental confusion, and irregular heartbeat.* Death from kidney or heart failure may occur. Such factors are especially likely to be present in anorexics who vomit or use laxatives. It is not uncommon, too, to find these electrolyte imbalances in individuals who outwardly appear relatively well. For this reason, and because of the potential gravity of an undetected disturbance, it becomes prudent to have suspected or possible imbalances specifically checked out medically.

Other abnormalities which occur regularly in anorexia include lowered body temperature (hypothermia); hyperactivity or lethargy; a slowed heart rate (bradycardia); low blood pressure (hypotension); low blood sugar; low white blood count, coinciding with an amazing resistance to infections (the afflicted individual may be the only family member to miss catching the flu); elevated cholesterol, which appears baffling since the intake of fat is reduced but which is actually due to the mobilization of body fat to be burned (the fat must get into the bloodstream in order for it to be used as energy); endocrine abnormalities, which can inhibit growth — although this too may be compensated for upon recovery, with growth simply occurring later than usual; swelling in the legs (peripheral edema) which although not common, may take place; swollen parotid (mumps) glands and submandibular or submaxillary glands, which give the appearance of chipmunk cheeks and are probably related to bingeing and/or vomiting.

Acetone in the urine can indicate lack of nutrition — the body is not receiving enough fuel to function and must metabolize its fat reserves. Also occurring are low plasma zinc; elevated blood urea nitrogen and creatinine, which indicate a state of dehydration; elevated liver enzymes, which are released when liver tissue is damaged; elevated amylase; repression of female sexual hormone secretory patterns to a pubertal or prepubertal level; and abolition or reversal of the normal daily rhythm of serum cortisol (an endocrine abnormality also commonly seen in people with depression or chronic stress). Feelings of sexuality also subside with starvation.

---

*Supplements of potassium should be taken only under medical supervision.

Many other abnormalities exist in laboratory findings, but to date, the significance of these abnormalities is not known. With weight gain, most of them disappear. The fact that some abnormalities remain, however, raises the question of causality. Research is continuing in this area.

Comparison of Anorexic Bingers and Nonbingers

As mentioned previously, some anorexics continuously curtail their food intake and never engage in binge-eating, while other anorexics alternate between binges and fasts (or severely restrictive diets). Some rather striking differences separate those anorexics who binge from those who do not. Let's take a look at some of the similarities and differences between these two groups as shown in Table 1-1, page 18.

Generally, anorexia nervosa that is not accompanied by bingeing tends to afflict younger age groups than anorexia accompanied by the binge symptom. A pre- or young adolescent is more likely to develop anorexia nervosa without the bingeing. While we have found a number of students on our campuses who first began the bingeing behavior during high school, to our knowledge the bingeing symptom rarely afflicts those younger.

Nonbingeing anorexics display fanatic self-discipline, while bingers display less self-control and more impulsivity. This impulsivity is reflected not only in binge-eating, but in alcohol and drug abuse, compulsive stealing, and more suicide and self-mutilation attempts. In addition, a greater incidence of vomiting and laxative abuse occurs among bingers, and is generally thought to be a reaction to their episodes of overeating. However, some evidence exists that the vomiting may lead to the binges; that is, knowing that one will vomit to get rid of the food allows one to go ahead and binge. If this option or a similar one is not available, the binge is far less likely to occur.

Bingers show greater psychic distress. A study by Casper et al. (1980) reports that anorexic patients with the symptom of bingeing tend to be more depressed, anxious, guilt ridden, and preoccupied with food than nonbingers. Bingers have more bodily complaints of aches and pains, and experience more trouble sleeping. Also, a number of their scores on the MMPI* are elevated.

---

*Minnesota Multiphasic Personality Inventory.

TABLE 1-1. Comparison of Anorexic Bingers and Nonbingers.*

Nonbingers	Bingers
1. Younger age of onset	1. Older age of onset
2. Fanatic self-discipline	2. Less self-control and more impulsivity
	• More stealing
	• More alcohol and drug abuse
	• More suicide attempts and self-mutilation
	• More vomiting
	• More laxative abuse
	• Higher Pd scale on MMPI
	• Binge-eating
3. Depressed but little overt psychic distress	3. Greater psychic distress, guilt
	• More depressed, anxious, labile in mood (especially after bingeing)
4. Withdrawn	4. More outgoing
5. Sexually naive	5. Often sexually active
6. Tirelessness (until illness is advanced)	6. May complain of fatigue
7. Feel cold; low blood pressure and slow pulse rate	7. May feel hot, sweaty after binge
8. Periods of deep sleep; dream sleep reduced	8. More sleep disturbance
9. Denial of hunger	9. Stronger appetite complaints (though not necessarily hunger per se)
10. Deliberate eating	10. Rapid eating
11. Less maternal obesity	11. More maternal obesity
12. Lower original normal body weight	12. Higher premorbid weight and more premorbid obesity
13. Denial of problematic eating	13. Awareness that eating pattern is abnormal
14. Steady weight loss	14. Frequent weight fluctuations
15. Less concern with sexual attractiveness	15. Great concern with appearance and sexual attractiveness
16. Course of the illness may be a single, but lengthy, episode	16. Course of the illness is usually chronic and intermittent over a number of years
17. Fewer somatic complaints	17. More somatic complaints (headaches, stomach problems, dizziness)
18. Better relationship with father	18. Poor relationship with father more common
19. Frequently oppose treatment	19. Favor treatment more often
	• May be due to greater emotional strain and feeling out of control
20. Eat low calorie, low fat foods only	20. Eat high calorie foods during binges

*This is a compilation of research to date. This information must be viewed as preliminary and should be updated periodically.

Nonbingers tend to be more withdrawn and introverted than their bingeing counterparts who are more outgoing and sensitive to others. Likewise, nonbingers are typically sexually naive and out of touch with their sexuality, while bingers are often sexually active and concerned with physical attractiveness and attention from the opposite sex.

Anorexics are noted for their remarkable tirelessness (at least until the illness has progressed to an extremely advanced state). Those with the additional bingeing symptom, though, are more likely to complain of fatigue.

Bingers report stronger appetites than nonbingers who are able to ignore and even deny hunger (Casper et al., 1980). They eat rapidly, particularly during binges, when a large amount of food is consumed in a very short period of time; nonbingers more often engage in eating rituals which are very deliberate, such as arranging and rearranging food on a plate, eating without allowing food to touch the lips, chewing food a requisite number of times, and so forth.

Casper also found that a higher rate of maternal obesity exists for bingers, who are also more likely to have been overweight themselves prior to the onset of the illness.

For the anorexic who does not engage in binge-eating, weight loss usually takes place in a steady, progressive, unremitting manner. The individual's illness may consist of a single, albeit lengthy, episode. When accompanied by bingeing, the disease tends to take a more chronic, intermittent course, persisting over a number of years.

While the nonbinger tends to deny the existence of a problem in connection with eating behavior and frequently resists treatment, the binger is more likely to favor treatment. This may be due to feeling out of control and to the greater emotional strain.

Nonbingers generally eat low calorie, low fat food, while bingers consume high calorie food during their binges. Poor father-child relationships are reported to occur more often in the lives of anorexic bingers than nonbingers. Anorexia accompanied by the bingeing symptom is less likely to result in complete recovery (Andersen, 1981; Hsu, 1980).

The information available to date is preliminary, and this comparison has been stated in generalities. For instance, in the Casper et al. (1980) study, 86 percent of the anorexic bingers are described as outgoing as children in contrast to only 57 percent of the nonbingeing anorexics. Even though this difference is reported to be at the .01 level of significance, we must remember that more than half of the nonbingers are also described as outgoing. This demonstrates the importance of keeping in mind that stated characteristics are generalities only and that each individual is unique.

A variety of subgroups exist within the classification of anorexia nervosa. In addition to bingers and nonbingers, another subgroup has been identified. This subgroup consists of individuals who resort to vomiting, regardless of whether they always restrict their food intake or binge. Characteristics have recently been isolated for these vomiters in several studies. In the Casper study, vomiters were reported as more hostile, worried about becoming compulsive eaters, fearful of becoming fat, selective in their food preferences, aspiring toward a thin body, and likely to overestimate sizes. Vomiters were more likely to exhibit strange food-related habits, to gain less weight by the end of the assessment period, and to come from a higher socioeconomic background with more highly educated fathers. Other subgroups may exist which have not yet been identified.

CAUSES

As yet, no one really knows the specific etiology of anorexia. It probably develops in response to a combination of factors. We do know that the onset of the disorder tends to be associated with stressful life situations accompanied by a lack of adequate coping skills, adolescence, cultural factors, possible biological predisposition, family dynamics, and other medical/physiological considerations. Additionally, it has been proposed that a lack of meaningful peer relationships may also be an exacerbating factor. It is difficult though to distinguish causation from association. While several theories exist regarding causation, these theories are not definitive; rather, they constitute well-educated guesses based upon clinical observation. In other words, though we have learned much about anorexia nervosa over the years, much remains to be resolved — including causal factors. Keeping this in mind, let us now look at each of the items proposed as potential causes of the disorder.

Stressful Life Situations

Therapists have repeatedly observed that the development of anorexia nervosa often begins with a stressful life situation for which the individual does not possess adequate coping skills. This life situation may take the form of a rejection or perceived rejection, a loss of some kind, a sexual encounter, or some other adverse event. Note that the peak ages of onset also happen to coincide with the transitions from junior high to high school and from high school to college.

Change in general, as mentioned earlier, is especially stressful for anorexics. Even small changes can send an anorexic into a tailspin. This rigid attitude is exacerbated by the drive for perfection, and the worry over performing well and being accepted and respected in the changed situation.

Anorexics reason, however, that the one thing they *can* do which is under their total control is lose weight. This they can do perfectly — better than anyone else — and in so doing, they earn some self-respect and a "specialness" as far as other people are concerned. Academic striving may take on a desperate air for the same reason, but it is never convincing *enough,* just as the initial goal for weight loss is never good enough. "Just a little bit more and then everything will be perfect" — so goes the magical thinking of the anorexic. For her, unable to solve life's more complex problems, the grading system and the numbers on a scale provide concrete measures of success. One former victim of the disorder revealed the following during an interview with a reporter for the university newspaper: "I grew up wishing my life could be different, always trying to control and manipulate it to the way I felt it should be. I harbored this overwhelming responsibility to solve the problems around me. I couldn't of course. But I could control my weight. It was like gaining control over something no one else could" (Tornell, 1980, p. 5). The anorexic's difficulty with change may also be a reflection of the family's style of handling change. If the family is not able to deal with change in a flexible way, certainly the child will have difficulty in doing so.

Adolescence

Anorexia is, in the vast majority of cases, a disorder of adolescence — a period of particular vulnerability to all kinds of problems. Thus the disorder is often viewed as a reaction to the stresses of puberty. For females, the hallmark of puberty is physical development which results in an obvious change of shape and, of course, menstruation. Some professionals have theorized that anorexia nervosa is a rejection of female sexuality and an attempt to retain "little girl" status by warding off the adolescent's physical development.

This theory has been challenged by those who contend that it is the entire *role* of a woman which is being rejected. Possibly, becoming an adult woman may be perceived by some younger females as unattractive. Women often lack positive role models, and the role models which are available to them frequently have little self-esteem or status. For a female, becoming an adult may be viewed as a loss of status (Goff, personal communication).

Clearly there are developmental tasks other than sexuality which the anorexic avoids by choosing to remain a "child." First, intimacy issues are problematical for the anorexic, who is terrified of making mistakes or being rejected. In our experience, even those anorexics who are sexually active are not typically "intimate" with their partners. A lack of honesty and assertiveness characterizes the relationships; very little risk taking is allowed their inner person. Perhaps the sexual activity is, in fact, the result of an inability to assert themselves in the sexual area.

Secondly, assuming an adult role with its accompanying responsibilities may seem nearly impossible to an anorexic, especially if she is a young person at an age in which feelings of inadequacy and low self-esteem are standard. There is no clear-cut route to follow into adulthood. The individual who becomes anorexic is usually extraordinarily accomplished at being a "good little girl." Her rules for good behavior are quite clear, and she has mastered them remarkably. This is familiar territory — her territory — but the rules governing success in the world as an adult woman are enigmatic. Societal expectations and women's roles have changed dramatically in recent years. The "good little girl" does not automatically become the "good little womn" anymore, especially when academically talented (which these girls usually are). Having been such a good little girl, in fact, in some ways inhibits one's ability to become a successful adult. Being overly compliant and unassertive lends difficulty to making autonomous decisions and achieving goals. By allowing others to make all her decisions for her, she has developed neither the skill and self-confidence to make independent decisions nor the ability to tolerate making a mistake. She has not had the chance to learn that mistakes are seldom disastrous.

These adolescent years are a time when important choices must be made from an overwhelming number of options. There is no "one right way" of viewing the world and doing things. The world is no longer totally black and white; an unsettling gray has begun to creep in. For instance, the adolescent discovers that the one-and-only perfect career doesn't exist; neither does the one-and-only perfect mate. Instead, a number of possible career choices might be fulfilling, while none may be "perfect." Similarly, a number of potential "Mr. Rights" might exist, but none will be flawless. The path leading to success is not at all well defined, and for women especially, the route is problematical.

Note again that the two most common ages for developing anorexia nervosa coincide with points of transition: the 14 year old is often moving from a junior high setting to high school, while the 18 year old is graduating from high school and going to college. However, one can develop the disorder at an older age. One of Lesegue's patients was a 32-year-old woman. Dally and Gomez tell us that an "essentially similar" condition was described by the British physician John Ryle before the Second World War in women between 31 and 59 years of age. Dally and Gomez go on to state that they themselves have treated a number of patients over the age of 40.

Culture

Let us take a look at cultural considerations which relate to females, the primary victims of anorexia nervosa. First, anorexia nervosa is almost exclusively a disorder of Western culture; the disorder affects primarily the middle and upper classes (or individuals from upwardly mobile families). In most Western societies, a strong cultural emphasis is placed on success. Women formerly achieved their status through affiliation: a woman was the "daughter of . . ." or the "wife of . . .". Women took on the social status of the men in their lives. Today, new demands of success, independence, and sexuality confront women. These demands not only are new, but often contradict other traditional demands that exist simultaneously. Women are consequently thrust into a state of transition. Most women have been raised with traditional values and expectations which are now being challenged and modified. While roles for women and the means of attaining success are more varied, they are also more ambiguous. Thus many females find themselves caught up in the "Superwoman" syndrome, and carry overwhelming and unrealistic expectations for themselves, trying to be all things to all people.

Little wonder, then, that girls who are already perfectionist people pleasers and inexperienced decision makers may have extraordinary difficulty navigating the course into adulthood. These girls may be overwhelmed by feelings of powerlessness to affect their own destiny. This is, in fact, what is often reported to us by college age anorexics: the inability to make choices; the fear of making a wrong choice; the terror of not being respected and admired; the ache of wanting, yet not knowing how, to be this ultrarespected, self-confident, successful adult who is always happy and approved of by everyone. The cultural emphasis on success, then, when combined with the ways in which females are socialized and with women's lack of a clear-cut route to adulthood, can be viewed as contributing to the development of anorexia nervosa.

Two other potent cultural influences affect the increasing incidence of this disorder as well: (1) a burgeoning consciousness of nutrition and physical fitness, and (2) a national obsession with calorie counting and slimness. In the last two decades, our nation has become increasingly conscious of the importance of nutrition and physical fitness. Sales of vitamins and health foods have skyrocketed. Refined sugar and white flour are losing favor. Additives and preservatives in our food have been attacked as poisonous chemicals. Anything labeled "natural" sells at the supermarket. While not everyone's eating behavior has changed radically, clearly our society is more conscious of its diet and health in general — which is certainly not bad. Since 1968 the nation's incidence of cardiovascular deaths has decreased.

However, even health issues are willingly compromised for the wonderful world of slimness. Witness of public outcry when cyclamates, artificial sweeteners, were banned by the federal Food and Drug Administration on the basis of being carcinogenic. In no way were people about to surrender quietly the opportunity to guzzle low calorie soda, even if it did supposedly cause cancer. The liquid protein diet is another case in point. Even after this diet was linked to the deaths of several women, some individuals continued to use the product in an attempt to lose weight. A thin body was here deemed to be more important than a healthy one. In our food-oriented society, the thought of simply "going without" does not entice. People want to eat, drink, and be merry, but they want to be thin too. We pay huge amounts of money to eat more food that we need and then pay again for the privilege of exercising it off.

This brings us to our next point – the role of physical fitness. Estimates are that one in every three people is 10 or more pounds overweight. Concern over obesity and fitness has mounted during the last 20 years. Food is abundant and the necessity for physical labor has declined. In the 1960s, the fitness level of Americans, including children, was declared to be at an all-time low. A national effort was put forth to raise the fitness level of school children, and adults were encouraged to do likewise. Since that time, aerobic exercise, among other things, has been shown to be an effective anti-stress agent, a protection against heart attacks, an antidote for depression, and a means for achieving a natural "high" or feeling of well-being. Health and exercise clubs are now in vogue, and a certain amount of social status comes with the membership card. Even business deals are transacted on the racquetball court or over the tennis net. Physical fitness is in! Because of this wide interest in fitness, however, the anorexic's obsession with exercise and nutrition might easily be overlooked or dismissed.

Interestingly enough, women alone have become thinner in the last 20 years. Women constitute 95 percent of the membership in diet organizations. This is not really surprising when one considers the strong fashion dictates for the slimness of women. The message, primarily aimed at the female population, is that we must be slim in order to be attractive, popular, healthy, accepted, sexy, and desirable in the work force.

Where are these messages coming from? How do we know our society has an extreme focus on thinness? A person has only to turn on the television set and view the vast array of commercials for diet pills, diet pop, diet foods, diet beer, and diet clubs. In these commercials, both the men and the women are shown to be extremely thin, beautiful, popular, and happy. Our newspapers and magazines are overflowing with diet information, in both the advertisements and the feature articles. At the same time, we are deluged with messages luring us to eat, eat, eat. The covers of women's magazines alternate between pictures of pencil-thin models and enticing desserts! The neighborhood junk food palaces institute major promotional campaigns promising us a great day if we chow down their malts, fries, and burgers. So to "treat" ourselves, we are to eat heartily, but woe to the woman who doesn't somehow manage to maintain a slim, trim body in the process. Even kindergarten children have been shown to prefer a thin rag doll to a fat one (cited in Wooley et al., 1982).

Besides an obvious emphasis on thinness, the media and fashion industry seem to de-emphasize the desirability of the female curve. Small busts and very narrow hips are popularized; boyish figures are presented as the norm. The authors recall, as teenagers, a time when female curves were relished, not hidden or dieted away. Jayne Mansfield and Marilyn Monroe were considered beautiful then. Today our ideals are in the opposite direction. Compared to present-day models, Jayne and Marilyn were fat! A study of *Playboy* centerfolds in the last 20 years shows smaller waists, hips, and thighs presented as the ultimate in female attractiveness. Even more ridiculous is the recent trend of taking young, preteen models whose bodies have not yet fully developed, dressing them seductively, applying makeup to their faces, and presenting them as the "ideal woman" in advertising. One example of the extreme negation of any feminine curves came from a bulimic woman who stated, "I will never get pregnant. I couldn't stand to look so fat."

Why, oh why, should we negate the very curves that our bodies naturally develop? Is this also a negation of our femininity? Is it a nonacceptance of who we are as women? Kim Chernin, in her book *The Obsession: Reflections on the Tyranny of Slenderness* (Harper and Row, 1981), analyzes this societal phenomenon. She sees a parallel between women seeking to achieve their personal rights along with equal career opportunities and society negating femininity as a way to control women. We recommend reading this book to gain a more in-depth view of this cultural perspective.

Our male children experience the reverse of this stress on slimness. The cultural emphasis for boys is to develop their body mass, to grow "big and strong." Again, in the example of television commercials, the male is generally depicted as macho, dominant, and physically strong. For instance, in one commercial the male is shown deep-sea fishing, pulling in a huge fish while a female stands behind him watching in awe. Most males do not aspire to being "90 pound weaklings"!

This difference in the physical aspirations of young females and males is dramatically demonstrated in two different studies, one carried out in California and one in Sweden. In California, Huenemann et al. (1966) found that male and female high school students were equally dissatisfied with their bodies — the males perceiving themselves as too thin and small, and the females seeing themselves as too heavy. In actuality, only 25 percent of the women were at all overweight, but more than 40 percent considered themselves to be so. In spite of the reality, 65 percent of the ninth grade girls and 55 percent of the twelfth grade girls were trying to lose weight. Likewise, only 25 percent of the males were actually underweight, but the majority, again, were attempting to gain weight or muscle.

Similarly, in an extensive study undertaken in Sweden by Nylander,* male high school students seldom felt fat, while more than half of the female students felt fat (cited in Jones, 1981). This was despite the fact that 97 percent of the students were of normal weight — a remarkably lean group! This difference in perception of body size between female and male students accompanied by the differing cultural values for the opposite sexes, may help account for the fact that anorexia nervosa is a much rarer occurrence in males than in females.

The societal messages that have been discussed for both males and females fail to portray the importance of the inner person: a well-integrated personality; the ability to care about ourselves and others; social and communication skills; and a strong, unique identity. Society's focus is mainly on the physical proportions of the body. The pervasive message is: a person's worth is determined by his or her body weight and body measurements.

In conclusion, we believe that it is not by mere coincidence that the increasing incidence of both anorexia nervosa and bulimia occurs at a time when society strongly stresses the importance of a slim body for women. A goodly amount of stigma attaches to being overweight in our society, and the individual faces tremendous social pressure to maintain a trim body. Ours is the first generation of children that has been brought up by mothers in Weight Watchers.

The most evident models for young girls, besides their calorie conscious mothers, are professional models who are paid to starve themselves for the honor of gracing our magazine and television ads. No wonder shocked parents discover 6- and 7-year-old daughters

---

*Since dieting is often a precursor to the development of anorexia, it is significant to note that in the Sweden study, 25 percent of the females who dieted went on to develop three or more negative side effects of a physical and/or psychological nature.

standing in front of mirrors, complaining they are too "fat." Even the very young feel the impact.

Biological Predisposition

One phenomenon of the disorder, as previously stated, is that its victims are primarily female. While cultural and other factors may account for the unique pressures placed on women which encourage anorexia, it has also been suggested that women may be biologically susceptible since they have been shown to be far more likely than males to experience appetite fluctuations in response to stress (Krumbacher and Meyer, cited in Jones, 1981).* We also know that as a result of socialization, females are more inclined than males to inhibit negative feelings. When these negative feelings are not directly discharged in some way, the result is internal stress. This stress certainly might interact with and exacerbate the biological phenomenon.

Earlier we discussed various physiological abnormalities that have been found to exist in diagnosed anorexics. Most of these abnormalities disappear with weight gain, but the fact that some remain cannot be ignored. Generally speaking, if an organic defect exists, it is most likely related to the hypothalamus, since many of the symptoms associated with anorexia could also occur with a hypothalamic disorder. Furthermore, it has been clearly established that disturbances in hypothalamic function exist in anorexia nervosa (Lucas, 1981; Vigersky, 1977; Weiner, 1982). In one of the most impressive literature reviews of anorexia nervosa that we have found, Kelly Bemis (1978) of the University of Minnesota cites a study carried out by R. A. Mecklenburg and colleagues which focuses on hypothalamic functions in patients with anorexia. The authors of the study conclude:

> At least three possibilities exist. It may be that starvation damages the hypothalamus, that psychic stress somehow interferes with hypothalamic function, or that the manifestations of anorexia nervosa, including the psychological aberrations, are relatively independent expressions of a primary hypothalamic defect of unknown etiology. (p. 609)

---

*We suggest that appetite fluctuation in women might also be a learned response.

So we have a case of the chicken and the egg: which is the producer and which is the product? Does the anorexia produce the physiological changes or vice versa? Are the two factors unrelated or do they feed one another, creating an ever circular state? This mystery remains.

Family Issues

A familial predisposition for developing an eating disorder appears to exist. An excess risk of developing anorexia occurs for an individual if any other family member has had the disorder or if either parent is excessively thin or obese. Whether or not this fact is due to a hereditary link has not been established. Family histories often reveal the presence of other conditions which are associated with hereditary factors — conditions such as depression, obesity, diabetes, and alcoholism. On the other hand, if anorexia as an illness is hereditary, we would expect identical twins to be similarly afflicted. In actuality, identical twins are not necessarily similarly plagued (Bruch, 1969; Lucas, 1981). This predisposition, then, has been suggested to be more the result of family environment, but the total facts of the matter are yet to be determined.

Anorexics do tend to come from families which express a concern over food issues. This concern may be the result of the special dietary needs of a family member, an emphasis on nutrition, and/or previous power struggles over eating. The family may also have used food for purposes other than nourishment. Eating may be used when members face problems or unpleasantness, as a sign of love and caring for the providers, to fill time, or to keep the family together and "happy." Some families, for instance, when confronting problems react to them by eating (or not eating); other families may require members to show their love and acceptance by eating food prepared for them. In the case of one of the authors, visits to a particular grandmother were highlighted by the meal ritual. The grandmother would spend days cooking great amounts of food and would hover over each person, watching to see that everyone ate well and dishing extra food onto plates after family members had finished eating. If the food was not eagerly accepted, she protested that we must not like her cooking or that we needed to eat more for our health. One thing was clear: we *must* eat more. The grandmother's behavior became a family joke, and newcomers to her meals were warned to arrive famished and to make their first attempt to quit eating while still hungry. In this way they would be able to eat the extra helpings Grandma dished out and still leave without feeling totally ill or insulting her! Obviously, the family can be a significant factor influencing the consumption of food for reasons other than nourishment.

In the family of one anorexic client, a premium was placed on all of the family eating exactly the same thing. If one person (particularly a parent) had a serving of a particular item, everyone had to have the same in order to "keep the peace," *and there was no flexibility regarding this.* It seemed a show of family solidarity, with no allowance for individual preferences or circumstances.

Certain parental personalities have been described in the literature. Mothers are often portrayed as dominant, intrusive, and frequently having episodes of depression, while fathers are described as aloof or passive. However, we have known instances in which this was reversed. Alcoholism is at times present in one or both parents, as is the obesity or exceptional thinness mentioned before. No single set of parental personality characteristics, however, has definitely been shown to exist universally.

Some clinicians and researchers are convinced that family dynamics play a critical role in the disorder. Dr. Mara Palazzoli of Italy has spent the majority of her professional life treating victims of anorexia. After investing great time and energy in treating afflicted individuals with traditional psychoanalysis (without particular success), she began to treat the clients' families as well. In this arena, success was met with, and remarkably so.

Salvadore Minuchin, an American expert on family systems, and his colleagues have described the internal politics of a typical anorexic family. (We would encourage you to read their work directly.) The family features proposed by Minuchin et al. (1978) which encourage anorexia are enmeshment, rigidity, overprotectiveness, and lack of conflict resolution.

The enmeshed family is often viewed by outsiders as very "close," with family members highly involved and concerned with one another. Great importance is attached by the family to all changes and upsets, which are immediately attended to (identical happenings in another kind of family may go relatively unnoticed). This attentiveness can result in impairment in the development of individual identity or autonomy. When everything is a "big deal," one may learn not to make waves lest the boat tip.

As children grow and change, and as outside circumstances change, so must families. Change is always stressful because it requires readjustment or replacement of familiar, comfortable ways of doing things and treating people with new, unfamiliar patterns. For instance, a child who once rushed home from school or activities eager to relate the daily happenings may, with the advent of adolescence, become less open and more desirous of privacy. Rather than taking part in the usual family activities, the child may express a preference for exchanging the family's company for that of a friend. One of our own mothers shared the surprise and disappointment she felt when her daughter approached the teenage years, a time the mother had anticipated as an opportunity for mother and daughter to become closer. This mother thought her primary care-giving relationship would be exchanged for a more cooperative friendship relationship with her daughter, who was old enough now to enjoy many of the mother's hobbies. The mother had looked forward for years to the time when the two would be able to do such things together. As it turned out, the daughter did in fact enjoy the same activities but was not at all interested in doing them with her mother. The mother's realization of the developmental changes taking place in her daughter is demonstrated in her statement, "Just when I thought we could be great friends and do all these things together, I found out I wasn't needed anymore! You had your friends instead." Fortunately, in her wisdom, the mother quietly stepped back and allowed her daughter the choice and freedom to grow more independent. That decision required, among other things, flexibility.

If a family is unable or unwilling to change, to be flexible, it demonstrates rigidity. Upon encountering stress or pressure, the family may simply become less flexible than before, doing what it has always done, only more so. Such a family no longer fosters continuing growth and development but rather, as Minuchin states, "becomes a cage."

The parents of an anorexic tend to be overly protective of their child, monitoring her every need and action. Since every action and event in such a family is evaluated by others' reaction to it, this child develops a self-consciousness and an excessive concern for perfection. She is extraordinarily sensitive to cues from others and is an approval seeker — a characteristic which leads to difficulty in acting independently.

The familial overprotection is seen to inhibit the development of autonomy in the child. Minuchin et al. (1978) state:

> Large areas of her psychological and biological functioning remain the subject of others' interest and control long after they should have become autonomous. This control is maintained under the cloak of concern, so that the child cannot challenge it. (pp. 59–60)

They go on to contend:

> ... disagreement and even initiative become acts of betrayal. The denial of self for another's benefit and family loyalty are highly valued. The concern for mutual accommodation without friction produces an environment in which differences are denied and submerged. (p. 60)

Since accommodation and "keeping the peace" are so highly valued in anorexics' families, conflict is not dealt with openly. Instead it is avoided or detoured. If problems are not acknowledged and dealt with directly and mutually, family members can experience no meaningful resolution. Thus another hallmark of the anorexic family is the lack of conflict resolution.

In addition to these four characteristics of family functioning, Minuchin mentions two other details that have repeatedly been confirmed in our own experience with anorexics: difficulty in dealing with peers in terms of developing close relationships and a strong involvement of grandparents (or aunts and uncles) within the family to create coalitions.

Hilde Bruch similarly identifies family issues among her anorexic patients. The central issue in Bruch's view is the overall sense of ineffectiveness and powerlessness on the part of the patients. They do not see themselves as initiators but as reactors; they react not to their own desires or needs, but to those of others. Bruch believes the genesis of this disturbance lies in the early parent-child relationship. She describes "model" families wherein the anorexic child has not been encouraged to develop her own individuality and autonomy. The parents' sense of what is appropriate takes precedence over the child's needs. Nothing but compliance is tolerated. In Bruch's view, anorexia may represent a child's valiant attempt to claim control of her life and to achieve an identity of her own.

Arthur Crisp and his colleagues have suggested that anorexia may be maintained by the family's needs. The family's sickness may be displaced onto the patient. A study carried out by Crisp, Harding, and McGuinness in 1974 found that as the anorexic patient recovered, the level of neurosis in the parents increased significantly. Minuchin et al. (1978) also saw the anorexia as being used to detour conflict (no other problems can come to attention) and to bring the family together in their concern.

Furthermore, the anorexia brings a great deal of attention to the child and can be self-perpetuating. Giving up the attention and the "specialness" that anorexia guarantees can be a major hurdle in the patient's recovery process.

Family dynamics which coincide with the onset of anorexia nervosa have been discussed widely in the literature. A number of writers have given extensive descriptions of how the anorexic family operates. Most of these descriptions are based upon clinical impressions and observations rather than controlled studies. While such impressions may be valid and are certainly useful, we cannot say with certitude that they typify the anorexic family. The fact that some writers have failed to find any consistent pattern cannot be ignored. Moreover, the precise cause-and-effect relationship is difficult to determine. Did the presence of the eating disorder create the existing style of family interaction, or did the style of interaction encourage the anorexia? Certainly, having an anorexic child places tremendous stress upon the family and would tax even the healthiest family's emotional reserves. On the other hand, a consistent family history would refute the notion that family interaction is a response developed in reaction to the eating problem. Possessing an awareness of the kinds of family dynamics which may promote anorexia can be decidedly helpful in treatment, in helping parents develop healthier methods of coping with their anorexic child, and also in facilitating prevention of the disorder through education.

Peer Relationships

The client's lack of meaningful peer relationships has been theorized to be an essential feature in the genesis of anorexia nervosa. Delores

Jones (1981) confirms in her award winning paper, "Structural Discontinuity and the Development of Anorexia Nervosa," that anorexics have an absence of close friendships. When any relationship is developed by anorexics, it is usually with only one person at a time and even then is short-lived. This behavior pattern is probably true of male anorexics as well. Male patients in England were found to be inhibited and nonassertive, and notably did not belong to a "gang" (Crisp, 1980).

Jones tells us that most people have between six and ten close friends, as well as another thirty acquaintances with whom they interact regularly. She asserts that in Western societies, adolescent peer groups are vital in easing the individual's transition from child to adult status. Of the anorexics' transition process, Jones states:

> On the one hand they must discard the patterns of behavior acquired with the family since they are no longer functional, and on the other, adopt modes of conduct more appropriate to the external world. Because these behaviors and modes of orientation are not immediately self evident, there is a lag between the abandonment of old behaviors and the discovery of new ones. This hiatus is characterized by a high degree of uncertainty, since individuals are without a well defined normative structure to guide their behavior. In such a situation, there is a marked decline in autonomy and a concomitant increase in the formation of personal dependencies. (pp. 238–239)

During this time, peer relationships are essential. It is no longer appropriate, and is in fact counterproductive, for the family to be the source for meeting the adolescent's needs. Adequate peer networks provide "a connecting link between the particularistic family structure and the universalistic occupational and other nonfamilial spheres. They serve as channels for the learning of various general role dispositions essential for effective participation in the main institutional spheres of adult society" (Jones, 1981, p. 240).

The anorexic who tends to be overly involved with, and dependent upon, her family to the exclusion of outside relationships is at a severe disadvantage. Jones views the disorder as

> . . . an attempt to cope with the seeming irreconcilable conflict between societal expectations for adult behavior and the individual's

inability to respond appropriately to these demands. Because the anorexic has no adolescent peer group to help her make the transition from the private to the public sphere, she is effectively imprisoned within the family. However, because her adult size creates expectations for more independent behavior, her continued attachment to the family is regarded as inappropriate. The anorexic resolves this conflict by losing weight so that in terms of size and biological functioning, she becomes a child again and can legitimately remain within the family. (p. 241)

This point of view is consistent with the fact that the disorder is rare in those societies wherein the transition to adulthood is not marked by ambiguity, but rather has clear-cut, traditional role expectations.

While we have discussed a number of possible causal factors in the development of anorexia nervosa, we reiterate that no definitive statement can be made at this time regarding the etiology of this disorder. We would contend that it is highly unlikely that any single one of these factors will prove to be "the cause" of anorexia. Rather, it is far more probable that anorexia nervosa results from a combination of interacting factors.

INCIDENCE

How common is anorexia nervosa? For many years anorexia was considered extremely rare. One of the first serious endeavors to study patients with this disorder was made at the Mayo Clinic in the 1930s. Prior to that time, anorexia victims were often incorrectly diagnosed as having primary pituitary disease (as previously discussed). Even as recently as 1970, the sole information regarding anorexia nervosa given to a graduate counseling class attended by one of the authors, was the statement that anorexia was a rare disorder and would probably never be encountered. Certainly, with so little knowledge, such an encounter could easily go unrecognized even if it occurred! To this day we know of graduate programs in counseling, psychology, and social work which do not address anorexia nervosa or bulimia. However, this situation is, we hope, improving.

In the last 20 years we have seen a dramatic increase in diagnosed cases of anorexia nervosa. Several possible explanations for this occur. A number of excellent research projects and treatment programs have finally been described in professional publications. The popular press and other media have also taken a keen interest in this unusual disorder. Hence, mental health professionals, physicians, dietitians, and the general population are much more familiar with the problem. This exposure factor would certainly account for part of the perceived increase in anorexia diagnoses. Previous inadequate records, lack of agreement regarding diagnosis, and inconsistent criteria for diagnosis of anorexia nervosa also contribute to our inability to assess accurately the changes in incidence. Additionally, we have no idea about the number of individuals who were victims of this disorder and did not come to medical attention. Nevertheless, the medical evidence that does exist reveals a significant increase, and practitioners widely hold that anorexia nervosa is increasing both in its identification by medical and mental health personnel, and in its actual frequency.

The Anorexia Nervosa and Related Eating Disorders Organization (ANRED) estimates that approximately one in every 100 white females between the ages of 12 and 18 suffers from anorexia. Roughly 10 percent of anorexics are male. Females afflicted with this disorder then outnumber males nine to one (Anderson, 1981).

In addition, anorexia appears to be more prevalent in affluent societies, in upper and middle class families, and among whites — although this is not to say that it cannot occur elsewhere. One particularly striking fact, however, is that the disorder develops strictly in the face of plenty. Only where food is abundant and available do we find anorexia nervosa.

RECOVERY

Fortunately, even though we are not at all clear about the exact causes of anorexia nervosa, recovery from the disease is possible. Recovery is a multifaceted occurrence, achieved in varying degrees from marginal to complete, and involving not only a gain in weight but also a return of the menstrual period and social/emotional development. Clinical studies and articles reporting recovery rates can be confusing and contradictory, and they must be viewed carefully. One reason for this caution is that differing criteria are used to designate recovery. Therefore, we must ask *in what ways* anorexic individuals have recovered. For example, some researchers only consider weight gain as a measure of health. The fact that forced weight gain as a sole method of treatment may terminate in suicidal behavior is not acknowledged in the statistics. Additionally, while restoration of normal weight is clearly of prime importance, it also happens to be a relatively easy task when the individual is hospitalized. Enabling the patient to maintain the gained weight outside of the hospital is far more difficult. Thus the length of time that elapses prior to follow-up is another vital consideration. Longer-term follow-up studies report higher mortality rates, frequent rehospitalizations, continuing psychological impairment, inadequate marital/social adjustments, and obviously lower recovery rates. On the other hand, with the improved treatment methods that have recently evolved and with earlier detection of the disorder, the anorexic's recovery is becoming more hopeful.

With these warnings in mind, let us now look at some of the statistics. (The following statistics are a combination of various studies.) The good news is that, nutritionally speaking, we can expect 50 percent of diagnosed and treated anorexics to recover completely within two to five years. If we include as well those anorexics who will show some improvement, we can anticipate nutritional improvement or recovery in two-thirds of the anorexic cases (Bliss and Branch, cited in Bemis, 1978). Approximately 90 percent of treated anorexics go on to become employed. Moreover, between 50 and 87 percent of these anorexics regain menstrual function (Hsu, 1980). Generally, after body weight has stabilized, approximately one year or more is required for menstruation to resume. Even for those anorexics who do not experience the return of menstrual periods, the possibility of bearing children remains, since ovaries may still be active.

Unfortunately, not all the news is good. Anorexia can become chronic. Even when it is arrested, lingering problems are common. As many as half of those afflicted have a relapse (Moldofsky et al., 1978), and up to 38 percent may have to be rehospitalized within two years (Dally, cited in Bemis, 1978). We must be careful not to assume that this is necessarily negative, however, and so become discouraged. Rehospitalization *can* be another step toward recovery. Sometimes recovery requires several setbacks before real progress is apparent. Nevertheless, approximately 18 percent of diagnosed anorexics do remain ill and unchanged (Hsu, 1980). Death from complications of the disorder or from suicide has been estimated to occur in anywhere from 3 to 25 percent of the cases (Bemis, 1978).

Psychologically, approximately 50 percent of anorexia victims upon follow-up show significant impairment, being plagued with phobias, depression, and so forth. Less than half demonstrate adequate marital/social adjustment, which indicates perhaps a need for treatment programs to focus more attention on the development of relationship-building skills (Hsu, 1980).

Another phenomenon of concern in anorexia treatment is that some anorexics who gain weight exaggerate their eating behavior in the opposite direction, going on to become compulsive overeaters. As compulsive eaters, this group either will be fat to the point of obesity or will develop bulimia. (We will deal further with the syndrome of bulimia as a distinct eating disorder in Chapter 2.) While this reversed eating behavior is not thoroughly understood, it nevertheless points out the necessity for reinforcing only appropriate eating in the course of treatment and by the family. This need will be dealt with further in Chapter 3 which addresses treatment issues.

Because the statistics cited are the result not of one unified study but rather of a compilation of studies, it seems very difficult to know clearly the final outcome of anorexia nervosa research. Differing criteria are used by different authors to define recovery; follow-ups occurring in the literature take place over varying spans of time; methods of treatment are not identical; and no distinction is made between those anorexics who indulge in eating binges and those who do not. This last point is important because current evidence suggests that differences exist between the two subgroups. These differences not only are lost when no differentiation is made but also may confound the overall results.

So what else do we know about anorexia except that some get a lot better, some get a little better, and some don't get better at all? Most of the research literature seems to agree that poorer recovery rates are associated with a greater weight loss, an older age at the onset of the illness, and the presence of binge-eating and/or purging (vomiting, laxative abuse). In addition to these factors, the duration of the illness seems to play a role in recovery. The longer an individual has been anorexic, the poorer is her prognosis. That is, an individual who has been anorexic for ten years will have a more difficult time recovering from the disease than one who has had the disorder for only one year (Hsu, 1980).

In terms of recovery outcome, perhaps the above-mentioned characteristics of the victims are themselves better predictors than is any particular method of treatment. Since it is important to get such individuals into treatment early, before weight loss is extreme and the illness has a chance to become firmly implanted, it would seem worthwhile to address ways in which to make an early identification of the disorder.

EARLY IDENTIFICATION AND PREVENTION

Anorexia victims are often well-mannered children who take school seriously and who are seemingly successful. Consequently, we are shocked to discover that they have such a strange problem. The disease may seem to have emerged out of the blue, without warning. Yet, if we are attuned to the dynamics of this disorder, we find warning signals — red flags, so to speak. If we keep on the lookout for these, perhaps we can intercept the development of this vicious illness.

What kinds of behavior signs are telltale? We have already stated that dieting, for example, is a common precipitating factor and is moreover an activity engaged in by a large number of young teenage girls. Does that mean that all young girls who diet are vulnerable to developing anorexia? Not necessarily. However, combined with other factors, dieting may very well indicate such a vulnerability. Frequent dieting may place young girls at a higher risk for developing an eating disorder. Weight loss appears to be an antecedent of bulimia and, as stated, is the primary factor in anorexia nervosa. A "red flags" list can be found in Table 1-2. This list is by no means exhaustive, and you may find additional signals. While none of the factors we mention is necessarily indicative of anorexia in and of itself, the *combination* of factors occurring over an *extended* period of time must be attended to. Furthermore, the presence of a combination of these factors indicates, but does not guarantee, the presence of an eating disorder. If an eating disorder is not present, clearly a problem of some kind exists, which merits your attention.

Possibly the richest area in which to direct our efforts is that of prevention. Since virtually nothing has been written on this topic, we are all left to our own devices. We feel that research in this area is urgently needed and a most worthwhile undertaking. The thrust

TABLE 1-2. Red Flags for Early Identification.

1. Loss of menstrual period
2. Dieting with relish when not overweight
3. Claiming to "feel fat" when overweight is not a reality
4. Preoccupation with food, calories, nutrition, and/or cooking
5. Denial of hunger
6. Excessive exercising; being overly active
7. Frequent weighing
8. Use of laxatives and/or vomiting to control weight
9. Leaving for the bathroom after meals (secretive vomiting)
10. Strange food-related behaviors
11. Complaints of feeling bloated or nauseated when eating normal amounts of food
12. Intermittent episodes of "binge-eating"

of our own prevention efforts in the university setting has primarily been that of education.

Education regarding eating disorders can be carried out in various ways; detailed examples can be found in Chapter 5. In addition to becoming educated about eating disorders, female students especially can be encouraged to learn how they have been socialized toward such illnesses and how to challenge unhealthy cultural messages. Classes taught from a feminist perspective, such as Women's Studies courses, have been valuable to some of our anorexic and bulimic students. With offices located on the college campus, we do not have much direct contact with parents. This, however, is a most important audience to meet. We believe it is essential to educate parents as to (1) the nature of eating disorders, (2) the growing-up needs of their children, (3) healthy modes of family functioning, (4) the importance of building self-esteem, etc. It has been said that one of the most important things a parent can do for an anorexic child is to let her (or him) win an argument. To take this a step further, why wait until the child is anorexic? Parents must be made aware of such matters.

An individual who feels confident and good about herself is unlikely to develop anorexia (or other mental health problems). One extraordinarily committed pediatrician we know makes a point to attend at least one school or extracurricular event of each of her patients in order to acknowledge that child and let her know that she is noticed and important. Can you imagine the impact it would have upon you

— a child — if your doctor took the time to come to an event specifically to see you? This same physician greets every child she meets on the street (or wherever) with interest and an attempt to give a meaningful compliment on something other than physical appearance. We all have similar kinds of opportunities. Some of us have opportunities to impact not only individuals but systems such as schools and churches. Creating mentally healthy environments is obviously an antidote not only for eating disorders but for a host of other problems as well.

REFERENCES

Bemis, K. Current approaches to the etiology and treatment of anorexia nervosa as a disease. *Psychological Bulletin* 85(3):593–617 (1978).

Bennett, W. and Gurin, J. Do diets really work? *Science* 82:42–50 (March 1982).

Boskind-Lodahl, M. Cinderella's stepsisters: a feminist perspective on anorexia nervosa and bulimia. *Journal of Women in Culture and Society* 2(2):342–356 (1976).

Bruch, H. Perceptual and conceptual disturbances in anorexia nervosa. *Psychosomatic Medicine* 24(2):187–194 (1962).

Bruch, H. Anorexia nervosa and its differential diagnosis. *The Journal of Nervous and Mental Disease* 141(5):555–566 (1966).

Bruch, H. Anorexia nervosa in the male. *Psychosomatic Medicine* 33(1):31–46 (1971).

Bruch, H. *Eating Disorders.* New York: Basic Books, 1973.

Bruch, H. *The Golden Cage: The Enigma of Anorexia Nervosa.* Cambridge, Mass.: Harvard University Press, 1978.

Casper, R., Eckert, E., Halmi, K., Goldberg, S., and Davis, J. Bulimia: its incidence and clinical importance in patients with anorexia nervosa. *Arch. Gen. Psychiatry* 37:1030–1035 (September 1980).

Chernin, K. *New York Times Magazine* 28 (October 11, 1981).

Chernin, K. *The Obsession: Reflections on the Tyranny of Slenderness.* Harper and Row, 1981.

Crisp, A. H. *Anorexia Nervosa: Let Me Be.* New York: Grune and Stratton, 1980.

Dally, P. and Gomez, J. *Obesity and Anorexia Nervosa – A Question of Shape.* London: Faber and Faber, 1980.

Diagnostic and Statistical Manual of Mental Disorders, 3rd ed. American Psychiatric Association, 1980, Washington D.C.

Duddle, M. An increase of anorexia nervosa in a university population. *American Journal of Psychiatry* 123:711–217 (1973).

Garfinkel, P., Moldofsky, H., and Garner, D. The heterogeneity of anorexia nervosa. *Arch. Gen. Psychiatry* 37:1036–1040 (September 1980).

Hedblom, J., Hubbard, F., and Anderson, A. Anorexia nervosa: a multidisciplinary treatment for patient and family. *Social Work in Health Care* 7(1):67–86 (1981).

Hsu, L. Outcome of anorexia nervosa: a review of the literature (1954 to 1978). *Arch. Gen. Psychiatry* 37:1041–1046 (September 1980).

Huenemann, R. L., Shapiro, L. R., Hampton, M. C., and Mitchell, B. W. A longitudinal study of gross body composition and conformation and their association with food and activity in a teenage population. *American Journal of Clinical Nutrition* 18:325–38 (1966).

Jones, D. Structural discontinuity and the development of anorexia nervosa. *Sociological Focus* 14(3):233–245 (August 1981).

Keys, A., Brozek, J., Henschel, A., Mickelsen, O., and Taylor, H. L. *The Biology of Human Starvation*, Vols. 1 and 2. Minneapolis: University of Minnesota Press, 1950.

Lucas, A. R. Anorexia nervosa. *Contemporary Nutrition* 3(8) (1978).

Lucas, A. R. Toward the understanding of anorexia nervosa as a disease entity. *Mayo Clinic Proceedings* 56:254–264 (1981).

Mecklenburg, R. S., Loriaux, D. L., Thompson, R. H., Anderson, A. E., Lipsett, M. B. Hypotholamic Dysfunction in Patients with Anorexia Nervosa. *Medicine* 53:147–159 (1974).

Minuchin, S., Baker, L., Rosman, B., Liebman, R., Milman, L., and Todd, T. A conceptual model of psychosomatic illness in children. *Arch. Gen. Psychiatry* 32:1031–1038 (August 1975).

Minuchin, S., Rosman, B. L., and Baker, L. *Psychosomatic Families: Anorexia Nervosa in Context.* Cambridge, Mass.: Harvard University Press, 1978.

Palazzoli, M. *Self Starvation.* New York: Jason Aronson, 1978.

Palmer, R. L. *Anorexia Nervosa: A Guide for Sufferers and Their Families.* New York: Penguin Books, 1980.

Papalia, A. and Bode, J. Perspectives on the anorectic student. *Journal of College Student Personnel* 224–228 (May 1981).

Rizzuto, A., Peterson, R., and Reed, M. The pathological sense of self in anorexia nervosa. *Psychiatric Clinics of North America* 4(3):471–485 (1981).

Russell, G. Bulimia nervosa: an ominous variant of anorexia nervosa. *Psychological Medicine* 9:429–448 (1979).

Schwartz, D. M., Thompson, M. G., and Johnson, C. L. Anorexia nervosa and bulimia: the socio-cultural context. *International Journal of Eating Disorders* 1(3):20–36 (1982).

Slade, P. D. and Russell, G. F. M. Awareness of body dimensions in anorexia nervosa: cross-sectional and longitudinal studies. *Psychological Medicine* 3:188–199 (1973).

Thoma, H. On the psychotherapy of patients with anorexia nervosa. *Bulletin of the Menninger Clinic* 41(5):437–452 (1977).

Tornell, G. *Alum News,* Moorhead State University, 80(4) (Winter, 1980).

Weiner, H. The problem of anorexia nervosa: psychobiological considerations. *Phenomenology and Treatment of Psychophysiological Disorders* 143–154 (1982).

Wooley, O. W. and Wooley, S. Editorial: The Beverly Hills eating disorder: the mass marketing of anorexia nervosa. *International Journal of Eating Disorders* 1(3):57–69 (1982).

Zeeman, E. C. Catastrophe theory. *Scientific American* (April 1976).

2
Bulimia

MY DAY

Thursday, December 9th*

I slept in . . . got up at 5:45 A.M. instead of 5:30. Big test, gotta study! (I started studying for this one last Sunday.) Took a *hot* shower (I'm so cold these days). Oh, I wanted to stand there longer and let the hot spray penetrate my scalp (my head throbbed with pain) but had to get going, had to study, had to give Sharon some notes before I started my day — before breakfast. Slapped on makeup (my eyes, so red — dark circles, so deep . . . me pretty? They're all lying.) Covered all that up.

6:30. Another cigarette . . . more coffee. I had exactly 15 minutes to — relax?

7:00. Damn — I always have to wait for the cafeteria to open. Breakfast, finally. Eggs, toast, peanut butter, bananas, cereal, juice — I went over the "limit" *again*. Shit, did I care? Took four doughnuts and two rolls, wrapped them up and stuffed 'em in my pockets. (I'm so good at that.) Bathroom — threw up.

7:30. Listened to the weather in the lounge — had to know it for the test (Geography test . . . gotta study!). Stuffed the doughnuts and rolls down my throat, drank water, and threw up.

7:45. Coffee and study time (smoke, read, sip). I knew that Geography by heart — not good enough though.

10:30. Break. Relax? Had two bags of cookies. Pace — pace — pace.

11:00. Lunch. Brought my notes with me, read some more (again). Two fishwiches, salad, chips, soup, cake, ice cream, milk . . . threw up, drank water, threw up again.

12:00 noon. Test time. Ten pages — 50 minutes. Not enough time . . . PANIC. The instructor kept saying "Gotta go — times

---

*A day in the life of a college student with bulimia.

up . . . . Gotta go – times up . . . . Gotta go – times up." I *knew* the answers; I knew *beyond* the answers! All I could hear was "Times up"; I blew it. I wanted to cry? yell? I don't know – it's so unfair! I didn't guess at the answers, so I couldn't get done in 50 minutes. Ten pages in 50 minutes! "Times up" (I wish it was sometimes – today). Just me and him in the room. "I know the answers," I said. "I know you do; it's so frustrating." He smiled, "Have a good weekend." HE SMILED! How could he!

1:02. I walked out, head throbbing. I hated . . . me! I couldn't think anymore . . . nothing mattered.

1:30. Quickly got my purse and drove to the shopping mall. First, gas up – stopped at Taco Johns. Two soft shells, refried beans, natchos, and an apple grande. Safeway – drank Mountain Dew and cashed a check. Shopping mall – threw up. Bought a sweater, purse, mittens – treat myself? Ha! I didn't care about any of those things.

3:30. Lunch? Dinner? Who knows? Who cares? Salad bar, mushroom burger, fries, pie, milk. Threw up; coffee and cigarette.

5:00. Perkin's. Blueberry pancakes, eggs, sausage, hashbrowns, hot chocolate. Drove back to school. Threw up. Talked to Ben (he tried cheer me up; I acted "cheered up"). Up to room. BOOM. Tears, anger, hatred flooded me. Joan heard me; tears stopped. I bitched, like any other student. Appropriate, I thought.

5:30. Dinner. Fish, fries, salad, corn, bar, ice cream, chocolate milk . . . down the can.

6:15. Talked to Ben. Of course, I started with my true feelings, then I rambled on in my "intellectual, compassionate, caring" style.

8:00. Candy bar on the way out; I walked to the parking lot. Torn – so torn. Cold, wet from rain, and alone. Hmmm – Denny's or stay here? Pace, pace, pace. Denny's it was. Chili, BLT, grilled cheese, fries, milk. Threw up. Pretended I was waiting for Sally; must have asked the waitress four times if she had seen her. A girl asked me to join her and friends. "Ahhh, I really must find my friend," I lied. Pretended to have called Sally, then I left. Dairy Queen – sundae and parfait. Home; threw up.

9:30. So weak, numb.

11:45. A *diet* Squirt and here I am. I hope I lose weight; I hope I disintegrate.

****

A week later − test results . . . shock! I earned (?) an A . . .
highest score on the first part, second highest on the second. So
. . . could have been an F . . . . I don't *feel* it . . . just stuffed it in
my notebook and it's gone now − it was never there.

(Anonymous)

INTRODUCTION

Bulimia has been called the sister ailment of anorexia nervosa. Victims of the two disorders share many of the same behaviors and concerns, especially the intense fear of becoming fat. They assess their
worth by the numbers on the scale or by how far their stomachs pro-
trude. Both groups tend to strive for perfection and success.

Bulimia, however, is characterized by compulsive binge-eating and
purging (self-induced vomiting, laxative abuse, diuretics, etc.). Food
becomes an obsession and addiction − an escape from the pressures
of life. However, the prospect of keeping unwanted calories in their
system is so terrifying to bulimics that they vomit or use another
method to eliminate the food. Very often bulimics alternate fasting
with bingeing. Unlike anorexics, those caught up in the syndrome of
bulimia *usually maintain a normal or near normal body weight,* perhaps are even somewhat overweight, with the primary symptom being
gorging rather than starvation. Bulimia tends to run a chronic course
often interspersed with periods of remission, while anorexia is more
often a single episode.

During periods of remission, however, eating is seldom normal for
the individual afflicted with bulimia. The remission is from binge-
eating and purging only, not from dieting behavior. Relinquishing
the purging behavior and the control over weight which it provides
leads to an intensification of the bulimic's fear of gaining weight. Thus,
very little is eaten, meals are skipped, and fasting is self-imposed. Although quite a few people who are not bulimic also occasionally engage in binge-eating and vomiting, for victims of bulimia the behavior
becomes a compulsive ritual which consumes their lives. Decisions
must be made how to get the food and how to get rid of it. For many,
every waking moment is food centered. In order to maintain secrecy,
dishonesty with others becomes a necessity for bulimics. The guilt
associated with this disorder can be overwhelming and can lead to

even more binge-vomiting. Life thus becomes a devastating cycle of bingeing and vomiting (and/or laxative abuse, exercise, etc.).

DIAGNOSIS

Bulimia literally means "ox hunger." The diagnostic criteria set forth in the DSM-III (1980) are as follows:

A. Recurrent episodes of binge eating (rapid consumption of a large amount of food in a discrete period of time, usually less than two hours).
B. At least three of the following:
    (1) consumption of high-caloric, easily ingested food during a binge
    (2) inconspicuous eating during a binge
    (3) termination of such eating episodes by abdominal pain, sleep, social interruption, or self-induced vomiting
    (4) repeated attempts to lose weight by severely restrictive diets, self-induced vomiting, or use of cathartics or diuretics
    (5) frequent weight fluctuations greater than ten pounds due to alternating binges and fasts
C. Awareness that the eating pattern is abnormal and fear of not being able to stop eating voluntarily.
D. Depressed mood and self-deprecating thoughts following eating binges.
E. The bulimic episodes are not due to Anorexia Nervosa or any known physical disorder. (pp. 70–71)

While the presence of purging is not necessarily required for the diagnosis of bulimia according to the DSM-III, such purging occurs in the vast majority of cases and is usually equated with bulimia in most of the clinical and popular writings (Mitchell and Pyle, 1982).

Only recently has a distinction been made between anorexia nervosa and bulimia. Additionally, the relationship between the two disorders remains a controversial issue. Consequently, we confront several problems.

First of all, a significant problem exists with the term itself. In Chapter 1, we mentioned the existence of bulimia as a possible symptom within the context of anorexia nervosa. That is, a large number of anorexics periodically break their fasts and go on eating binges. This behavior is usually followed by purging so that calories ingested will not be retained and there will not be any resultant weight gain. Because of this consistently low weight, the diagnosis of anorexia is retained in such cases.

In this chapter we refer to bulimia as an illness related to, but distinct from, anorexia nervosa. Obviously using the same term for both a symptom of anorexia and a separate syndrome or illness leads to great confusion — this is one of the problems in the professional literature. Usually no distinction is made between bulimia within the context of anorexia nervosa (this is the *symptom* of bulimia) and the separate syndrome of bulimia, a disorder distinct from anorexia nervosa. Similarly, the literature on anorexia frequently does not differentiate between those anorexics who only restrict their food intake and do not have the symptom of bulimia, and those who do have this symptom.

Three major subgroups have been delineated to date: (1) individuals with anorexia nervosa who continuously restrict their food intake, never indulging in binge-eating; (2) individuals with anorexia nervosa who intermittently engage in binge-eating (this symptom being called bulimia); and (3) individuals with bulimia (the syndrome) who are not underweight and are therefore not anorexic. Movement from one condition to another is possible and quite common, usually occurring in the direction of category (1) upward. Many former victims of anorexia become bulimic. Occasionally the reverse will occur, with an individual afflicted with bulimia losing substantial weight and then being diagnosed as having anorexia nervosa. These distinctions will in all likelihood prove to be important. We hope to see an improvement in terminology in the future. This is not to say that other terms have not been used to describe the bulimic condition — quite the contrary. Over the years, authors have coined and used a variety of terms such as bulimia nervosa, bulimia syndrome, bulimarexia, dysorexia, the gorging-purging syndrome, and secondary anorexia. Until the 1970s, however, bulimia was usually considered to be symptomatic of anorexia nervosa and was not recognized as a separate entity. The Third Edition of the *Diagnostic and Statistical Manual of Mental Disorders,* published in 1980, officially designated bulimia as the term of choice and established it as a separate eating disorder. Yet even the standards set forth by the DSM-III are problematical and need redefinition. Note that anorexics who experience episodes of binge-eating fit all the diagnostic criteria established for bulimia except the last one: that the bulimic episodes are not due to anorexia nervosa! This means that any individual with early anorexia symptoms and binge-eating episodes would be diagnosed as bulimic until an extreme weight loss had been attained. Likewise, anorexics in the process of gaining weight may graduate into the bulimic state. Thus we can find individuals moving from one diagnosis to another.

The controversy over the relationship between anorexia nervosa and bulimia is far from settled. Some authorities in the field see the two disorders as fundamentally different and requiring different treatment approaches despite the similar behavior patterns. Others view the disorders as related, emerging from the same origins. The inconsistency in use of terms, lack of separation between the disorders historically, and different views of the illness have confounded research and hindered the development of treatment as well.

INCIDENCE

We have far more knowledge about anorexia than about bulimia, since bulimia has only recently been recognized as a separate entity and attended to by mental health professionals. Yet it is bulimia that is more widespread. Although its actual incidence has not been clearly established, evidence exists that bulimia is alarmingly prevalent, certainly far more so than anorexia. Craig Johnson, director of an eating-disorder treatment program at Michael Reese Hospital in Chicago, estimates that up to 20 percent of the college population fit the bulimia criteria, based on results of a study Johnson and a colleague conducted. In 1976 a study was also conducted at the University of Pennsylvania: half of the women in the sample reported using laxatives to control weight and 14 percent engaged in induced vomiting. The National Association of Anorexia Nervosa and Associated Disorders (ANAD) estimates that between 20 and 30 percent of college women engage in bulimic behavior.

While bulimia predominantly affects females, the disorder is not peculiar to women. According to ANAD statistics, 5 to 10 percent of bulimia's victims are male. As one might expect, many of these men are involved in sports or professions in which weight plays an important role, such as wrestling. Induced vomiting might seem, for example, to be a relatively innocuous trick for meeting weight requirements, but in vulnerable individuals, this behavior can trigger a vicious cycle which becomes a trap for the victim. Together, these statistics indicate that thousands of college students today struggle with the disorder. While some of these individuals may temporarily experiment with bulimic behaviors without becoming full-fledged bulimics, clearly many others do develop a long-term, serious problem. At the University of Washington, researchers found that 5.4 percent of all women coming to the psychiatric clinic were initially diagnosed as having bulimia. Researchers saw this as a conservative estimate of the actual incidence, since therapists discovered other cases with initial problems of a different nature. Many women, for example, sought help for their depression rather than for the over-eating which could accompany it. Then, of course, many individuals needing care may not approach the psychiatric clinic for help at all. A great deal of shame and secrecy may attach to bulimia in a way that precludes one's seeking professional help. Additionally, lack of public information regarding the disorder and its treatment certainly reduces the likelihood of an individual's seeking help for it. Why seek help for a problem which society says doesn't exist? Moreover, if treatment is not available or is not known to be available, the logical conclusion for the victim to make is that he or she is alone in this affliction.

A case in point took place after an article on eating disorders and an interview with one of the authors appeared in a local newspaper. The following day we received a long-distance telephone call from an older woman who had suffered with bulimia for nearly 30 years. Until reading the newspaper article, this women had assumed that she was a freak and that no one else had ever experienced such a bizarre problem. During her years of bulimia, this woman had seen several doctors for treatment of the physical complications which resulted from purging. However, she never directly told the doctors what she did that led to these complications and, in fact, may not have totally recognized the relationship herself. Her doctors were baffled about why she continued to have these internal problems. She alluded several times to the fact that she "had trouble eating," but her doctor unwittingly brushed aside this cue with the comment "You look okay to me," meaning that she did not look undernourished or obese. The matter was dropped.

The woman consulted a psychiatrist for her depression and low self-esteem, but the eating disorder was never addressed there either. When asked if she had told the psychiatrist about her eating behavior, the woman replied, "Oh, yes. Well, not exactly. I dropped a lot of hints, but he never said anything about them. I thought if something like this existed in other people, he would have known and told me about it. After that I just couldn't bring myself to tell him exactly what was happening; it would have been just too humiliating." This woman's approach is not unusual. Bulimics are not known for their directness or assertion skills! Moreover, they do not look ill. Alertness, followed by matter-of-fact investigation, is generally required for the recognition of bulimia.

Our own experience in the university setting bears this suspicion out. Five years ago anorexia and bulimia were virtually unknown on our particular campuses. Students at our schools apparently did not experience these problems. Then one day two young women came into the counseling center very concerned about their roommate who had been steadily losing weight, had become withdrawn, and seemed very depressed. The young women were afraid their roommate might have cancer or some other horrible disease. The roommate denied that anything was wrong with her, but at a height of 5 feet 10 inches, she weighed less than 100 pounds. She claimed to feel fat. The roommates were perplexed and fearful for her life — she looked to them as if she might die. They knew something was wrong but had no idea of what or of how they could get her help. This emaciated student provided our first direct confrontation with anorexia nervosa. Needless to say, she also provided a great deal of motivation to learn as much about the illness as possible.

After scouring the literature and becoming more familiar with eating disorders, we found ourselves recognizing other cases of anorexia and bulimia that were right under our noses. We simply had not been aware of the problem. As we began to see other students with these types of eating problems, however, another need surfaced. People around the victims were also being impacted by the illness and needed support in dealing with the afflicted individual. In residence halls, for instance, roommates, floor members, student resident assistants, and residence hall directors were all very concerned about the possibility of doing or saying the wrong thing and being responsible in some way for making the bulimic's or anorexic's situation worse; they wondered how to help the student with the illness, and so forth.

The needs of these other people resulted in development of in-service programs, particularly for residence hall and health center staff who were in key positions to become aware of individuals who might be experiencing such problems. As staff people at the university became aware of eating disorders, they also began to recognize the warning signs for what they were. Bags of vomit in trash cans, for instance, did not necessarily mean that someone was just weird or had an un-ending case of the flu. This new staff awareness generated a number of appropriate referrals to the counseling center.

Likewise, after local newspaper articles were published or presen-tations made to various groups concerning eating disorders, we would be beseiged with telephone calls from students and nonstudents si-lently suffering from one of these eating disorders, usually bulimia. We must emphasize that had we not spoken out publicly or had we waited until we were "experts" before doing so, we might still be under the mistaken impression that such a problem did not exist at our schools!

We know that bulimia affects a much greater number of people than we once realized. Exactly how many people are affected re-mains as yet unclear. The shame and secrecy associated with bulimia are of such magnitude that even anonymous questionnaires are not always truthfully answered. Afflicted individuals are even less likely to consult health or mental health professionals directly. The hidden nature of the disorder precludes referrals by friends or family since the victims do not look sick and certainly do not voluntarily share their "secret." A lack of awareness and understanding on the part of professionals compounds the problem, and treatment is often inac-cessible. This state of affairs makes it extremely difficult to assess the true incidence of bulimia.

Age

Bulimia usually begins in late adolescence or the early twenties. The most frequent age of onset is said to be 18 years, a time when most people are under a great deal of pressure to make major life decisions and transitions. However, bulimia can also occur at younger ages. Research indicates that bulimia generally begins between the ages of 15 and 18 years (Pyle, Mitchell, and Eckert, 1981). Some college students we have seen report previous anorexic-like behavior at a younger age. Then, under parental pressure to eat, these individuals resort to bulimic behavior instead. This seems to them to be the perfect solution: a way to have their cake and not have it, too.

The age of onset does not seem to be a prognostic indicator as it is with anorexia. In anorexia, the younger the patient, the easier the recovery is thought to be. This is not necessarily the case with bulimia. In fact, in some clinicians' experiences, the reverse seems to be true; there seems to be more difficulty in treating young adolescents who are still living at home than those who are old enough to live independently (Pyle, personal communication). As yet, prognosis on the basis of age remains largely a matter of conjecture.

CAUSES

Probably one of the most repeatedly asked questions is, Why do people ever develop something like bulimia? Unfortunately, the answer to that question, like so many others, is not known. Most of what was said in Chapter 1 about the genesis of anorexia is thought to be true of bulimia as well. Low self-esteem, a combination of societal emphases on slimness and success particularly as related to women, certain family characteristics and dynamics, and presence of stressful life situations with an accompanying lack of appropriate coping skills, deficits in autonomy and assertiveness, and various biological considerations — all appear to play important roles (Boskind-Lodahl, 1976; Mitchell et al., 1982). Weight loss appears to be a major factor in the development of bulimia (Pyle at al., 1981) and is the most apparent precursor to the disorder. Some researchers speculate that a destructive diet may cause malnutrition or depression which in turn triggers bulimia. However, some bulimic women claim to have dieted sensibly, while others have started bingeing and vomiting after weight loss due to surgery or illness, and still others have begun the behavior after being treated for chemical dependency (and maintaining sobriety; Goff, personal communication).

The psychoanalytic model views both eating disorders, anorexia and bulimia, as results of a sex role conflict. The anorexic may be rejecting femininity and the bulimic may be overly identifying with femininity. Some authors feel that bulimia originates basically from a desire to give way to sexual impulses combined with a fear of losing control.

A fear of rejection is also frequently discussed as a source of bulimic symptoms. Perceived or actual rejection by the opposite sex may precipitate the onset of the disorder (Boskind-Lodahl, 1976; Pyle et al., 1981).

Marlene Boskind-Lodahl White (1976), who began to study and treat the disorder in 1974, views it from a feminist perspective. She states that ". . . these women have already learned a passive and accommodating approach to life from their parents and their culture. This accommodation is combined with two opposing tensions: the desperate desire for self-validation from a man, and an inordinate *fear of men* and their power to reject" (p. 354).* The bulimic is seen as surrendering her personal power to men, as defining herself and her success by the approval and love of a male. Naturally this has implications in the sexual arena, an area of particular vulnerability. Wanting desperately to please the men in their lives yet not believing in their ability to do so, female bulimics experience strong sexual conflict. However, this conflict is not viewed by Boskind-Lodahl as a rejection of femininity, but rather as a fear of sexual rejection, of "not being good enough to please a man."

The four males treated by Boskind-Lodahl (1976) displayed similar characteristics:

1. They expressed low self-esteem; feelings of inadequacy and helplessness.
2. They were extremely dependent passive individuals who tried to please parents through academic achievement.
3. They felt fearful and inadequate with women, were unable to sustain relationships, and had been rejected in adolescence by a female.
4. They described their parents as extremely repressive.

A clinical study by Casper et al. (1980) suggests that lack of control over a strong appetite might contribute to the development of bulimia. However, the authors point out that the strong appetite is not related to hunger alone. While bulimics may be more conscious of hunger than are other individuals, appetite is not necessarily the driving force behind their bingeing, since bingeing often occurs when hunger is not experienced — bingeing thus occurs in relation to other stress instead. Patients in the Casper study, as well as clients of ours, report

*Reproduced with permission from Boskind-Lodahl, Signs 2:2(1976) pp. (342-356) © The University of Chicago Press.

that overeating relieves upsetting emotions or thoughts as well. Kim Chernin (1981) reflects upon her own experience with bulimia: "Many of life's emotions from loneliness to rage, . . . can be felt as appetite . . . . Standing in front of the refrigerator, I realized that my hunger was for larger things, for identity, for creativity, for power, for a meaningful place in society" (p. 39).*

While we know that bulimics are, for example, plagued by a diminished sense of self, an underlying fear of rejection, and a fear of being unable to resolve their problems in any effective way, we also know other poeple, similarly troubled, who do not develop bulimia in response to these problems — perhaps they become alcoholic or are afflicted with other psychological maladies. Bulimia's determining factors are, as yet, unclear. Researchers generally accept, though, that bulimia like anorexia is a complex disorder unlikely to erupt from any single cause. Most likely the interplay of a number of factors is involved in bulimia's development, but these factors have yet to be definitely identified.

PSYCHOLOGICAL ASPECTS OF BULIMIA

Bingeing and purging are used, among other things, as mechanisms for escaping negative feelings and stressful situations. It is important to note that the bulimic individual is not usually aware of these feelings, particularly while she is engaged in the binge-purge cycle. Thus one of the challenges of therapy is heightening the client's awareness of feelings so that the underlying needs might be identified and addressed.

In fact, some practitioners claim that as long as clients still engage in bulimic behavior, what they do feel is not "real" at all; that is, true feelings have been diverted and distorted to such a degree by the bulimic behavior that they are no longer recognizable. Instead, bulimics' attention and energy are usurped by feelings which are byproducts of the binge-purge cycle (food-related relief, guilt, anger, etc.). Some counselors contend that only during abstinence from bingeing-purging can clients begin to experience authentic responses to situations in their lives. As one recovering bulimic stated, "I didn't become aware of any emotions until I tried to stop it [bulimia]."

---

*Reprinted with permission from *The Obsession,* by Kim Chernin, © 1981 by Kim Chernin. Published by Harper & Row, Inc., New York, N.Y.

Therapeutically then, we must keep in mind that abstinence creates a special vulnerability and a consequent need for much support.

The bingeing and purging cycle plays a primary role in the lives of bulimia victims. While this cycle may disgust even the bulimic, it is also clung to and cherished. It becomes very comfortable. For one thing, the cycle provides structure and takes up time. In our experience, clients with bulimia face free time with trepidation. Bingeing and purging provide a structure for managing that time. Thus, other decisions do not have to be made; people do not have to be dealt with. Moreover, many bulimics report the behavior as extremely reinforcing in and of itself. The behavior can be a way of relaxing. In fact, invitations to participate in other activities are often declined in order to preserve the opportunity to binge.

To digress for a moment, we might add that if an individual has decided that he or she wants to indulge in bingeing and purging, anything which interferes with this decision can be extremely upsetting. At the university, for example, students on meal contracts are free to eat as much as they choose, and mealtimes are flexible. Commonly, those students with bulimia choose to eat alone and at times when traffic is slow in the dining area. In this way, such individuals can eat as much as they want without attracting attention and can hit the bathroom immediately afterwards to throw up in solitude — or at least without friends listening. If, however, someone should attempt to join them at this meal, the bulimics might well be thoroughly enraged by the intrusion. Similarly, if something interferes with the act of throwing up afterwards, the individuals are panic stricken.

One interesting and rather humorous situation has occurred as a result of this consistent desire for secretiveness. The dining hall on one of our campuses has several quite private dining niches set apart from the other tables. Naturally, these niches are very popular among the bulimic population and a veritable race for these favored spots can result! While the competition for niches and the accompanying hostility can become quite intense, another fascinating development has taken place. We have had students show up at the Counseling Center for help as a result of being intercepted at the pass, so to speak, by some of our clients who have begun the path to recovery. These recovering clients often clearly recognize other students as being bulimic (even though they may have never spoken to one another) by the telltale nervousness, the way in which food is approached, the amount of food taken, the seating chosen, and so forth.

For some individuals, the bulimia seems almost to take on a life of its own, operating not only in response to stress but also as an independent habit. Times arise when the behavior is not planned or thought about, but merely done. On campus, some of the common triggers are candy machines or shops that sell sweets. Our students report spontaneous bulimic episodes which are spurred not by hunger or stressful events, but by habit — which brings us to our next point.

A striking similarity exists between bulimia and chemical dependency. Gretchen Goff of the University of Minnesota's Outpatient Psychiatry Department proposes that bulimia be viewed as an obsessive fear of fatness combined with an addiction to food. The renowned Dr. Arthur Crisp of England sees binge-eating as an addiction also — a carbohydrate addiction requiring ever increasing amounts of carbohydrates and resulting in both physical and psychological dependence.

While we are not aware of any definitive evidence of physical dependency, we do find the addiction model quite useful in understanding and treating bulimia. In *How Much is Too Much: Healthy Habits or Destructive Addictions,* a paperback gem by Stanton Steele, the author describes addiction as a "habit gone out of control" (p. xii) and asserts that one susceptibility to addiction is a "readiness to believe in magical solutions to problems. A magical solution is one which cannot affect the actual situation, but which reassures the person none the less" (p. 17). The magical solution for the anorexic is losing weight. For the bulimic it is eating without gaining weight. The characteristics of an addictive experience as set forth by Steele are as follows:

1. It eradicates awareness . . . of what is hurting or troubling him . . . .
2. It hurts other involvements . . . the person then turns increasingly toward the experience as his one source of gratification in life . . . .
3. It lowers self-esteem . . . .
4. It is not pleasurable . . . . There is nothing pleasurable about the addiction cycle . . . what is "pleasurable" about addiction is the *absence* of feelings and thoughts that lead to pain . . . .
5. It is predictable . . . [providing] a sureness of effect. (pp. 5–6)

Steele goes on to state that an addiction exists when a person is no longer able to make choices.

Bulimia clearly fulfills Steele's criteria for an addiction. First, the binge-purge cycle temporarily wards off the pain, anxiety, and consciousness of the person's immediate problem. When a potentially upsetting situation occurs, a bulimic turns to food to ward off the anxiety that this situation would otherwise cause. For the bulimic, this turning to food usually entails more than the sole act of eating. A whole sequence of events is activated and the immediate problem is temporarily blocked out. First, the food must be obtained. Next, a place — preferably a private place — must be found in which to eat this food. The food is then rapidly consumed, usually with little or no enjoyment. Then, for vomiters, a place must be found to eliminate the eaten food. The regurgitation also makes it possible for the individual to gorge further. Guilt and self-disgust set in and often spur the repeat of the cycle. In an academic setting, for example, exams nearly always trigger episodes of bingeing and purging, the bulimic's "magical solution." Intense anxiety sets in over the upcoming tests. The student binges to combat the anxiety, then throws up to at least in part allay anxiety over weight gain. As a result of this diversion from studying, the student is now further behind in course work. This leads to increased anxiety which leads to further overeating, and so on. Only after going through this cycle anywhere from one to a number of times does the student finally get down to studying.*

Besides allowing the individual to escape the primary problem at hand, bulimia fulfills Steele's second criterion for the addictive experience: namely, hurting other involvements. The binge-purge cycle consumes a tremendous amount of energy and time. Life for the individual becomes increasingly food oriented, and binge-purging soon comes to take priority over all else, including close relationships, school, jobs, budgetary considerations, health, honesty, etc. In many cases, bulimic students must drop out of college because they have no time or energy left for studying. The preoccupation with food and weight may also grow to the point of making study impossible even when the time is available. The bulimic "habit" also requires money. Overdrawn checking accounts and financial difficulties are not unusual occurrences. Although bulimics tend to be highly principled in general, stealing is common (usually for the purpose of acquiring food).

---

*Vomiting also allows the individuals to continue functioning (i.e., take the exam). A binge without vomiting can render some individuals physically unable to take an exam. As ability to vomit is developed, the bingeing increases in size and usually in frequency as well.

People have lost jobs and have gone bankrupt as a result of bulimia. One woman earning $40,000 per year was forced to declare bankruptcy because of her $100 per day food bill. Another was unable to hold a job because her time at work was spent eating and trying to borrow money from fellow workers.

Health considerations are specifically attended to later in this chapter, but the point is appropriate here as well that bulimia certainly has a negative impact upon the physical health of its victims.

Relationships with other people also suffer. While bulimics tend to be more extroverted than their anorexic counterparts who are not bulimic, their relationships nevertheless tend to be superficial and lack genuineness. They are adept at distancing themselves from people even while seeming to be very friendly and sociable. The bulimic's underlying fear and belief is, "If this person really gets to know me, he or she won't like me."

The secretiveness associated with bulimia leads to dishonesty even in primary relationships. For instance, women report dreaming up excuses to get rid of boyfriends or spouses long enough to engage in binge-vomiting episodes. The typical lack of assertiveness and the avoidance of dealing with negative feelings further impede the bulimic's development of close, intimate relationships. Additionally, the constant preoccupation with food intrudes. It is difficult to participate in conversations, for example, when all one can think about is food. A comment or two may be thrown into conversation occasionally so that the preoccupation won't be so obvious, but often conversation has little meaning for the bulimic individual.

The more frequently bulimic behavior is engaged in, the more entrenched it seems to become as a strong, and perhaps sole, source of gratification in one's life. The individual's range of alternatives for dealing with problems and anxieties becomes narrowly restricted to this one mode of avoidance (which may in turn be combined with some form of substance abuse, such as alcoholism). Clearly then, bulimia affects other areas of its victims' lives in a negative way and fulfills the second criterion for addiction.

Thirdly, self-esteem takes a dive as the bulimic sees that she cannot stop doing something that hurts her. This particular disorder/addiction is also viewed as weird or disgusting by the victim herself, which leads to even more guilt and self-hate, thus decreasing self-respect even further.

Fourthly, bulimia is not a pleasurable affliction. While bulimics certainly like food, they do not generally take real pleasure in the food consumed during a binge. There is no active savoring of it. In our experience, most report that the food is so rapidly consumed that it is not even tasted.* As one woman reported, "After the first bite or two, it could be cardboard and it wouldn't matter." Certainly nothing is innately pleasurable about purging either, although purging is clearly anxiety and guilt reducing for bulimics.

Moreover, in our society we eat for reasons other than sustenance. The eating ritual has tremendous social overtones: we share food with friends, we celebrate with food, and so forth. However, the victim of bulimia binges in isolation. The victim experiences no sense of joy in what she consumes or eliminates — relief, perhaps, but never joy. We must interject here that we have seen several cases of bulimic roommates who did, in fact, binge together. It was their "secret." However, most of these relationships deteriorated as the two individuals began to compete with each other and resent one another.

Finally, bulimia generally provides a predictable experience. There is no uncertainty or risk of failure.† It is private and the effect is known. The person faces no need to deal with the confusion that the rest of the world presents. A comment by a former victim of the disorder illustrates this predictability:

You know exactly what you are going to do. You might not feel good about getting up and throwing up, but you know you're safe. You're going to get up and that's what you are going to do; and that's what you're going to do all day long. You might be uncomfortable with it, but you are also comfortable with it.

There is security in the known.

This leads us to two other qualities we have frequently observed in conjunction with bulimia and anorexia: inflexibility and a tendency to overdo things. The way in which these eating-disordered individuals often approach exercise and academic work, for example, also takes on the attributes of addiction. Steele (1981) states,

---

*Since fasting or dieting usually precedes the binge, the binge is reinforced by a real need for food.
†Some anxiety may be experienced by those who are not yet proficient at vomiting and are unsure that they will be able to regurgitate the food.

As an addictive involvement deepens, it becomes less enjoyable. This does not lessen the strength of the person's attachment to the involvement because the addict's goal is not pleasure but constancy. He is seeking primarily to have the same experience every time. We know this not only because he does not want — in fact, he eschews — variation, but because he engages in the activity more as a way of avoiding other things than because of its intrinsic value. Chief among the things he is avoiding is the sense of inadequacy. (p. 28)

The self-imposed exercise and study regimens which some bulimics and most anorexics put themselves through certainly reflect the qualities of addictive involvements. The regimens tend to be rigid and joyless compulsions which cannot be eliminated without panic. The behaviors are not comfortably varied to fit circumstances, mood, or the needs of others: they are designed to elicit admiration and to insure a successful image. However, the eating-disordered individuals themselves remain unconvinced and self-dissatisfied.

Because study and exercise are both socially acceptable — and even desirable — activities, the excessiveness of such behavior might easily be overlooked. Furthermore, clients may tend to downplay the extent of their involvement with these activities. A "few exercises" may in actuality be several hours worth; not getting "any studying done" may mean cutting back an hour or so. It is imperative for the therapist to discover how the individual approaches these other activities so that the addictive tendencies can be countered and a healthy approach to life fostered.

Substance abuse (especially alcohol, barbiturates, and amphetamines) has been noted by many to be frequently associated with bulimia.* In a study done at the University of Minnesota Adult Outpatient Psychiatric Clinic, bulimic women reported using alcohol for the purposes of avoiding the depression associated with the binge-purging, to relax, and to delay or prevent overeating (Pyle, Mitchell, and Eckert, 1981). Goff (unpublished manuscript) theorizes that the two behaviors (substance abuse and binge-purging) reinforce one another and furthermore "create a new and more destructive syndrome of their

---

*Alcoholism and drug abuse have been noted as affecting 25 to 40 percent of the bulimic population as compared to 10 percent of the rest of the population (Banaszynski, 1981).

own" (p. 11). She emphasizes the need to address both of these "addictions" in treatment lest the client retreat further into one upon giving up the other. The area of substance abuse by bulimics is only beginning to be systematically studied, certainly, research in this area carries weighty implications for chemical dependency treatment centers.

We must point out that bulimia exists in varying degrees of severity. One person might spend much of the day engaged in bingeing and purging, perhaps even awakening at night to do more of the same; another may resort to binge-purging only once or twice a week or only upon going home for visits. If left untreated, however, one can generally assume that bulimia will become progressively worse.

The presence of bulimia does not imply that normal eating never occurs. Occasionally, periods — maybe even weeks or months — of "normal eating" and/or fasting are interspersed with the binges. For some, so-called normal eating becomes equated with living "perfectly": exercising perfectly, studying or working perfectly, eating perfectly. The requirements for perfection vary from person to person. Eating perfectly for one may mean ingesting very small amounts of low calorie food, not eating between meals, and absolutely consuming no sweets. For another (healthier), a well-balanced three-meal day, including a fruit snack, might be allowed. The point is that no slips are allowed by the bulimic and that even one slip, whether an unplanned handful of popcorn, missing a class, or a distressing encounter with another person, can upset the whole apple cart and trigger another bulimic episode. For such people, only two modes of living exist — the "perfect" mode and the "bulimic" mode.

A variety of methods may be employed to manage weight: appropriate eating, dieting, exercise, fasting, saunas, diuretics, laxatives, vomiting, amphetamines, chewing without swallowing (spitting the food out), and so forth. When do these behaviors become pathological? Certainly one of the keys to this question is the issue of control. Is the person in control of the behavior, or is the behavior in control of the person? The overall effect upon the person needs to be assessed. Steele suggests raising additional questions similar to the following:

1. Is the behavior compulsive or is real satisfaction present?
2. Does it have negative consequences?
3. Is there flexibility — can the behavior be varied in response to physical conditions, scheduling changes, or mood?

4. Can it be modified to meet the needs of others?
5. Can it be eliminated without panic?

We are probably not yet even aware of the full spectrum of eating disorders. Anorexia and bulimia have only recently come to the attention of most counselors and therapists. Of the two, anorexia is the more familiar. We have only begun to *recognize* bulimia, let alone untangle its mysteries. In clinical settings, other atypical eating problems surface as well. A significant number of people do not fit the criteria for either anorexia or bulimia, yet experience similar problems — people such as those who are extremely preoccupied with food and weight and have many other characteristics in common with anorexics and/or bulimics but who have not yet indulged in the extreme behavior. These people have a psychological focus on food but do not display the overt behaviors.

It is vital that we see the individual rather than the category or diagnosis. We must ask what purpose this way of thinking or behavior serves for this *particular* individual, and must not overly concern ourselves with whether or not the person fits exactly the designated criteria for diagnosis.

Regarding this discretion in diagnosis, we must make mention of a current trend spreading across college campuses called "pigging out." As we understand it, this event is a group social activity — a throwback to ancient Roman orgies. The goal is to gorge as much as possible, then induce vomiting in order to make room for further gorging. This phenomenon is quite different from bulimia, since the circumstances and reasons for it are not at all the same. "Pigging out" is a social trend like cramming a crowd of people into a telephone booth or swallowing goldfish. One of the authors overheard a conversation that went something like this:

"We went and pigged out last night. Boy, did we eat."
"Did you get rid of it?"
"Yes."
"Good girl."

No secretiveness, shame, or guilt is involved with this activity. It doesn't impact any other area of the person's life. The individual manifests no preoccupation with weight or food in general. The behavior takes place only in the group setting and with group approval. This is bizarre activity certainly, but it is not bulimia. This does not imply that such activity is totally harmless. In fact, such behavior is potentially dangerous for those who are vulnerable to developing an eating disorder — and we are seeing cases of this happening — but we can't assume that everyone who participates in this "pigging out" activity is a victim of bulimia. Again, we reiterate the importance of assessing each case individually to determine the function that such behavior serves.

PHYSICAL EFFECTS OF BULIMIA

The toll bulimia takes is a heavy one. In addition to psychological considerations such as depression, which is very common and of course entails the risk of suicide, bulimia causes other physical side effects. Laxative abuse can damage the colon and can inhibit the ability to evacuate naturally. Frequent vomiting may result in tears in the esophagus and hiatal hernias, although this is rare. Urinary infections and impaired kidney function have been reported. More commonly, bulimia leads to chronic indigestion, facial puffiness, swollen glands, bloodshot eyes, irregular menstrual periods, sore throats, and myriad dental problems. Dry, tender skin and lethargy may also occur, and EEG abnormalities have been reported in association with bulimia. Callouses on the fingers and hands have been noted from inducing vomiting, although this is not frequent. Overloading the stomach may result in its overexpansion, which could cause stomach rupture. A binge consisting of sugary foods followed by vomiting can result in a dive in blood sugar due to an insulin dump reaction.

Of special concern are the fluid and electrolyte abnormalities that result from vomiting and laxative/diuretic abuse. Since these are internal effects not readily recognizable by the observer and since bulimics tend to be close to normal body weight, they do not appear ill. Consequently, physiological imbalances, which are both common and potentially life endangering, are easily overlooked until they progress in severity to the point of the individual's collapse. For this reason, we recommend that a medical assessment be carried out, including urine and blood tests.

While it is important to keep these considerations in mind, we do not want to be alarmists. A friend and colleague of ours binge-vomited for 28 years. Although she required extensive dental work and experienced weakness, dehydration, and aching jaws, she was able to function fairly well throughout those 28 years. Even in the grips of chronic bulimia, she maintained reasonable health and gave birth to four healthy children! (We might add that she has been free of bulimia for several years now.)

Although this woman escaped the serious health effects previously detailed, critical complications can and do occur. Therefore, it is important to educate victims and alert them to symptoms which can indicate imbalances, dehydration, and a need for medical attention (see Chapter 1). Also, measures the individuals can take to counteract these deficiencies should be spelled out.

If bulimic behavior is not accompanied by the usual associated characteristics, a referral to a physician is in order since it is imperative to examine for other disorders which might be confused with bulimia — disorders such as frontal lobe tumors, parkinsonism, schizophrenia, partial complex seizure, hypothalamic tumors, encephalitis, Kleine-Levin syndrome, or Huntington's chorea.

TABLE 2-1. Comparison of Bulimia and Anorexia.*

Anorexia	Bulimia
1. Refusal to maintain recommended minimal weight	1. Normal or near-normal weight • May be overweight
2. Afflicts younger age agoup	2. Afflicts older age group
3. Loss of menstrual period	3. Menstrual period may or may not be lost; irregularities common
4. Distorted body image common	4. Usually don't have a distorted body image
5. The existence of a food-related problem is generally denied	5. Eating is recognized as being abnormal
6. More self-control	6. More impulsivity • Alcohol and drug abuse common
7. Anemia and vitamin deficiencies rare	7. Anemia and vitamin deficiencies uncommon but not as rare
8. Vomiting less pervasive	8. Greater incidence of vomiting and other purging behavior
9. Eating rituals	9. Generally appear to eat in a normal manner when not bingeing and when eating in public
10. 4–25% mortality rate	10. Mortality rate undetermined

*Very little research attention has been given to the occurrence of bulimia in the normal weight individual. Research activity has just recently commenced in this area. Therefore, most of our information regarding the syndrome of bulimia is extremely tentative.

TABLE 2-2. Red Flags for Bulimia.

1. Excessive concern about weight
2. Strict dieting followed by eating binges
3. Frequent overeating, especially when distressed
4. Bingeing on high calorie, sweet food*
5. Expressing guilt or shame about eating
6. Being secretive about binges and vomiting
7. Planning binges or opportunities to binge
8. Feeling out of control
9. Disappearing after a meal
10. Depressive moods

*We have also had clients who binge on salads or other foods.

REFERENCES

Andersen, A. Psychiatric aspects of bulimia. *Directions in Psychiatry,* Lesson 14:1–7 (1981).

Banaszynski, J. Bulimia — self destructing victims use food for naught. *Minneapolis Tribune* (July 5, 1981).

Bennett, W. and Gurin, J. Do diets really work? *Science* 82:42–50 (March 1982).

Boskind-Lodahl, M. Cinderella's stepsisters: a feminist perspective in anorexia nervosa and bulimia. *Journal of Women in Culture and Society* 2(2):342–356 (1976).

Boskind-Lodahl, M. and Sirlin, J. The gorging-purging syndrome. *Psychology Today* 50–52 (March 1977).

Casper, R. C., Eckert, E. D., Halmi, K. A., Goldberg, S. C., and Davis, J. M. Bulimia: Its incidence and clinical importance in patients with anorexia nervosa. *Archives of General Psychiatry,* 37:1030–1035 (Sept. 1980).

Chernin, K. How women's diets reflect fear of power. *New York Times Magazine* 38 (October 11, 1981).

Chernin, K. *The Obsession: Reflections on the Tyranny of Slenderness.* Harper and Row, 1981.

Diagnostic and Statistical Manual of Mental Disorders, 3rd ed. American Psychiatric Association, 1981.

Eating binges. *Time* 94 (November 17, 1980).

Goff, G. M. Bulimia: status and considerations of health care (unpublished manuscript, 1980).

Keys, A., Brozek, J., Henschell, A., Mickelsen, O., and Taylor, H. L. *The Biology of Human Starvation,* Vols. 1 and 2. Minneapolis: University of Minnesota Press, 1950.

Lucas, A. Bulimia and vomiting syndrome. *Contemporary Nutrition* 6(4):1981.

Lucas, A.   When friends or parents ask about "pigging out." *Journal of the American Medical Association* **247**(1):82 (1981).

Lucas, A. R.   Pigging out. *Journal of the American Medical Association* **247**(1): 82 (1982).

Mitchell, J. and Pyle, R.   The bulimic syndrome in normal weight individuals: a review. *International Journal of Eating Disorders* 61–73 (1982).

Pyle, R. L., Mitchell, J. E., and Eckert, E. D.   Bulimia: a report of 34 cases. *Journal of Clinical Psychiatry* **42**:60–64 (February 1981).

Rosen, J.   Bulimia nervosa: treatment with exposure and response prevention. *Behavior Therapy* **13**:117–124 (1982).

Steele, S.   *How Much is Too Much.*   Englewood Cliffs, New Jersey: Prentice-Hall, 1981.

Van, J.   Binge and bust: an eating phenomenon. *Chicago Tribune* (Sunday, October 25, 1981).

3
Therapeutic Approaches

A variety of treatment modalities have been used successfully in the treatment of eating disorders. However, the development of treatment strategies is in its infancy, and agreement has yet to be reached on the optimal treatment techniques.

Research that has been done to date makes a comparison of treatment methods difficult. Because of the newness of the field, the criteria which have been used both for diagnosis and for recovery have not been consistent. Additionally, follow-up studies which have been carried out regarding treatment outcome for anorexia have taken place over varying lengths of time. The short-term follow-ups, such as those of six months, indicate higher recovery rates than the long-term follow-ups of two or more years. We cannot attribute this difference to the mode of treatment alone; the passage of time may be a significant factor. Characteristics of the subjects under study also vary widely. Some researchers have been highly selective regarding the clients they choose to treat, while others have included in treatment outcome studies the most difficult, intractable cases for whom other treatment programs have failed. Research on treatment for bulimia remains virtually nonexistent. Issues such as these make meaningful evaluations and comparisons between treatment methods difficult. Fortunately, current research efforts are underway which take factors such as these into consideration.

Major Treatment Approaches

The major approaches utilized in the treatment of anorexia nervosa and bulimia are hospitalization, individual psychotherapy, family therapy, and group therapy. Medication, self-help groups, and nutritional consultations are adjunctive to the primary forms of treatment.

Our presentation in this chapter will address the treatment of anorexia neryosa and bulimia separately. However, much of the section on anorexia can be applied to bulimia as well.

TREATMENT OF ANOREXIA NERVOSA

Initially, nutritional rehabilitation is necessary and of primary concern in the treatment of anorexia nervosa. Several ways exist to restore adequate nutrition. The method of choice will depend upon the severity of the illness at the time of intervention. Generally, it is best to use the least restrictive approach that works. The client should be invited to collaborate in all decision making regarding her treatment to the greatest extent that she is capable. This requires enormous delicacy on the part of the therapist, who essentially has the awkward role of "enforcer" even while advocating choice.

In those instances in which the illness is intercepted in its early stages before weight loss is extreme, it may initially suffice:

1. to explain, or have a dietitian explain, the nutritional needs of the body and the effects of starvation (while anorexics are wizards at calorie counting, they often are unaware of actual nutritional requirements) — see Appendix H for a listing of starvation effects;
2. to explain the purposes the illness can serve, and discuss common fears and anxieties associated with the illness (in particular, discuss their fears — the relief of being understood can go a long way toward establishing rapport and trust);
3. to contract for stabilization of weight and set a limit which, if trangressed, will result in medical intervention (usually hospitalization).

Within this general framework, a wide variety of techniques might be employed to achieve these ends depending upon the orientation of the therapist.

Importantly, reassure the anorexic that you do not want to see her get fat and that care will be taken not to produce excessive or rapid weight gain; stress rather a gradual return to a target weight which the client will later be able to choose in partnership with you, the therapist. Initially, however, the goal is simply stabilization of weight. This approach leaves the individual with the freedom to choose how she will maintain her weight and where (outside or inside the hospital) — but not "if" she will maintain it. The client may or may not desire outside help to establish an eating plan for herself; this choice can be offered for her to decide. In other words, the client will be allowed to be in control of as much as she is capable. If she proves to be "out of control" and continues to lose weight, the necessary controls will be provided by others until she is able to resume the responsibility herself.

This treatment format establishes the nutritional recovery process and lays the foundation for later additional attention to normalizing eating habits, widening the choice of foods, and eventually increasing weight (versus stabilization). Concomitant attention should be given to emotional and family issues, but for the sake of simplicity, we will limit our discussion here to nutritional issues.

If, on the initial visit, the client is already quite emaciated, a decision must be made about whether she should initially be treated on an outpatient basis or immediately hospitalized.

No hard-and-fast rule holds for determining the range of allowable weight loss. The general consensus seems to be that if 15 percent of the client's original weight has been lost (including the weight she would normally have gained due to growth), she should at least be seeing a physician regularly. If the client's weight is 25 percent below what it should be, hospitalization is imperative. In the marginal and in-between ranges, therapists must use their clinical judgment in consultation with a physician. Key factors to consider when making this decision are (1) the rapidity of the weight loss (rapid weight loss being the more dangerous); (2) the presence or absence of obesity prior to weight loss (an obese individual can tolerate a greater weight loss); (3) the physical status of the individual — this must be checked by a physician and includes testing for potassium deficiency, dehydration, cardiac irregularities, etc. (see Chapter 1); and (4) the presence or absence of starvation symptoms. If the victim already suffers the cognitive and emotional effects of starvation, effective psychotherapy is impossible until those effects have been reversed.

The best that can be hoped for at this advanced stage is to establish a relationship of trust and to help the client understand the nature and effects of the disorder, as well as the necessity for hospitalization.

Hospitalization

Hospitalization provides, at the very least, separation from the family (and the ongoing struggles about eating) and from anxiety-producing stressors in the patient's life; it also ensures adequate nutritional intake. Hospitalization may additionally provide individual and/or group psychotherapy, training in coping skills which are aimed at raising self-esteem and confidence (such as assertiveness, rational thinking, relaxation techniques), and family therapy. Medication may also be employed. Additional outpatient treatment is usually necessary and provided upon discharge.

In Great Britain, the hospital regimen advocated by Dr. Arthur Crisp entails bed confinement, a 3000-calorie diet with normal amounts of carbohydrates, and a target weight appropriate for the individual patient's height at the age she *developed* anorexia nervosa. No other food is allowed beyond the 3000 calories. After the target weight is reached — usually between 8 and 12 weeks — the patient is gradually allowed to be up and about and is given increasing responsibility for her food intake and gradual weight gain. This treatment plan is coupled with individual psychotherapy, eventually including family and group therapy.

The Mayo Clinic's Residential Treatment Unit in the United States differs from this plan (as do many others) in that patients are not confined to bed and the diet tray initially provided is calculated to maintain the patient's weight upon admission. Periodically calories are increased slightly to achieve weight gain. Meals are closely supervised. As the patient improves, she moves to a different dining room where meals are served family style with the patient serving herself under gradually decreasing supervision. The patient is eventually allowed to choose a target weight within a range appropriate for her age and height. This weight must be achieved and maintained before discharge. Additionally, the patient has to eat with relative ease and without counting calories. Ongoing psychotherapy revolves around issues such as autonomy; development of a more accurate body image; recognition of, and differentiation between, internal physical sensations (such as hunger and satiation) and emotional states; as well as any other aspects of the patient's functioning.

Milieu therapy* is also incorporated into the hospital program. With patients typically remaining in the hospital from three to five months and living closely with other adolescents during this time, a good deal of experience is gained in confronting and dealing with interpersonal conflicts and issues. All of this is attended to therapeutically. Family counseling is included in this treatment plan to varying degrees and is seen as particularly critical for those patients who are returning to their original homes. After discharge, follow-up therapy continues on an outpatient basis.

In some hospitals, hyperalimentation or tube feeding may be employed with extremely severe cases. Hyperalimentation is the most drastic measure and entails inserting a catheter into the jugular vein. A solution consisting of adequate amino acids, glucose, vitamins, and electrolytes is then fed through the catheter. The jugular vein is chosen for this procedure because it empties directly into the heart and provides a sufficient volume of blood to dilute the solution as rapidly as possible. This procedure requires a physician knowledgeable about the metabolic abnormalities often present with anorexia nervosa so that such a drastic intervention can be successfully employed. Hyperalimentation is frowned upon by many medical practitioners because of possible infections and the accompanying danger of overhydration and resultant cardiovascular stress. Additionally, it has been criticized as further relegating the anorexic to the powerless state that she is so desperately attempting to escape. Most treatment centers find this intervention unnecessary as well as distasteful, although a few proponents remain. Tube feeding is a less drastic method of providing nourishment. The procedure is not pleasant and requires voluntary assistance from the patient. A tube is inserted by the physician through the nose and esophagus to the stomach. Nutrients are administered in liquid form via this route. Although the gastrointestinal tract is more functional with this approach, the patient is nonetheless put into a passive state.

As can be seen, hospitals differ in their treatment programs, and we suggest that therapists familiarize themselves with the approach taken by those hospitals nearest to them. For more detailed information

---

*Milieu therapy attempts to develop trust, assurance, and personal autonomy by providing the appropriate interpersonal contacts within the environment.

regarding these regimens and their theoretical bases, we recommend the reference works listed at the end of this chapter.

One last comment regarding hospitalization. Some workers in the field propose that hospitalization *always* be utilized in the treatment of anorexia. One author considers treating seriously ill anorexics on an outpatient basis antitherapeutic and a form of collusion with the patient's denial of her illness (Thoma, 1977). Without doubt, hospitalization makes treatment more manageable, comprehensive, and efficient – particularly when the hospital has an established program for treating eating disorders. On the other hand, research has established that recovery can also be effected in *some* cases without hospitalization. If hospitalization is deemed unnecessary, therapy can be carried out on an outpatient basis as long as the individual's condition does not deteriorate beyond the limits established.

Individual Therapy for Anorexia Nervosa

Most of the literature concerning the treatment of anorexia nervosa focuses on inpatient treatment. We have just now obtained, during the writing of this chapter, a copy of an exceptional article which addresses outpatient treatment. "A Multidimensional Psychotherapy of Anorexia Nervosa" by Garner, Garfinkel, and Bemis (1982), published in the *International Journal of Eating Disorders,** should be a "must" for all therapists encountering eating disorders.

Various types of individual psychotherapy have been applied to the treatment of anorexia. These usually depend upon the theoretical orientation and training of the therapist. The psychotherapy might be carried out on an outpatient basis or, as stated previously, as part of a hospitalization program. The aim of psychotherapy is to resolve the underlying psychological issues and to restore proper nutrition.

At one end of the psychotherapy continuum is the classical psychoanalytic approach which, while still occasionally employed, has come under fire as being singularly ineffective (Bemis, 1978; Bruch, 1973; Palazzoli, 1977). An emphasis solely on interpretation and insight without specific attention to weight has the poorest track

---

*Reprint information can be obtained from Craig Johnson, Ph.D., Editor, International Journal of Eating Disorders, Michael Reese Medical Center, Psychosomatic and Psychiatric Institute, Chicago, Ill. 60616.

record for nutritional rehabilitation. The use of interpretation with anorexics and the inactive role of the therapist are decried by critics. One of the major problems encountered here is that patients have great difficulty becoming involved in this type of treatment and leave prematurely.

One of the most widely recognized authorities on anorexia in this country, Hilde Bruch, operates out of an ego psychology framework and emphasizes a "fact-finding" and trust-building approach to treatment. Attention is given to identity issues, changing faulty self-perceptions, and improving interpersonal relationships.

Cognitive restructuring (i.e., changing thought patterns) and a variety of behavioral approaches are commonly employed in the treatment of anorexia. These approaches are generally aimed at increasing self-esteem and confidence, developing autonomy, challenging irrational or "anorexic" thinking, and teaching other coping skills. Trance therapy (free association in a trance state) has also been reported as being somewhat successful (Zeeman, 1976).

The behavior modification approach, on the other end of the continuum, focuses specifically upon weight gain for the anorexic to the exclusion of underlying psychological issues. For example, a client's gain in weight is rewarded with increased privileges and positive reinforcement. Emotional and family issues are not addressed. This approach is notable for its quick and often dramatic success in restoring weight. Unfortunately, these results are not always positive in the long run since pitfalls can be associated with rapid weight gain.* Some clients continue to gain weight and become obese, and still others resort to suicide rather than accept normal weight. A common criticism of behavior modification is that its effects do not generalize to situations outside of the treatment setting. For instance, some patients gain weight in order to be released from the hospital — so that they can once again reduce. Thus, critics claim that the cure is only temporary and may in fact exacerbate the condition. These critics believe it essential to deal with the underlying issues such as feelings of inadequacy and resentment of others' expectations, so that these issues can be resolved, and increased assertiveness and independence can be developed.

---

*Certainly not all practitioners utilizing this approach strive for rapid weight gain. Perhaps what is being criticized is the inappropriate application of behavior modification techniques.

In actual clinical practice, of course, it is the rare therapist who adheres strictly to one treatment approach alone. Most of us select, modify, and combine as we go along — incorporating those ideas and approaches which have worked for colleagues, fit into our own personal style, and address the needs of our clients. This flexibility and eclecticism appear to be critical in the treatment of anorexia nervosa. The current prevailing view regarding the development of anorexia is that it is a multidetermined disorder erupting not from any single cause, but from a combination of factors. Recent literature in the area repeatedly emphasizes the importance of implementing a multifaceted therapy approach which deals with the various aspects of the disorder (Crisp, 1980; Garner et al., 1982; Hedblom, Hubbard, and Andersen, 1981; Lucas, Duncan, and Piens, 1976).

Whatever the theoretical orientation or specific techniques employed, successful treatment programs share certain factors. Alexander Lucas et al. (1976) of the Mayo Clinic report these factors to be as follows:

1. There is one primary therapist who exerts a strong influence over the patient or there is a close-knit treatment team who use a consistent approach and who are identified by the patient as a cohesive group;
2. there is a genuine commitment to the patient, who is approached as a unique human being;
3. there is continuous long-term involvement with the patient;
4. there is understanding of both the physiological and psychological components of the disorder, and treatment ignores neither of these components; and
5. there is awareness of family and other environmental influences that help or hinder the patient's progress, and these influences are considered in the treatment plan. (p. 1034)*

One of the primary goals in the treatment of anorexia nervosa is obviously to eliminate malnutrition and normalize eating patterns. While this is certainly not the only treatment goal, the initial stage of treatment tends to be much more food related than the later stages in which a deliberate shift is made away from food and weight to issues of feelings, independence, self-defeating cognitions, and development of interpersonal skills. While a certain amount of interplay

---

*Reprinted with permission from *The American Journal of Psychiatry,* vol. **133**:9 p. 1034. © 1976 The American Psychiatric Association.

occurs among these stages, elimination of starvation factors is a prerequisite, since the starvation will itself color the victim's experiences.

The initial focus of treatment is threefold: establishing a trusting relationship, gathering information, and educating the client. Of these three, establishing a trusting relationship is clearly the most pivotal element. This relationship is central to the therapeutic process; without it, therapy cannot proceed. While this attention to relationship building may seem obvious in that it is at the heart of all psychotherapy, building the relationship can be an exceptionally challenging task with the anorexic client. These clients are noted for their moroseness and negativism, their resistance to therapy, and their ability to sabotage progress. Unlike other clients, for the most part anorexics do not want to give up their symptoms, and they perceive the therapist as an adversary. Even in the less common instances in which an individual voluntarily seeks therapy and has not assumed a hostile stance, there remains a resistance, albeit a masked one, to the recovery process. Thus we cannot overemphasize the fact that until a collaborative relationship or therapeutic alliance has been developed, the client will reject the therapist as just another one of the many individuals who are attempting to "fatten her up."

Gathering information about the client entails assessing to what degree food and weight have impaired the individual's functioning. Empathic discussion of eating patterns, preferences, rituals, obsessions, and emotions related to food intake takes place. This discussion not only will provide information but can further the development of a trusting relationship. The client's amount of exercise, vomiting, purging, or other methods of managing food should also be explored, and a baseline of food intake and purging behaviors should be obtained. Exploration of the history of the weight phobia as well as the family history and personalities, is in order. This information can also be obtained through the use of questionnaires, followed up by discussion (see Appendix G for a sample questionnaire).

Educating the client about the nature of the eating disorder (including physical and psychological effects, commonly held fears and beliefs, etc.) and the goals of treatment is another component of the initial stage of treatment. Such education enables the client to gain some understanding of what is happening to her and also demonstrates that the therapist has a sense of what the client is experiencing. Furthermore, this education gives the client some good solid information, free from the emotionality which marks so many of her interactions over this issue, and appeals to her intellect. Often it is only through this intellectual realm that collaboration with the therapist is initially possible.

Dr. Arthur Crisp of Great Britain outlines the elements of his first encounter with anorexic patients in *Anorexia Nervosa: Let Me Be.* This encounter usually takes place in an outpatient department following a meeting with the patient's parents. Crisp begins by acknowledging that the anorexic may likely see him (the therapist) as similar to, and in collusion with, her parents — as being interested only in her weight gain. Acknowledging this sets the stage for establishing oneself as separate and different from others in her life (nevertheless, there is a recurring and frustrating tendency for the client to react to the therapist "as though" he or she were someone else, usually a parent).

Crisp then describes the disorder of anorexia nervosa, some of the purposes it serves, and the typical concerns of its victims. He goes on to explore family issues — attending to alignments within the family, changes effected by the advent of the patient's puberty, the effect of other family members leaving home, and so forth. The client's fear of weight and the course it has taken are also explored. When, and under what circumstances, did the fear begin? What fluctuations in weight occurred and under what circumstances did the fear get worse? (Crisp points out that the weight phobia may be denied by some anorexics at this stage.) He presents the task at hand as being "to grow up — biologically and psychologically." This "growing up" requires normal weight for two reasons: (1) psychological change is not possible until weight is restored, and (2) biological maturation — which also requires the restoration of weight — is necessary before the problems associated with the transition to adulthood can be effectively addressed. Crisp explains to the victim that her freedom, at this point, is limited to how she manages food and weight, whereas therapy will facilitate other freedoms — those associated with feelings, relationships, and adolescence.

Discussion of the meaning low weight has to the anorexic will help identify the role it plays in this particular individual's life. For instance, in what ways might low weight help to fend off some frightening issues of adolescence? Garner et al. (1982) suggest the following question: "Although I understand that you would prefer not to gain weight, if you were to gain, at what point would you begin to experience panic?" Garner often finds the answer given to be that weight which would signal the return of menstruation and normal hormonal functioning. This response may open the door for further discussion about fears of growing up. Whatever weight is stated, it is important to ascertain what meaning the answer holds for the individual.

After some degree of trust has been established between the therapist and client, it becomes possible to explore the meaning of weight loss in the client's life and to acknowledge the fact that the loss, regardless of how much it is, is never satisfying enough and does not bring the happiness which was anticipated. The weight loss will never be good enough because *that is the nature of the illness.* While the client's weight loss has usually been rewarding in that people notice and comment upon it, the weight loss has not met the client's other needs and moreover has increasingly become the sole focus of her thoughts. The prospect of being unable to continue the weight loss becomes scarier than ever. The successful dieting which started out as a lift and a thrill with an accompanying sense of accomplishment becomes a terrifying burden — for in order to remain successful one must continue to lose weight, which grows harder to do and requires constant vigilance. While this realization by the client does not necessarily diminish the potency of weight-related issues or result in any immediate behavior changes, it does in some cases allow the individual to glimpse, often for the first time, that the promises offered by weight loss are not being realized and that, infact, she is becoming increasingly unhappy and entrapped by the very thing that was supposed to liberate her. This realization can be an important step in enabling the client to join forces, at least on some level, with the therapist. While she will probably still want to lose weight and/or avoid weight gain, through this realization she can at times begin to see the irrationality of her endeavors and to identify the "tricks" which the illness plays on her thinking.

One way to get at this fact is to ask the client what her original target weight was when she first began to diet. How did she think she would feel upon reaching this weight? What were her feelings, in fact, upon reaching it? What led her to continue to lose weight — and how much more does she believe she needs to lose? How will life be different at that weight? Usually what emerges from such questioning is the belief that people will like her more, notice her more, and that she herself will feel successful and admired for being able to accomplish that weight goal. Many people attempt to lose weight unsuccessfully. As a result of her success, attention does indeed come her way — initially in the form of "compliments" or comments, later in the form of concern over the ever downward spiral of weight loss. These experiences serve to reinforce the notion that this is the way to be noticed and to be acknowledged as a unique individual. As one college student stated, "When I was in high school I had lots of things I was good at, even though I didn't think so at the time. But now all I have is this: being thinner than everyone else. I know I'm too thin and I don't always like the way my clothes hang on me, but yet I do like it because it makes me different. If I gained weight I'd be average — just like everyone else." This "specialness" is exceedingly difficult to give up. Furthermore, the weight loss is reinforcing in and of itself, and provides a sense of mastery. It is this fact which makes the treatment of anorexia so difficult.

Once a trusting relationship has been established, the patient should become a partner in decisions and plans pertaining to weight. Garner et al. (1982) emphasize that the therapist should outline the following points:

1. The patient must be convinced that the therapist's motive is not control but the reduction of her overall suffering,
2. Low weight, seen by the anorexic as a sign of "control" must have been re-interpreted as precisely the opposite — a sign that she is *out* of control,
3. It must be understood that outpatient therapy can only proceed if the patient's weight does not fall below a certain minimum . . . . (Garner, p. 32)

If the client's weight is already dangerously low and other physical or psychological complications have set in (as discussed in Chapter 2), hospitalization is obviously necessary. The therapist's task at this point is to develop some sense of collaboration with the patient so as to make this decision, at least in some way, a joint one. The reason for hospitalization certainly needs to be explained, and the necessary reassurances must be given that this move is not designed to make her fat and that, in fact, excessive weight gain will not be allowed. Explaining what hospitalization will entail will relieve some of the anxiety associated with encountering the unknown. Often clients express fears of being with "all those crazy people" and possibly of being seen by others as "crazy" also. The client can be reassured that she is not crazy but is in need of physical care; that starvation impacts the way we think and feel, emotionally as well as physically; that everything undertaken on her behalf will be thoroughly explained; and that she will be included in the decision-making processes as much as possible and to the extent she is capable. Every effort should be made to avoid hospitalization's being misconstrued as a punitive measure or as a means of exerting control *over* her — rather it is a means of allowing her to reestablish *self*-control and regain her health. Many clients are able to see, when this is pointed out and their personal experiences are reflected upon, that they have lost their freedom in their approach to food and perhaps in other areas of their lives as well. For those who deny this, however, the fact can still be demonstrated that the client is indeed out of control — although she does not believe herself to be — by employing a strategy suggested in the Garner article. This tactic is presented as an "experiment" in which the client is to attempt to gain 2 pounds per week for two weeks to ascertain her degree of "control." "For many patients, failure will graphically illustrate that they are *not* able to force their weight up, even as a temporary measure to prevent hospitalization. At this point the focus should be to attempt to elicit trust and a sense of collaboration in the hospitalization" (Garner et al., 1982, p. 32).

Various media have recently devoted much attention to eating disorders. As a result of this publicity and heightened public awareness of the problem, clients are more often coming for treatment before the illness has advanced to the point where hospitalization is necessary. In these instances, outpatient treatment is more likely to be employed. This assumes that the victim is maintaining her weight at or above a previously agreed upon minimum. Treatment simultaneously involves providing structure and setting limits on the one hand, and encouraging freedom and independence on the other. This approach can be likened to a free society which requires a certain amount of structure lest there be chaos and resulting infringements on personal freedoms. Likewise, for the anorexic, freedom is not possible with continuing dietary chaos. The latter consumes the consciousness. One cannot be free, for example, to engage in a meaningful conversation if all one can think about is food or how one looks.

Most writers in the field suggest establishing a target weight range of 3 to 5 pounds versus a specific target weight, and explaining to the client that everyone's weight normally fluctuates to some degree and that it is unrealistic to aim for one specific number on the scale. We tell clients that people need a minimum of 1200 calories daily or the body will react negatively. If the weight they have chosen does not allow this number of calories, renegotiation is required. One cannot recover and learn to approach food normally while in a constant state of hunger.

For those clients who are troubled by binge episodes (and it is this that usually concerns the sufferer rather than food avoidance), we have found it useful to help them see the connection between strict dieting or fasting and the eating binges: namely, that the dieting sets them up for binges (possibly a built-in survival mechanism). One of the first steps in eliminating the binges, and it is only the first, is to approximate a "three square meals a day" approach. (Sometimes eating six smaller meals is easier since the amount of food eaten at any one time is then less.) A healthy nutritional state requires eating a balanced and adequate amount of food. As long as clients restrict their food intake, they can probably count on recurring binge episodes. This knowledge will sometimes enable and motivate an individual to tolerate an increased intake of food.

Two critical points which elicit panic in anorexic clients have been identified in the ascent to normal weight.

The first is when they initiate their ascent. The second is at the critical weight (body fat) level necessary for the resumption of menses (Frisch and MacArthur, 1974) At this threshold, patients are confronted with the mature shape that they have been dedicated to avoiding (Crisp, 1965). Pleas for renegotiating a weight below this should be met with firmness on the part of the therapist. The therapist must avoid being seduced or worn down into allowing an unhealthy weight. The patient should be reassured that only under special circumstances, such as if she were able to sustain normal menstrual functioning at a slightly lower weight, should the range goal be modified. The patient's desire to remain below this level should be interpreted in psychological terms. (Garner et al., 1982, p. 33)

Another critical point occurs upon reaching the weight of 100 pounds. Three digits seem to be much more formidable to the anorexic patient than two digits.

Some clients express a need for assistance in determining what to eat in order to effect a gradual weight gain. Some will be very open in expressing the fact that they no longer even know what a "normal" meal is like or have the ability to assess how much food is actually too much and how little is truly not enough. Recording the kinds and amounts of food eaten and then discussing this with a dietitian can be very helpful to a client in learning what constitutes normalized eating. Some of these clients will want a "diet" to follow, that is, specific meal plans which are laid out for them and will not require on-the-spot food decisions that generally lead to confusion and panic. For these clients, a diet provides an element of safety: structure and "permission." University students, for example, are often overwhelmed by the number of choices and the ready availability of food in the cafeteria. Knowing beforehand exactly which offerings they will choose can alleviate a great deal of anxiety, particularly for the individual with the additional symptom of bulimia.

Other clients can meet this need for structure by devising their own meal plans in accordance with certain guidelines established by the dietitian or therapist. The reduction and diabetic exchange lists are commonly used for this purpose, along with instructions to include servings from each of the four food groups (meat, milk, cereals/breads, fruits/vegetables). Two pamphlets we recommend when using the exchange method are:

1. *Exchange Lists for Meal Planning,* American Diabetes Association, Inc., 2 Park Avenue, New York, N.Y. 10016;
2. *It's a Weighty Problem,* edited by Barbara North and Marlys Connell, College of Home Economics, North Dakota State University, Fargo, N.D. 58105.

For laxative abusers, a high fiber diet can be "prescribed" as a laxative substitute, with an accompanying explanation given regarding the negative effects of the abuse — notably, laxatives do not rid the body of calories as is usually assumed. By the time food reaches the part of the gastrointestinal tract which laxatives affect, the calories have already been absorbed. What is lost is not true weight, but water which the body needs. The high fiber diet will act as a natural laxative, relieving constipation but avoiding negative side effects.

We have found structuring mealtime in other ways to be advantageous at times: that is, having set mealtimes and establishing ahead of time with whom one is going to eat. For those clients who are living at home, the cooperation of the family may have to be solicited in meal planning. These strategies, however, are not helpful until the client is committed to recovery and is willing to put the information to use.

Generally, guidelines chosen for dietary assistance should eventually include the normal variety of foods eaten by the client prior to the development of the eating disorder. Although vegetarianism or low sugar diets may seem relatively reasonable and can be worked around, some clinicians contend that in cases of anorexia these diets should not be condoned and that interest in them should be clearly attributed to the disorder. Small quantities of all "forbidden foods" (i.e., foods the anorexic refuses to eat and views as unsafe) are to be included in the diet. Janice Hedblom and her colleagues at Johns Hopkins Hospital will allow the individual a bit more leeway in the choice of food, but limit exclusions to three food items. We believe that as long as the individual is eating a balanced diet and gaining the required weight, she should be allowed to use her own "plan." Some clients will have extremely rigid eating requirements for themselves though, and when this interferes with balanced eating or weight gain, the requirements must be discontinued or appropriately modified.

The client will likely resist eating even small amounts of the forbidden foods due to the fear of losing control and thus gaining excessive weight. To counter these fears, we first explain to the client that in actuality very few anorexics go on to become obese after treatment, particularly if they do not have a history of obesity prior to the onset of the anorexia. Secondly, we promise that if the client should experience a loss of control and continue to gain beyond a normal weight, intervention will be made in the form of hospitalization. In this way, others will assume the responsibility for providing the "control" until she is able to do so herself. As stated previously, this kind of commitment is vital and reassures the client that the therapist's intent is not to make her "fat" and that uncontrolled weight gain will be taken as seriously as uncontrolled weight loss. Thirdly, we explain that physiologically the client is in a state of starvation and that her fears of being unable to stop eating are attributable to this biological state. Once she is properly nourished and able to maintain a healthy weight, this fear and obsession with food will gradually diminish. This approach is in line with Garner's suggestions.

Clients also frequently ask, "If I'm eating this little and not losing more, how can I eat normally and not get fat?" This question can be answered with an explanation that this process is not well understood but that the body has somehow adapted to the reduced food intake and is in a self-protective state. The current theory is that calories are not the sole determinant of weight. The body appears to have a built-in control system or "set point" for regulating the amount of fat carried. This set point is different for each person and is determined primarily by heredity. If the amount of fat being stored deviates in one direction or another, physiological changes are activated in an attempt to keep the fat level fairly constant. Long-term dieting results in slowing the metabolic rate, among other changes, which results in calories being burned much more slowly. When the body is renourished it will be able to utilize far more food without excessive weight gain.*

Therapists repeatedly observe that one of the features of anorexia nervosa most resistive to treatment is the unusual attitude toward food and weight. This attitude tends to be long lasting and recurring in times of crisis, although this is not always the case. The therapist has the challenging task of navigating a careful course between encouraging weight gain and/or maintenance, and avoiding reenactment of the power struggle that has probably taken place with family and/ or friends. To keep weight from becoming the focus of therapy, many writers have suggested having a physician see the individual for the purpose of monitoring weight and a therapist see the individual for psychotherapy. We utilize the services of registered dietitians for the purpose of monitoring weight. The weighing can be carried out on a weekly basis and the client informed of her weight. Some clients do better, however, not knowing their weight. In these instances,

---

*Gaining weight beyond the set point is as difficult as losing. Studies in overeating have shown maintaining higher than normal weight to be quite difficult even when calorie intake is tremendously increased. This information can be comforting to the client who is troubled with periodic binge-eating. For a more thorough explanation of set point theory, we highly recommend, for both therapists and clients, the Bennett and Gurin (1982) article listed in the references.

the client can be weighed facing away from the scale reading, being informed of her weight only if she is in trouble in terms of gain or loss of weight. Clients should also be forewarned that some abdominal discomfort and bloating may occur as they begin to increase the amount of food eaten and retained. This is a normal occurrence and an exceedingly frightening one to the client. Reassurance must be given that these temporary phenomena will gradually diminish as the body readjusts. We encourage clients to wear loose clothing (sweat pants are popular among college students), avoid mirrors, and get rid of the scale.

Oftentimes, after the client has managed to gain some weight, her "skinny" wardrobe will heighten her anxiety. If she wears her old clothing, its tightness will emphasize her weight gain. Even if she doesn't wear this clothing, it will beckon to her as long as she owns it. Giving away or selling such clothes is usually tremendously difficult for clients. They want to "pack them away" instead. However, as long as such clothes remain available in any way, they will be a temptation. Why keep them unless they will be worn again – an occasion which would herald a relapse? The recovering client needs to plan for continuing recovery rather than relapse.

We have found the elimination of self-weighing to be helpful on several counts. It breaks the client away from this source of repeated reinforcement for her low weight and/or the anxiety provoked by even diminutive gains; it frees up the time that is usually spent weighing and reweighing (some of our students have had difficulty making it to their classes on time because of trips to the health center scale between each class); it eliminates problems resulting from the lack of calibration between the physician's scale and the client's own scale; and it allows *opportunity* to focus on something other than weight (which is not likely as long as the client is ritualistically weighing herself and using this as her measure of self-worth for the moment/hour/day). This procedure also ensures that the anxiety and/or relief experienced as a result of weighing-in can be dealt with immediately and therapeutically.

A word of caution is in order, though, for whoever is doing the weighing. Beware of pronouncing judgment on the scale reading – that is, of showing great pleasure or displeasure. Rather, ask the client for *her* evaluation. What does this mean to *her*? Allow *her* to do the evaluating. This not only furthers exploration of psychodynamic issues and allows for greater freedom in self-expression and evaluation, but also reaffirms the fact that the professional is not going to take on a domineering role — telling the client what should or should not feel good to her. Furthermore, this attitude shows interest in her *experience* of the event rather than the event itself.

In the university setting, we have used campus physicians and/or dietitians to deal primarily with weight and food: to establish the minimum weight and do the weighing, to carry out nutritional education, to work out individually tailored meal plans, and so forth. These professionals also provide another reality base in addition to the therapist regarding food, weight, and body image. We have found working with dietitians particularly helpful because of their nutritional knowledge (and the anorexic's intellectual respect for this) and their spending the time necessary to develop specific eating programs.

Physicians can be helpful not only in monitoring the physical status of clients but also in lending authority and further credibility to the need to gain weight. A great deal of care must be taken in the choice of a physician. It is absolutely essential that the physician chosen be one who is willing to establish with the patient a relationship marked by warmth, understanding, and a willingness to explain and answer questions. A remote, distancing physician can be harmful to the recovery process. Preferably, counselors should choose a medical collaborator who is knowledgeable in the area of eating disorders or at least willing to learn about this field. A contact by the therapist should be made with the physician prior to referral. Naturally, close contact must exist among all those involved with the client so that they can function as a unified team. If the professionals involved do not operate as a close-knit team, there exists the distinct danger of being played against one another. Crisp warns us of the anorexic's regressed personality structure and tendency to split people into "good" and "bad." The anorexic may also attempt to draw others into a reenactment of the relationship with parents. Clinicians may find themselves, for instance, being cast into the roles of the "good mother" and "bad father" (or vice versa) and doing battle with one another as the client comes with tales of woe about her experiences at the hands of another team member. However, if a collaborative relationship has been established among team members and a consistent approach utilized, this situation is less likely to occur and can be dealt with more effectively if it should arise.

While weighing may be done by other professionals, both weight and psychological issues must be dealt with directly in therapy. Experienced practitioners generally accept that it is not appropriate, and in fact can be dangerous, to avoid dealing with weight per se. Further, dealing with food and weight in therapy sessions offsets the potential problem of the client's continuing to separate mind and body issues. However, care must be taken not to let therapy sessions become just one more opportunity to obsess about food.

One of the authors began work with eating-disordered clients by focusing mainly on their eating. This work was rather unsuccessful. Clients spent their time in the office talking about what they ate, how much they ate, how they ate it, how it was cooked, the number of calories, and so forth. They enjoyed, and in fact reveled in, the telling of this, but they made precious little progress. Today we believe that eating needs to be attended to, but with a dietitian or self-help organization. In therapy sessions, then, rather than the focus being placed on developing meal plans or monitoring weight, it is centered on the cognitive distortions and fears; on establishing the meaning and function of food and weight in the individual's life; on emotional issues, reactions to everyday happenings, and so forth.

The article by Garner et al. (1982) suggests that therapists have clients engage in "corrective experiences," that is, participate in activities that have been avoided. They encourage clients to differentiate between "anorexic" and "appropriate" behavior, and to practice the latter even before giving up the former.

> For example, anorexics typically develop peculiar eating habits. They cut food into small pieces, vacillate between menu selections, eat in isolation and only choose foods which they label as "safe or dietetic". While these are partially starvation related, some aspects are often maintained in the period immediately after weight restoration. The therapist may enlist the patient's commitment to decide consciously, in advance of a meal, to eat in a "non-anorexic" manner. If the patient is not successful, it may be pointed out that this indicates that she is not yet "in control" of her behavior since that would imply having some "choice". Success in this type of exercise gives the patient practice in "normal" eating and an opportunity to learn that this is not immediately followed by obesity . . . . (p. 29)

We will occasionally eat meals with clients in the campus cafeteria. This is in line with another of Garner's suggestions. This activity would never be for the purpose of "watching" or "checking up" on the client, but rather to support and model "normal" eating in a nonintrusive manner. Such behavior also reminds the client that the therapist is a human being too — even therapists have to eat! Obviously similar action should be attempted only under circumstances in which the client desires such a venture.

Occasionally we encourage clients to call us when they feel in crisis. Asking for help seems to be extremely difficult for many eating-disordered students, even with an invitation to do so. At times such supportive contact may be critical. The common fear of "imposing" can be partially alleviated by assuring clients that you *want* them to call if they feel the need, that you will be honest with them at the time of the call by telling them if you are not available at the moment, and that you will make arrangements to get back to them.

We may also invite students to call to share a particular victory. This contact serves to reinforce the immediate victory as well as the entire recovery process. The invitation conveys the message that it is not necessary to remain "sick" in order to merit our attention. This, by the way, is a significant issue and should not be overlooked. One therapist inadvertently reinforced his client's weight loss by seeing her more frequently when she lost weight. Fearful of losing the relationship with him should she recover, the client maintained a low weight (Garner et al., 1982). We make a point of addressing this topic directly with clients, letting them know that we won't abandon them as they gain weight and, in fact, that is when our work will really begin.

Eating-disordered clients possess a set of rather pronounced personality traits which impair overall coping skills. These include obsessive-compulsive traits, depressive traits, and anxiety/social avoidant traits (Bemis, 1978). However, not all clients possess the same traits to the same degree. What may be an issue for one may not be for another. Thus, within the homogeneity of the disorder, a great deal of diversity exists. Therapy involves addressing the issues that contribute to, and maintain, each particular client's disorder.

With this fact in mind then, we will describe problem areas common to anorexia nervosa — reiterating that these cannot be indiscriminately ascribed to all anorexic clients.

Cognitive Distortions

According to nearly every author in the field, one of the most critical tasks facing the therapist and the anorexic client in the recovery process is the correction of cognitive distortions, that is, faulty thinking and beliefs. Distortions and irrational beliefs are numerous in anorexics and must be directly but gently challenged. The client needs to learn to "think" differently, to exert control over her thoughts in such a way that new patterns of thinking emerge when faced with stress; erroneous beliefs have to be identified and modified. On the one hand, the client's experiences need to be affirmed as currently authentic for her, and on the other hand, alternative ways of viewing the world and herself need to be taught with great patience. Cognitive distortions include the client's misperceptions about her body — both its size and its biological functions (for instance, anorexics often have strange ideas about what happens to the food they eat, imagining that it goes "directly" to their thighs, hips, or abdomens). Hilde Bruch's explanation of psychotherapy is "a process during which erroneous assumptions and attitudes are recognized, defined, and challenged so that they can be abandoned. It is important to proceed slowly and to use concrete small events as episodes for illustrating certain false assumptions or illogical deductions. The whole work needs to be done by re-examining actual aspects of living, by using relatively small events as they come up" (1978, pp. 143–144).

A perfectionist mode of thinking is commonly found in clients with anorexia. These illogical or distorted thought patterns have been discussed by Burns (1980) in his article on the perfectionist. He lists the following thinking patterns:

1. *Dichotomous thinking.* All-or-nothing thinking in which perfectionists "evaluate their experiences in a dichotomous manner, seeing things as either all-black or all-white; intermediate shades of gray do not seem to exist" (p. 38). Some examples of this might be: "If I don't choose a major before school starts, I'll probably end up just being a bum" or "If I gain any weight, I'll be fat."

2. *Overgeneralization.* Perfectionists "tend to jump to the dogmatic conclusion that a negative event will be repeated endlessly" (p. 38). A client may have a small lapse in her eating and explain, "I'll never get better, my eating will never improve."

3. *Should statements.* When perfectionists fall short of a goal, "they harangue themselves, saying, 'I shouldn't have goofed up! I ought to do better! I mustn't do that again!' " (p. 38).

Two other reasoning errors have been identified as common to victims of anorexia: superstitious thinking and personalization (Garner et al., 1982). Superstitious thinking is believing in the cause-effect relationship of unrelated events. This kind of thinking may play a part in the emergence of anorexic behavior, with the client believing that weight loss will solve other problems in her life. Superstitious thinking can also lead to other bizarre behavior rituals. Personalization involves seeing one's self as the focus of other people's attention and taking things (events and comments) "personally" whether or not they are related to the self. Consider, for example, "Two people laughed and whispered something to each other when I walked by. They were probably saying that I looked unattractive. I *have* gained three pounds" (p. 16). To counter this thinking, the authors suggest the technique of decentering, which involves applying the same evaluative standards to others that are applied to the self. We can ask the client, "Does your admiration of friends or acquaintances directly correspond to their weights?"

Whatever form the irrational thinking may take, we try to help the client identify the thought patterns, rationally refute them, and replace them with more realistic patterns. (We talk more about this later in this chapter in the section "Identifying Anorexic and Bulimic Thoughts.")

One particularly tenacious distortion is that of body image. Anorexics display varying degrees of body image distortion, from severe to none. However, when the distortion is present, as it is in a great many cases, it does not appear to be amenable to alteration. We like Garner's alternative solution: a "reinterpretation" of body image. The idea here is that if we can't impact how a client *sees* her body, we can still impact how she *interprets* what she sees. This feature of anorexia can be explained as just that — a part of the disorder. The client's perception is not denied and is acknowledged as real for her; thus there is less likelihood of hostile disagreement. Body measurements, pictures, videotape feedback, and other objective kinds of evidence have been used to help demonstrate how the illness is affecting her self-perception. The therapist also must give direct feedback while acknowledging the client's differing perceptions. Self-help techniques can be taught to counter the "anorexic" thinking and perceptions. An example of this might be the statement, "Seeing myself as fat is due to my anorexia. It doesn't mean I *am* fat."

Feeling States

Although they have many misperceptions, anorexics also need to be encouraged to develop trust in themselves and their abilities, and to experience their feelings fully without shutting them out as inappropriate. The therapist should encourage risk taking, help the client to develop skills through corrective experiences, help the client to acknowledge feelings, and reaffirm the right to those feelings. While the therapy process must include correcting distortions in the client's thinking, so too must it install a sense of self-confidence.

Another of the primary therapeutic goals in treating eating-disordered clients is the genuine and appropriate expression of feeling. Some individuals are not able even to *identify* feelings, much less to express them. Others are aware of their feelings but lack the skills and/or belief system which would support the expression of those feelings. Furthermore, feelings can seem quite overwhelming and frightening.

This is not to say that eating-disordered clients don't ever describe feeling states. Complaints of "depression," for example, are common – and the client may indeed be depressed. However, some other unexpressed feeling may hide behind these feelings of depression (if we assume that the depression is not due to nutritional factors). For instance, we may find anger and frustration to be the actual basic feelings underlying the depression, just as we do with other depressed clients. Then again, a client may feel extremely sad and may not feel free to express this, doubting its legitimacy.

Anxiety and anger are two emotions which are likely to be particularly troublesome to the anorexic individual and require consistent attention. However, this attention should not be of a confrontive nature. Rather, in cases where the identification of feelings is difficult for the client, it would be well to heed the advice of Hilde Bruch (1973):

If there are things to be uncovered and interpreted, it is important that the patient makes the discovery on his own and has a chance to *say it first* . . . . Such a patient needs help and encouragement in becoming aware of impulses, thoughts, and feelings that originate within himself. Only in this way can he . . . become alert and alive to what is going on within himself. (p. 388)

The therapist acts as a co-detective searching out the unknown, rather than as the expert with ready explanations and labels. The process of self-awareness and acceptance in the client can be further facilitated by a self-disclosing therapist who shows his or her "humanness." A therapist who is willing to share, for example, instances of anger or embarrassment by specific example gives the client permission to feel and accept those same feelings. Sharing mistakes, describing those times we have really "botched up," can aid the client to also claim the right to imperfection.

Frequently, eating-disordered clients exhibit a tendency to "catch" feelings from others. That is, a difficulty exists in separating and maintaining one's own feeling state from that of others. This problem becomes notably apparent in therapy groups and is dealt with more extensively in the group therapy section of this chapter. Along the same line is the anorexic's tendency to react in accordance with what is thought to be expected or acceptable. Evidence of this behavior can be observed in the therapy situation when clients will respond, "Yes, that's how it is" or "Yes, that's how I feel" to a leading question. A colleague of ours states that whenever she hears this or a similar comment, she backs up and asks again, "Tell me how it was for *you*?" In so doing, she removes herself from the role of interpreter, keeping this responsibility on the client alone.

After the client is able accurately to identify and acknowledge her feelings, she can then be assisted in dealing with them in effective ways. At this point, coping skills such as assertion can be taught. The therapist can point out that the major coping response utilized by the client has been avoidance of food (or some other compulsive behavior such as excessive studying or exercise) but that other, more appropriate, responses are possible. By teaching clients these other response options and by emphasizing that they alone are responsible for choosing from several responses that one which is most adaptive to their actual needs, increased independence and effectiveness become possible, and can ultimately lead to greater self-confidence and self-esteem.

Therapists commonly observe that anorexics tend to base their self-esteem on high performance standards (including weight loss) which, for many, are successively upgraded as they are accomplished. In other words, in order to maintain the same level of self-worth, increasingly stringent requirements must be met. We stress to clients that self-worth is not dependent upon achievement. We encourage them to become more self-indulgent, learning to care for and be good to themselves. This is no easy task, since self-indulgence is in direct opposition to many societal messages which stress competition and accomplishment. At the university level, for instance, decisions to drop classes, take incompletes, and/or decrease study time — which can be signs of therapeutic progress for the eating-disordered student — fly in the face of traditional expectations for college students. Even in the area of recreation, clients with anorexia tend to participate from a performance perspective rather than from one of enjoyment. It is vital that anorexics develop sources of gratification not tied to evaluative standards: small activities which are done *solely* for personal enjoyment (a concept which is alien to many anorexics).

Evaluation by others is another basis for self-esteem. With the eating-disordered person, this evaluation often has become the major, or only, determinant of self-worth. Consequently, the anorexic's own interests and needs may be submerged in favor of meeting the real or imagined expectations of others. This tendency can manifest itself in varying degrees and, for some, impacts virtually every area of their lives from small daily interactions with others to major life decisions. "In these instances psychotherapy is aimed at reinforcing the patient's slow discovery of her own interest and gently challenging performances which seem to be strictly the products of others' expectations" (Garner et al., 1982, p. 24).

As therapy progresses, special "trouble spots" remain. For those clients who are sexually active, one of these trouble spots is, in our experience, the area of sexuality. One young college woman, for example, was an avowed feminist who articulated a strong viewpoint and value system that had been clearly and critically thought out and adapted to herself as an individual. This was not a case of simply buying what someone else had suggested to her. Yet this woman was unable to act in accordance with her philosophy in her relationships with men. She could discuss her beliefs with men, and maintain her independence and self-esteem in certain areas of her relationships, but not in others — particularly not in the sexual realm. While she would voice her desire not to engage in sexaul activity at certain times, she was not able to maintain her refusal in the face of continuing pressure by the man. She could acknowledge her rights on an intellectual basis but had an extremely difficult time claiming them. Her boyfriend was "sensitive" in this area, and she felt helpless in the face of his expectations — not to mention angry and violated. At this point, when feelings and rights are able to be acknowledged, a strategy such as role playing can be very effective in evoking behavioral changes.

Some clients, because of a fragile identity, often look to others for their beliefs, values, and modes of expression instead of looking inward and trusting their "guts." One client chose friends who were dynamic, successful, colorful, and opinionated, and then adopted their thinking as her own. She said, "Since they are successful, they must be right." We must also point out that this is not an all-or-nothing phenomenon. Clients may be quite confident and outspoken regarding certain values, beliefs, or decisions in one specific area and not in others. Then again, their actions may not back up their words, as in the case of the young feminist described in the preceding paragraph.

Family Issues

Another major aim of therapy with the eating-disordered client is to facilitate separation from the family and the development of autonomy so that the client may indeed "grow up." This point has been repeatedly emphasized in the literature pertaining to anorexia.

Historically, the treatment for anorexia nervosa has included literal, physical separation from the family. While this can be helpful for several reasons (and does not necessarily indicate poor parenting or that the illness is the fault of the parents), physical separation is not always essential. What is essential, however, is to enable the anorexic client to establish her own identity as an individual, separate from her family yet part of the family unit.

This process requires, among other things, the resolution of any developmental fears the client may have. Adolescence and its increasing demands may seem overwhelming to the child for a variety of reasons (delineated in Chapter 2). Whatever the reasons, anorexia is commonly thought to be a desperate attempt to stave off further development. One client reported that prior to developing anorexia, she had slept on her chest at night, hoping to inhibit breast development, and had refused to wear red or pink clothing because of the color association with menstruation. Losing weight proved to be more effective and reassuring to her. The client needs to understand the association between her fears and her anorexic behavior.

In some instances, work with the family may be necessary to promote its support of the client's autonomy. Sometimes parents, in their attempts to take care of their child, become overly involved and convey the message that the child is not capable of successfully handling life's problems. This attitude serves to reinforce the child's lack of trust in herself. Parents may also need help to allow and encourage the child to have thoughts and feelings independent from theirs. Other parents become so focused on their own problems that they do not provide their child with the support and direction needed. In these cases the child is, in essence, emotionally "orphaned," expected to operate independently too soon and without being prepared to do so (Hedblom, Hubbard, and Anderson, 1981).

Janice Hedblom and her colleagues outline the following principles in working with families of anorexia nervosa victims:

1. Approach families in a nonblaming way.
2. Assume that families have done their best.
3. Recognize that families are tired from stress.
4. Assume that families want to help.

Family therapy is addressed in greater detail in the next section of this chapter.

In summary, the treatment of anorexia nervosa must attend to both the physiological and psychological needs of the client. Close collaboration among the physician, therapist, and any other professionals involved in treatment is vital. The goals of individual psychotherapy are:

1. to establish a collaborative relationship marked by acceptance, understanding, and genuineness;
2. to provide education regarding the disorder;
3. to restore adequate nutrition and an acceptable weight;
4. to explore the meaning of weight loss in the client's life;

5. to reinterpret body image;
6. to develop other sources of gratification that are not tied to evaluation (by self or others);
7. to correct distortions of reality (erroneous assumptions, attitudes, and reasoning errors) and develop realistic expectations;
8. to develop the ability to recognize and express feeling states − and later develop effective coping skills;
9. to detach self-acceptance from performance and the evaluations of others;
10. to develop self-confidence (that the client's thoughts and feelings are valid and she can indeed exert the necessary controls in her life without overcompensating through excessive and rigid self-discipline);
11. to resolve developmental fears;
12. to foster the development of autonomy and separation from the family.

The therapist must have patience and be prepared to engage in a lengthy treatment process. She or he must be able to accept and treat each client as a unique individual with her own set of characteristics and needs within the framework of anorexia nervosa.

TREATMENT OF BULIMIA

As you know by this time, bulimia has only recently been established as a widespread phenomenon, and its treatment is not nearly as well defined as that of anorexia nervosa. The majority of bulimia research to date has focused upon investigating the prevalence of the disorder and delineating epidemiological factors. A paucity of information exists regarding the actual treatment of clients afflicted with the syndrome of bulimia. Although we note a flurry of professional activity across the country to develop treatment methods, those methods, for the most part, have yet to be described in the literature. While such descriptions will undoubtedly be forthcoming, it remains to be seen what the treatment modalities are and which of them will prove to be most effective.

In the meantime, increasing numbers of individuals with bulimia are approaching therapists for assistance. This section of the chapter attempts to provide the reader with some general and specific treatment strategies which can be used by the clinician. These strategies have been gleaned from the literature, from conversations with other practitioners, and from our own experiences.

First of all, much of what was presented in the previous section regarding treatment of anorexia nervosa can be applied to the treatment of bulimia as well. Bulimia is often accompanied by a significant amount of shame and guilt. A therapeutic relationship marked by warmth and a nonjudgmental attitude is critical.

Unlike anorexics, victims of bulimia are generally aware that their eating behavior is abnormal, and they may go to great lengths to conceal it from family and friends, often successfully. Initially, the bulimic's "secret" may seem like the ideal solution for weight control and/or other problems in life. As time goes on, though, the problems associated with the behavior (i.e., financial difficulties, maintaining secrecy, kleptomania, depression, etc.) take an increasing toll on the individual. It is as a result of this distress that the bulimic individual generally presents him- or herself for treatment. Consequently, the bulimic client is initially much more likely to be receptive to treatment than is the anorexic.

Cases also exist in which individuals are not voluntary clients but have come to the therapist under duress as a result of someone else's concern. In these cases — since motivation is the critical ingredient for recovery — the initial goal (as with anorexia) is to help the individuals become willing clients. Again, keep in mind the principles outlined in the preceding section (such as showing an appreciation for the client's plight and symptoms, expressing an interest in her view of the situation, and discussing the mechanisms involved in the disorder as well as its health complications). An assessment of the severity and extent of the client's food-related behavior must be made; this should include the frequency of eating binges, binge duration, the kinds of food eaten, when and where food is eaten, and how the binge is terminated. Methods utilized for weight control need to be identified along with their frequency of use. In the case of laxatives, the amount of usage should also be determined. Depression, social conflicts, and other sources of conflict should be evaluated. There is a special need for attention to substance abuse, family history of alcoholism and affective disorders, shoplifting and, with the depressed client, suicide potential. We might add that it is not uncommon for individuals with bulimia to underreport their symptoms. A complete medical evaluation is of paramount importance. The client's physical status must be evaluated so that the presence of any complicating factors can be detected.

Before suggesting tentative guidelines for treatment, we might first point out that appetite suppressants have not proven to be therapeutic. Likewise, hospitalization has not generally turned out to be effective in the long run for the treatment of bulimia (Pyle, personal communication; Russell, 1981) although it may be necessary to treat an accompanying depression. Hospitalization has been found to be useful as a temporary measure; that is, it provides an opportunity to at least interrupt the cycle (and for the rapidly deteriorating client this is essential) and regain control. Generally what has been found is that the bulimic individual experiences much relief and does quite well as long as she remains in the hospital. After exiting, however, this progress is rarely maintained, unless follow-up treatment is provided on an outpatient basis.

We recommend the following general guidelines for dealing with bulimic clients on an outpatient basis. Some of the strategies we use in treating bulimia are borrowed from those who work in the area of obesity and weight reduction:

1. Discussion of the pertinent issues (see preceding section and Chapter 2).
2. Explanation of the dangers involved in bingeing and purging.
3. Establishing a reasonable weight range and activity level.
4. Dietary instructions and education such as:

   (a) stressing the importance of eating regular meals and establishing daily routines, and
   (b) record keeping of food consumption, vomiting, and purging.

Sometimes a pattern emerges even when the client is sure there is none. Other times the bulimic behavior seems to operate independently. If the behavior is unrelated to emotional patterns, some pattern may still exist, such as opportunity to indulge in the behavior.

Most clients do not experience regular meals — they are either bingeing or severely dieting to make up for these binges. If, by chance, they eat a regular meal — for example, when they are with other people — they may follow it with a binge as soon as they are alone or "get rid of" the meal once it is eaten. The importance of eating three square meals per day in gaining control over binges needs to be explained. Most clients will recognize that their "dieting" never works on a long-term basis and that it increases their craving for food, setting them up for a future binge. It can be explained that this is a normal reaction to restricting food intake and that one of the first steps in elimination of binges is to begin to eat on a regular basis.

Individuals suffering with bulimia are also extremely concerned about gaining weight, and what has been said regarding this fear in the treatment of anorexia nervosa applies here as well (i.e., having a dietitian give them nutritional information and help them with meal planning; avoiding tight clothing, etc.; and countering cognitive distortions). While many bulimics want to lose weight, we stress beginning with weight stabilization, with the explanation that right now we need to focus on eliminating the binges (as well as the vomiting and/or purging). They will have enough to do without also trying to lose weight. Furthermore, the dieting itself will get in the way of progress. Later, if it is appropriate, they will be given help in choosing a "healthy" reduction diet: one that is designed to enable them to lose weight slowly and keep it off. We emphasize the importance of steering clear of fad diets which severely restrict food intake and which serve once again to raise the specter of eating binges and thus result in frustration. We reiterate time and again that they are undertaking a whole new life-style which does not include dieting or bingeing — a new approach to food.

5. Structuring the environment through time management and other kinds of planning (in extreme cases this structure may initially be in the form of hospitalization).

6. Emphasizing the necessity for the clients to exert control and choice — thinking about what it is they *really* want. Is it food or something else? If it is food, what kind of food (e.g., sweet or salty)? Discriminate between what is *truly* satisfying and whatever "is around." Give thought to the process of eating and be discriminating. Imagine beforehand how it will feel to eat the food, how it tastes, how one will feel afterwards.

Make binges a *decision* if they happen. Clients need to be encouraged to take control back and to realize that they *have* control. One technique we have found useful is to have clients wait a specified amount of time before initiating a binge and then writing, "I am choosing to binge" or "I am choosing not to binge," whatever the case may be. This reconfirms to clients the fact that they *do* have a choice and that the controls are indeed in their hands. The clients' choice is not limited only to bingeing or not eating anything. They can also decide simply to eat a small amount. (Most are very clear on what constitutes a binge for them.) Give permission to "eat" and stress the importance of "taking care of self," not allowing one's self to get overly hungry. Learning to eat in response to hunger (versus emotion) is critical. However, the fewer decisions that a bulimic needs to make about food, the less apt she is to binge — this is the primary rationale for developing a meal plan.

7. Utilizing cognitive-behavioral principles to deal with the fear of weight and other kinds of distorted thinking (as outlined in the preceding and following sections).

8. Facilitating the development of other coping skills such as assertion and relaxation techniques.

9. Use of behavioral techniques to prevent binge-eating, such as:

(a) Eating slowly. Hints such as putting the fork down be-tween each bite and chewing slowly can be helpful in slowing down the eating process. Instruct the client to make a point of *really* tasting and savoring the food.

(b) Eating with other people. Planning is necessary, not only of what to eat but with whom to eat. Planning to eat regularly with someone who is an appropriate eater has been helpful to some of our clients.

10. Planning meals and planning to avoid bingeing, yet tolerating "slips" which may happen. In planning to avoid binges, the issue of time must be addressed. Free time seems to pose a great problem. Careful attention must be given to this in planning, and alternatives have to be developed for handling free time. Slips must also be anti-cipated. When control is not maintained and the person "gives in," despair and guilt are likely to be the product. To short-circuit this situation, the therapist needs to indicate that a slip is predictable and forgivable. A slip is not the same as total failure and it does not have to continue to additional excesses. (This is further addressed in the section "Relapse Work" later in this chapter.)

11.   Identification of emotions and alternatives to binge-eating.

12.   Treatment for any other emotional problems which may exist.

13.   Treatment for chemical dependency, if necessary. Substance abuse is another problem that frequently afflicts bulimics and requires attention. Even for those bulimics who do not abuse alcohol, it often plays a role nevertheless in their eating behavior. For some, a drink or two lessens their resolve to deal with their eating in a responsible way and results in a binge. For others, it becomes a substitute for eating and a means of either avoiding a binge or avoiding the guilt associated with a binge. We believe it critical to discover and discuss the role alcohol or other drugs play in a client's eating problem, and to devise a plan for dealing with this.

14.   Examining ways in which the client has given power and control to society and the fashion industry to determine her worth as a person and as a female. Two books which clients have found meaningful and helpful in repudiating societal standards for body shape and in encouraging valuation of feminine curves are:

(a) *Fat is a Feminist Issue* by Susie Orbach, and
(b) *The Obsession: Reflections on the Tyranny of Slenderness* by Kim Chernin.

15.   Recommending group therapy and/or self-help groups. This item requires a comment. While we and others have successfully treated a number of students on an individual basis, it is the group approach which appears to be particularly promising in the treatment of bulimia, and the following section of this chapter will be devoted to that topic (Garner, Garfinkel, and Bemis, 1982; Lucas, 1981a, 1981b; Russell, 1979).

It is of vital importance that the client's collaboration be elicited throughout the treatment process. It is a well-known fact that, in general, effecting change is easiest when the people affected are involved in the decision making. These people are then more likely to be committed to the change process. Since motivation plays such a significant role in the recovery process, the client's input is imperative. Moreover, each client is unique, and treatment strategies must be adapted to that particular individual. Therefore, decision making should be left up to the client as much as possible, with the therapist providing information, encouragement, and an understanding of the issues involved. We might add that there is a tendency for clients to enter therapy thinking or hoping that the therapist will decide and do whatever is necessary to effect a "cure." The therapist sometimes needs to remind him/herself, as well as the client, that recovery lies in the client's hands and not the therapist's. The therapist can assist and encourage, but it is the client who must do the work.

Bulimia appears to have a more "addictive" quality than simple anorexia and seems to be more resistant to treatment (Casper et al., 1980; Crisp, 1980; Russell, 1979). Some clinicians in the field contend that if the addictive aspect of the behavior is not addressed, treatment is likely to fail (Goff, personal communication).

The recovery process is fraught with difficulties. Motivation is extremely difficult to maintain. The bulimic behavior is a potent and immediate reinforcer for itself. Bulimia is tremendously satisfying in the short run. The binge itself is extremely gratifying. It comes to be a way of taking care of oneself, whether as a planned reward for a hard day's work or as an impulsive solution for bad feelings. Vomiting and/or purging can also be satisfying in another sort of way — to eliminate the results of bingeing certainly, but also in some individuals to serve as an atonement and to relieve guilt. One of our clients reported, "I know this sounds weird, but I kind of *like* getting sick and being in so much pain from those laxatives. I mean — I deserve it." Her self-esteem was maintained through physical suffering. This dynamic has been noted by others also. While binge-purging is certainly one means of satisfaction, so is the flip side of the coin: dieting. Dieting is frequently referred to by clients as "being good" and is associated with an increase in self-esteem.

This same attitude tends to carry over into the therapy situation. As long as the client adheres to the contract developed, she sees herself as "being good" and keeps her regular appointments. If, on the other hand, she does not maintain the agreement, there is a strong tendency to avoid the therapist and to skip appointments. Furthermore, it is often difficult for bulimic individuals to allow themselves to get close to anyone. For these reasons, we find that keeping bulimic clients engaged in the therapy process can be difficult. Russell (1979) also notes sporadic client involvement in treatment.

One way we counter this trend is to initiate contact with clients when appointments are missed: let them know that we are interested in them regardless of their "performance," discuss with them the reasons for their absence, and invite them to return. The final decision is left up to the clients of course. Such contact serves two functions. First, it lets the client know that she is important and we notice her absence (some assume — and perhaps hope — they won't be missed). Secondly, since these individuals tend to be "avoiders" — they avoid unpleasantness, particularly in interpersonal situations — they have little skill in resolution of issues or conflicts. By initiating contact, the therapist refuses to collude with the avoidance behavior and further tries to reduce the anticipated unpleasantness. If the client does in fact return to therapy, and most do, the skipping diminishes considerably (it's no longer functional; contact occurs anyway). If the client chooses not to return — and we attempt to make this a guilt-free option — then there is at least the opportunity for closure and resolution. We can support the individual in her decision and let her know that our door will always be open in the future.

Maintaining motivation must be attended to consistently. This is probably the most difficult aspect of treatment. Of course, the reinforcement that the therapist provides in a global sense has a positive effect, to be sure. However, the competition is stiff. Once-a-week or even twice-a-week appointments hardly offset the continual daily exposure to the temptations of bulimia. One way to deal with this problem is to set up a reward system. This can be done in a variety of ways. The following strategy worked well for one of our clients who had established a "tradition" of going out for dinner every Friday night with a group of her friends. They would go to one of the local pubs which served an unending supply of cheese and crackers, with before-dinner drinks and an all-you-can-eat buffet. This event was inevitably followed by going home and engaging in a gigantic binge of several hours' duration. Through discussion with the client, it became apparent that one friend in particular was a food pusher who would encourage the client to eat more than she wanted. The client could hold her own until she had a drink or two. Then, willpower went out the window and she gave in. At the end of this time together, our client would have overeaten, but not terribly so, and she did not consider her behavior a binge. On her way home, though, she would stop at the grocery store, spend approximately 20 dollars or more on "junk food" (pizza, cake, cookies, ice cream, chips), go home, eat herself into oblivion, and then throw up. While it might seem that a change of "tradition" was in order, the client really did not want to give up these Friday night dinners. So we decided to try to work around this in some way, at least temporarily.

While several issues were involved here, for the sake of simplicity we will narrow our discussion to a portion of the plans developed and the reward system devised. Since the consumption of alcohol left the client vulnerable, and since she did not particularly enjoy alcohol, it was decided that she would substitute club soda with a twist of lemon. This provided a refreshing drink without alcohol (or calories), and it proved very enjoyable to her. In this way she did not feel deprived while the others had their beverages. After dinner, instead of going to the grocery store, she was to go to a magazine shop not affiliated with a grocery store and purchase one of her favorite magazines. This was a luxury in which she did not usually partake because of financial considerations. Initially she was reluctant to spend the money, but when it was pointed out that the magazine was significantly cheaper than the binge, she felt freer to indulge herself in this way. This option provided an enjoyable and rewarding alternative for her.

Continual dieting seems to have a counterregulatory effect, triggering compensatory overeating. There appears to be an actual physiological factor related to this effect. In addition, psychologically, the "forbiddenness" of eating certain foods seems to lead to a preoccupation with that which is being avoided. Energy must be directed toward it (i.e., thinking about it) in order to maintain vigilance *against* it; that vigilance in turn can lead to a feeling of deprivation and an increased yearning for that which is forbidden. In fact, this is a common counterproductive by-product of dieting for many of us. Explaining this can be helpful in getting the bulimic individual to attempt to eat small, prescribed amounts of forbidden foods (and keep them down) and to cease the dieting behaviors. Garner et al. (1982) state:

> In order to make the "forbidden fruit" less attractive, patients are encouraged to consume modest and pre-determined amounts of those foods that were previously the object of their binges. These

foods should be introduced to the patient as "medication" in the sense they will be helpful in reducing the psychological cravings and the feelings of deprivation. Patients should eat these foods even if they believe that they can do without. They should be taught to evaluate their thinking in order to identify any vestiges of their dichotomous method of dividing food into moral and immoral categories. (p. 37)

This certainly seems the most ideal way to go. However, there are also those practitioners who contend that, practically speaking, foods which always trigger binges should initially be avoided. Some therapists advocate giving up processed sugar and white flour (as does Overeaters Anonymous) as much as possible — realizing that bulimics are *not* "normal" eaters, just as an alcoholic is not a "normal" drinker. The bulimic, like the alcoholic, should initially eliminate the "binge triggers" from the diet (those foods which, if consumed, will always trigger a binge). At the same time, good nutrition must be maintained and care must be taken not to eliminate essential foods. While it would be preferable to reinstate "normal" eating completely, if this does not seem possible we may have to settle for what seems workable, on a temporary basis if not a permanent one. Again each case must be given individual consideration.

INDIVIDUAL THERAPY TECHNIQUES

Certainly there is a wide variety of specific therapeutic techniques and strategies the therapist can employ. In the following material we have included several specific individual therapy techniques which we have found helpful to our clients. Included in this section are: cognitive role playing, identifying anorexic and bulimic thoughts, relapse work, assertiveness training, resolution work, keeping a diary, and theory of change.

Cognitive Role Playing

We often hear the comment that there are difficult times during each day when the desire to binge or starve becomes stronger. Often these times are in the late afternoon, evening, or late night. We have found that mentally rehearsing the situation can be helpful in allowing the person to make constructive behavioral choices when the stressful time does occur. For example, June found that the 15-minute period immediately following supper, before she started her studying, was a very dangerous, stressful time. The urge to binge was very often triggered during this period. We asked June to think of other behaviors that could be chosen instead of bingeing during this time. She developed the following list:

1. Reading the newspaper in the lounge
2. Watching the evening news on television in the lounge
3. Making a phone call to a friend
4. Taking a walk
5. Visiting with friends in the dormitory

Once June had made the list, we asked her to choose one of the activities. She chose taking a walk. We then asked her to practice mentally visualizing herself walking from the dining center to her dormitory room, putting on her jacket, and walking out the door of the residence hall. She was to visualize this procedure several times during the day, before the evening meal, and right at the end of the evening meal. This technique can help clients to perceive the many options or choices they actually have other than bingeing or starving. Furthermore, the mental practice of the behavior will make it more comfortable when actually experienced.

The eating-disordered client always seeks more control over her life. This approach can give an immediate feeling of control. We instruct clients to use this approach for any situation that seems appropriate. Some find it very helpful; others do not seem particularly interested in it. Since practice is such an important aspect of this technique, the client must be motivated and willing to practice the imagery. She must also learn that if the original plan does not work (for example, June had to cancel her walk because of stormy weather), an alternative nonbinge/nonstarve plan must be devised. So June knew that if she couldn't take a walk, she would watch the evening news on television instead.

It is important that the client's choices are not all contingent upon the actions and cooperation of others. This keeps the responsibility for the behavior on the client. For example, if June had chosen visiting with friends (without an alternate plan), what would happen if the friends were busy? Frustration, loneliness, and possibly a real setup for a binge could occur. Taking a walk, on the other hand, does not depend on the availability of others.

An example of how this approach works can be seen in the case of Terry. Terry worked a shift that ended in the late afternoon. At the end of her work shift she would drive home, walk into the apartment and into the kitchen, stand in front of the refrigerator, and mentally argue over whether or not to eat something. She found that she usually ended up by eating something and then eventually bingeing because she had eaten food which she had not planned to eat.

The plan that Terry developed was as follows. She would walk into her apartment, go straight to the bathroom, wash her hands and face, brush her teeth, and then go into the living room and play her piano for a minimum of a half an hour. She found the piano playing to be very relaxing, and by the time she was through playing, she was calmer and it was time to eat supper. She had made the choice; she was in control. The more Terry practiced this, the stronger she felt. Furthermore, this stressful time turned into an enjoyable time each day. By mentally role playing, Terry allowed herself to experience the behavior before it happened, and therefore her task seemed more attainable.

Identifying Anorexic and Bulimic Thoughts

We ask clients to identify thoughts that lead to a binge or a period of starving. These are often irrational thoughts and are surprisingly similar for all anorexic and bulimic clients. The clients seem to accept these thoughts as true for them, and they then develop a case for bingeing or starving by building on these thoughts. The mere act of putting the thoughts into words can reduce their potency for the client. This might be compared to our differing thoughts and emotional reactions during the darkness of night and brightness of day. That which seems terrifying in the dark often seems quite manageable or even ridiculous in the light of day. Articulation of thoughts may at least serve as a "night light"! Unarticulated thoughts remain powerful and unquestionable beliefs. Putting a thought into words enables the individual to *realize* the assumption that is held and affords the opportunity to look at it critically with the support of the therapist and to make a judgment on it.

We first have clients identify their thoughts and become familiar with the kinds of thoughts that lead to bingeing or starving. They can do this by writing down their thoughts before, during, and after a binge or a starving period. This activity helps clients to expand their conscious awareness of the thinking patterns which are occurring and, hopefully, can break the automatic response to these irrational ideas. Once clients have identified these thoughts, we ask them to develop a list of the most common messages. We have them write these messages on the left-hand side of a sheet of paper that has a line drawn down the middle (see Figure 3-1, page 108). The opposite side of the page is blank.

The next step after identifying and writing down the thoughts is to learn how to refute them. Clients must learn how to challenge their thoughts, to investigate the validity of the messages that they give themselves, to question if the thoughts are true. For example, a client might have the following thought on her list: "I'm going to go ahead and eat it. I can always throw it up."

1. This thought can be challenged by raising the following kinds of questions:

- Is this really the thought I want to be thinking?
- What do I know about myself or my past experiences that says this may not be true?
- Is this thought helpful for my recovery?

The challenge thinking may go something like this: "Wait a minute! I am attempting to stop the vomiting behavior, and here I am telling myself to go ahead and throw up. No way! I don't want to throw up anymore, and therefore I choose not to eat this food. I probably will binge if I eat at this time. This is a bulimic thought — an irrational, destructive thought for me."

2. Practice is an important part of this technique. Whenever the thought comes into the person's awareness, she must challenge it and replace it with a more constructive thought pattern.

This technique becomes a way for the client to view and check her thoughts. By this method a person can then determine when she is thinking "anorexic thoughts" and/or "bulimic thoughts" and can develop the skill to change these thoughts constructively.

ANOREXIC/BULIMIC THOUGHTS	RATIONAL THOUGHTS
I'm going to go ahead and eat it. I can always throw it up.	Since I don't want to throw up, I probably shouldn't eat this food.
I need to binge to get rid of this anxiety and tension.	I am feeling anxious and I need to deal directly with these feelings. Bingeing doesn't solve anything.
I know I'll be happy if I lose 5 more pounds.	The last 5 pounds that I lost didn't make me happy.
If I don't eat I won't have to worry about throwing up.	But fasting usually leads me to another binge. I'm setting myself up again!
This eating disorder is not real. I can eat any way I please.	No I can't. I need to accept the fact that I do have an eating disorder. This is an important step for my recovery.

Figure 3-1 Anorexic and bulimic thoughts worksheet.

Relapse Work

A pattern that becomes very familiar when working with anorexic and bulimic clients is relapse. Relapse is different for each individual. Each will define the relapse in her own terms and according to her own behaviors; relapse occurs for each person in her own way. When the person is attempting to change a behavior such as bingeing and then engages in that very behavior, the experience is upsetting. The individual will often go into a destructive all-or-none thought pattern and may think, "I'm a failure. What's the use — why even try?" or

"I don't even care." So not only are relapse behaviors negative, but the thoughts which follow those behaviors are also.

The work of Allan G. Marlatt has been helpful to us in putting relapse behaviors into a perspective that is understandable. Marlatt and Gordon (1980) define two factors that play an important role in precipitating a relapse:

1. *A negative emotional state.* This occurs when a person has feelings of anger, frustration, boredom, loneliness, guilt, etc., with which they previously coped by using the behavior (for example, bingeing). A relapse can be precipitated by these feelings which the person copes with by falling back into the old behaviors.

2. *Overstepping skill level.* As clients work to develop new coping skills, they may encounter situations which their skill level is not advanced enough to handle successfully, and a relapse occurs. A person with anorexia nervosa, for instance, may be doing very well in terms of eating enough each day, but when a friend comes up and says, "Hey, are you gaining weight?" she may not yet have developed the ability to counter the anorexic thoughts which bombard her mind. If this countering skill has not been developed, the individual will most likely relapse. Often the relapse is a combination of steps (1) and (2).

Marlatt says that once the relapse occurs (bingeing, purging, and starving behaviors), the individual will react in a predictable but destructive pattern. She will develop extremely negative thoughts about herself, feel very bad, and view herself as totally unworthy or hopeless in any effort to get well. We call this the "back to square one" mentality. In this stage the individual does not give herself any credit for progress made, but only focuses on the relapse as proof of her unworthiness and her inability to recover.

Marlatt further explains that from these negative thoughts the individual proceeds to the next destructive thought stage, in which she plays down the importance of the goal (to stop bingeing/purging or starving). She develops a strong case, contending that she is OK in using the behavior and that recovery is not important or probable. Marlatt says that if the individual learns to view relapse in a different way, it can be very helpful in her recovery. The individual must look at the relapse as part of the positive skill development: only through relapse can the person learn how to develop new and solid coping skills. Marlatt explains that "changing a long time habit is like learning any new skill, like learning to ride a bike. If you fall off the bike once, you don't give up trying" (Goleman, 1982, p. 20*). It is the same with eating-disorder habits. Relapse is a chance to learn more about what leads a person into relapse and about what kinds of skill building will be necessary if recovery is to occur. Also, other words can be used in place of "relapse" — words such as "lapse" or "slips," which may have a less negative meaning for the client. This technique allows the client to understand the relapse process and learn to view it as a part of her eventual recovery.

We witnessed the following potential relapse experience in group. Jane had been abstinent from bingeing for two months. She was working with a dietitian on a slow weight loss program. "I don't know what is happening. I only have to lose 12 pounds to reach my target weight. I have a feeling that I'm going to sabotage myself and start gaining weight again. That has been my pattern in the past, but I don't want to do it this time. Why am I so afraid of being at my ideal weight?"

Another individual in group responded, "When I reach my target weight, I then have to be perfect in all ways — in all parts of my life. That is such a tall order. I can't possibly do it, so I rapidly gain the weight again." Everyone in group (all were bulimic) emphatically nodded their heads in agreement.

By identifying and understanding the situations which lead to relapse, and by continually building stronger coping skills, the individual can use relapse (or potential relapse) as a tool for her recovery.

Assertiveness Training

The word "assert" is a derivative of the Latin term *asserere* which means "to claim." Assertiveness is the ability to claim and stand up for one's rights while respecting the rights of others. It involves the ability to communicate one's thoughts and feelings in a direct, straightforward manner. Assertiveness skills are essential to the recovery of the anorexic and bulimic. We have yet to meet a person with an eating disorder who doesn't need to develop additional assertion skills. In a few instances we have seen people who seemed initially to be fairly assertive. However, upon investigation it quickly became apparent that deficits did in fact exist which were not visible initially. For instance, one might be quite assertive in a nonpersonal business

*Reprinted with permission from *Psychology Today,* © 1982 by Ziff Davis Publishing Co.

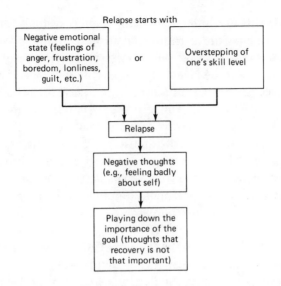

Figure 3-2 Relapse pattern.

situation yet have great difficulty asserting oneself in more personal relationships, such as with family and friends.

The anorexic and bulimic, because they tend to be people pleasers, oftentimes give up their personal rights and do not express their true thoughts or feelings in order not to hurt anyone else's feelings or get anyone angry with them. The fear is that if this precaution is not taken, the other person may not like them anymore. One of the typical beliefs which adds to this tendency is the belief that in order to be a worthwhile person, it is absolutely necessary to have everyone's total love and approval at all times. As long as this belief is held, assertion is nearly an impossibility.

Another belief common to many people but especially strong in eating-disordered individuals is that one must do things *perfectly* in order to be seen as a competent person worthy of respect. Such individuals often find it tremendously difficult to give themselves "permission" to make a mistake.

We recommend that clients read books on assertion and attend assertion training classes. These classes should include the following: learning and claiming individual rights and responsibilities; learning to differentiate between assertive, aggressive, and nonassertive behavior; identifying and challenging belief systems that interfere with assertive behavior; learning relaxation techniques for countering anxiety; and understanding the process of conflict resolution. Special attention should be given to role playing with specific practice in making requests, stating opinions, sharing feelings, and resolving conflict — all especially difficult for the eating-disordered client. The emphasis will of course need to be individually determined.

Assertiveness gets back to honesty, and it is this honesty that is invariably missing in the eating-disordered person's life. There is a vast array of excellent literature available on the topic of assertiveness. Books that we are personally familiar with and recommend for further information are the following:

- *Responsible Assertive Behavior: Cognitive/Behavioral Procedures for Trainers* by Lange and Jakubowski
- *Assertion Training: A Facilitator's Guide* by Colleen Kelley
- *Stand Up, Speak Out, and Talk Back* by Alberti and Emmons
- *The Assertive Woman* by Phelps and Austin
- *How to Be an Assertive (Not Aggressive) Woman in Life, in Love, and on the Job* by Jean Baer

For the therapist who is inexperienced but interested in providing assertion training, we especially recommend *Responsible Assertive Behavior* and *Assertion Training*. They will provide therapists with an overview of the topic and with various group formats complete with agenda, lecturettes, and exercises. *Stand Up, Speak Out, and Talk Back* provides guidelines for doing assertion training on an individual basis.

Resolution Work

A pattern that we see over and over in the eating-disordered individual is the avoidance of resolving issues, of tying up all loose ends, of finishing relationship issues, of getting a feeling of closure. We find instead that these individuals will carry these unfinished feelings around with them for years. What an emotional load that is! Learning to determine when something needs to be resolved is a skill that can and must be developed along with the assertive skills necessary to achieve resolution of the situation.

An example of this type of situation follows. Bonnie decided to go out shopping for the afternoon. She had been planning this for a while and was looking forward to it. When she left her apartment and went down to the garage to get her car, she found that another car was blocking it. Consequently, she could not get her car out of the garage. She knew who the owner of the other car was but did not want to approach this person. She became angry and upset because her plans were frustrated. She then went back to her apartment, feeling very deprived and sorry for herself, and proceeded to binge. A week later, in the office, she was still angry at what this person had done: namely, ruined her shopping trip and caused her to binge. While it had occurred to her to contact the owner of the car and ask him to move it, she didn't want him to get mad at her or to dislike her. So she found herself inhibited.

Retraining here obviously involves developing assertive skills, but other skills are also necessary. The person needs to learn the value of resolving a situation and putting it to rest. She also needs to learn that her irrational thinking, such as "I must be loved by all people all of the time," needs to be adjusted. If Bonnie had the necessary coping skills to deal with the situation directly, she probably could have avoided the binge.

Sometimes the situation involves another person who is willing to come into the office with our client. We have found this to be a good starting point for learning resolution skills. Furthermore, when the session is over, both parties usually feel better and have a sense of success and relief. We like to have clients dwell on these positive feelings and remember them. This reinforces the likelihood of trying the resolution skills again.

Keeping a Diary

We often ask our clients to keep a daily diary of (1) the type and amount of food eaten, (2) the time and place it is eaten, and (3) feelings and thoughts before, during, and after eating. We ask clients similarly to record purging behaviors, again noting time, place, feelings, and thoughts. The purpose of this is fourfold:

1. to heighten awareness of feelings,
2. to identify the kinds of thinking that leads to trouble so that appropriate counterstatements can be developed,

3. to provide a somewhat objective record of changes that do or do not occur,
4. to identify patterns.

Appendix E contains a chart that may be helpful for the client in monitoring her eating.

Theory of Change

Before becoming a counselor, one of the authors was a physical education teacher and intercollegiate coach. As she taught the skills necessary in various sports and activities, a progression in skill development became apparent. We have found this also to be true in skill building for individuals with eating disorders, and we have formulated the following theory of change.

Step one: Identification. It is important for the individual to identify the need for this new skill in her life; this provides motivation and a vested interest in treatment. This can occur in a variety of ways. For example, the client and counselor might determine that they will deal more directly with feelings of boredom because whenever the client gets these feelings, a binge is very likely. A plan is then developed whereby the individual can choose (1) to go to the library and study, (2) to call a friend, or (3) to take a walk when the feeling of boredom occurs. The client is aware of how to identify the feeling, what to do when the feeling occurs, and why the skill is needed. One last reminder is that the client must be motivated and want this plan as her own.

Step two: Missing the cue (choice point). Once the plan is developed, the individual must wait until the required situation occurs. Since many well-developed habits already exist regarding the aforementioned boredom situation, what usually happens is that the individual will get bored, do what she normally does (which is to start preparing to binge), and then at some point either before or after the binge, realize that she missed the boredom cue. This represents success; the person is definitely in the second stage of change. Step two is a critical stage because clients may feel as though they have failed. Just the opposite! They are into the second stage of change. Viewing such situations from this perspective is vital for continued motivation.

Step three: Attempting the skill — usually unsuccessfully. If the individual is honestly working on the identified skill development, after a few times of missing the cue and failing to start the plan, the individual will become bored and remember that she has choices at this point and that one choice is to implement the plan. The individual will attempt the plan but, because the skill level is very low, will very often be unsuccessful in her first attempts. For example, the individual may go to the library but binge anyway. This stage presents an opportunity for the counselor to educate the individual about how people learn: while they are developing their skills, they often are unsuccessful; in fact, they must be until they develop their skills. So it is not only OK not to succeed, it is a part of the skill development.

Step four: Attempting the skill — usually successfully. At this stage the individual has already practiced the skill of doing something productive when the boredom feelings occur, but the skill has usually not worked out and bingeing has occurred. However, through practice the individual has developed an awareness of the necessary skill level so that success starts to occur regularly. This is a stage in which support is necessary for the hard work involved in the change.

Step five: Continued practice of the new skill. This can be a dangerous time because the individual's confidence may outgrow the skill, and unless the individual continues consciously to practice the skill, she will revert to the old patterns of bingeing when bored.

What is helpful in viewing skill acquisition in this five-step way is that it allows for nonsuccess in the recovery process. In fact, failure is a requirement in this plan of change. Since most individuals with anorexia nervosa and bulimia are perfectionists, when they fail, they are very hard on themselves, think "What's the use!" and give up. If these individuals learn this pattern of change, they can fail and still be following the plan correctly. They can then fail and allow their failure to be acceptable despite perfectionist thinking.

Treatment Evaluation

How do you know when or if the eating-disordered client is getting better?

1. *Food intake.* One obvious parameter of health is normalized eating for both the bulimic and the anorexic. This is, in many ways,

the most important indicator of improvement but certainly not the only one. Often, the client's eating will become more normalized, but if changes have not occurred on other frontiers (e.g., cognitive, interpersonal), then the behavioral improvement with regard to eating will erode over time. Therefore, the therapist should regard the client's eating as an essential but not sole barometer of improvement.

2. *Cognitive changes and skill acquisition.* These changes are critical but more subtle. Has the client become more assertive, more aware of her feelings, and more able to express them directly? Are interpersonal relationships improving? It is a good idea to review with the client these more subtle changes and to provide tips for maintaining these changes. We strongly encourage clients to develop and maintain support systems for themselves after treatment is terminated.

FAMILY THERAPY

Nancy Bologna, Ph.D.
Clinical Psychologist
Southeast Human Service Center
Fargo, North Dakota

The following discussion of family therapy with eating-disordered patients is purported to serve as a "hands-on" guide to the practicing therapist. An array of theorists have addressed the use of family therapy in the treatment of eating disorders (Barcai, 1971; Bemis, 1978; Bowen, 1976; Bruch, 1973; Crisp, Harding, and McGuiness, 1974; Garner, Garfinkel, and Bemis, 1982; Haley, 1971; Kalucy, Crisp, and Harding, 1977; Minuchin, 1974; Leibman, Minuchin, and Baker, 1974; Minuchin, Rosman, and Baker, 1979; Russell, 1981; Schneider, 1981; Selvini-Palazzoli, 1974; Teyber, 1981), but it is beyond the scope of this book to review systematically the various theories. While many of the theorists suggest regular use of family therapy with anorexia, especially for younger clients (Caille, Abrahamsen, Girolami, and Sorbye, 1977; Conrad, 1977; Crisp, Harding, and McGuiness, 1974; Liebman, Minuchin, and Baker, 1974; Minuchin, Rosman, and Baker, 1979; Schneider, 1981; Teyber, 1981), others regard family therapy as supplemental to other treatment modes (Anderson, 1979; Garner, Garfinkel, and Bemis, 1982; Hersen and Detre, 1980). Piazza, Piazza, and Rollins (1980), in their proposal of a multidimensional formulation of the clinical course of anorexia nervosa, suggest the need to eliminate one specific treatment and to engage in a multimodal approach, depending on the degree and severity of the anorexic's clinical picture. Russell (1981) sees weight gain in the anorexic via hospitalization as the first stage of treatment for severe anorexics, with follow-up therapy consisting of treatment of the entire family. The author notes, however, that the efficacy of family therapy with eating disorders has not yet been empirically demonstrated. Garner, Garfinkel, and Bemis (1982) also propose a comprehensive multidimensional treatment for the eating-disordered patient. These authors recommend family therapy as the primary mode of treatment if the patient is 16 or younger and still resides at home.

Perusal of recent strategies with families of eating-disordered members reflects some general points that merit attention by the practicing therapist. First, there are very few methodologically rigorous treatment outcome studies which evaluate family therapy with eating disorders. Minuchin and his co-workers have been the most prolific in treatment outcome and document a recovery rate of approximately 85 percent, with follow-up extending from three months to nearly four years (Minuchin, Rosman, and Baker, 1979). However, many theorists suggest the need for more attention to reliable and valid treatment measures (Garner, Garfinkel, and Bemis, 1982; Hsu, 1980; Russell, 1981; Schwartz and Thompson, 1981; Wulliemier, 1978). Bemis (1978), characteristic of many of these theorists, states that ". . . although the treatment technique is too new to permit a conclusive assessment of its efficacy, the early results appear to be extremely promising, and the general emphasis on family involvement as an integral part of treatment seems well directed" (p. 602).

Second, there tends to be a heavy reliance among family therapists in this area on the "systems" model proposed by Minuchin. This model regards anorexia nervosa within the context of dysfunctional family communication. Several authors have described characteristic interactional patterns typical of families of anorexics, such as over-protectiveness, rigidity, enmeshment, and conflict avoidance (Caille, Abrahamsen, Girolami, and Sorbye, 1977; Conrad, 1977; Goodsitt, 1969; 1977; Liebman, Minuchin, and Baker, 1974; Minuchin, 1974; Minuchin, Baker, Rosman, Liebman, Milman, and Todd, 1975;

Minuchin, Rosman, and Baker, 1979; Schneider, 1981 ; Selvini-Palazzoli, 1974; Teyber, 1981). The goal of therapy is to disrupt and alter these dysfunctional patterns of communication so as to "free" the anorexic from the functional utility of her eating symptoms. In other words, the "systems" theorist assumes that the anorexic symptoms fulfill some important, albeit self-destructive, role in maintaining the family equilibrium. Garner et al. (1982) reflect on some of the possible functions of these symptoms:

> For example, the anorexic patient's symptoms may be functional in that they direct attention away from more basic areas of conflict within the family. They also may reflect ineffective parental controls which result from poor role definition within the family. In these cases, modification of the family's inappropriate communication patterns make the child's symptoms become unnecessary and permits the more fundamental areas of family conflict to be resolved. (p. 38)

Third, it should be noted that for the most part, research and theory on family therapy with eating-disordered patients tend to rely on anorexic rather than bulimic patients. This apparent bias in the literature is based on several factors besides the aforementioned one, that bulimia is just recently becoming recognized as a problem. First, the anorexic, because of the earlier onset of her disorder, is typically still living in the home. Consequently, interventions tend to include some alteration of the family context. As noted earlier, there do appear to be specific patterns of interaction common to the family of the anorexic which speaks to the need to alter these dysfunctional interactional patterns of communication. In addition, research has identified various personality disturbances in the families of anorexics (Blitzer, Rollins, and Blackwell, 1961; Halmi and Loney, 1973; Sours, 1974; Winoker, March, and Mendels, 1980). Consequently, family therapy has been used much more often with families of anorexics than with families of bulimics.

This discussion of the literature on family therapy with eating-disordered patients is not meant to be exhaustive; it merely provides the reader with a set of general guidelines and resources for further reading. The clinician, about to confront the difficult task of treating the anorexic and/or bulimic, is encouraged to read current and informed treatment approaches. Highly recommended are the "multifaceted" treatment packages which seem best able to deal with the overwhelming complexity of anorexia and bulimia (Garner, Garfinkel, and Bemis, 1982; Piazza, Piazza, and Rollins, 1980; Russell, 1981; Whipple and Manning, 1978). The clinician must make a decision whether to work with the individual alone, in a group context, or in family therapy. Further, the therapist must have a working knowledge of variables likely to affect the efficacy of the treatment of choice. Thus, to fully equip oneself, a familiarity with the theories and treatments is essential. In addition, communication with other clinicians regarding their application of various interventions can provide therapists with practical insight into helping the eating-disordered patients who are now knocking at their doors. The material which follows will combine many of the treatment strategies discussed in the literature and will endorse an eclectic approach. It is aimed at illuminating many of the dilemmas and decisions facing the clinician and providing the clinician with some general guidelines for treatment. This section is not aimed at presenting a new and/or distinct treatment approach but rather at familiarizing the reader with general concerns in treatment.

Assessment

A clinician's decision to engage the family of an eating-disordered patient in family therapy is based on a thorough assessment of two major factors: (1) the patient's clinical picture and (2) family characteristics. Each of these factors will guide the therapist in his/her initial decision to treat the family as a whole, as well as assist the therapist in deciding what particular set of therapeutic strategies would be most effective. Often, aspects of these two factors can be discerned even before the therapist sees the family in the first session (e.g., first telephone contact).

Patient's Clinical Picture

The first variable in the selection of family therapy is whether the patient is anorexic or bulimic. As noted earlier, there is a tendency among therapists to provide family therapy when the patient is anorexic and to recommend group therapy when the patient is bulimic.

This should only be regarded as a general rule of thumb, however, for often the bulimic does well with a structured, behaviorally based, family therapy approach. As previously mentioned, the earlier age of onset for the anorexic places him/her in a more embedded role within the family. Also, it has been noted that the precipitating event triggering the binge-purge syndrome in the bulimic is a change of life such as beginning college (Casper, Eckert, Halmi, 1980; Russell, 1979). Consequently, the bulimic patient is frequently already removed from the home.

A second major consideration is the patient's age, irrespective of the type of eating disorder. The younger the client, the more likely it is that family therapy will be helpful. Age may also guide the therapist in the set of therapeutic procedures she may wish to employ. The younger the patient is, the more behavioral, structured, and directive the intervention can be (Wells and Forehand, 1981). One family, referred to one of us by a physician, consisted of a 12-year-old anorexic female, her 14- and 17-year-old sisters, and her 9-year-old brother. The parents had been informed by one of the siblings that Kathleen, the anorexic, had been doing 150 sit-ups at night before going to bed, was running up and down the stairs when her parents weren't home, and was complaining constantly of "feeling fat." The girl had not yet shown any significant weight loss although she had begun to lose weight gradually over the previous six months. The parents had informed the physician that Kathleen was "an extremely picky eater" and noticed that she voiced signs of anxiety when she ate certain foods. The physician, accurately diagnosing early cognitive and emotional symptoms of anorexia nervosa, referred the family for family therapy. After several sessions during which a detailed assessment of the family dynamics was made, the therapist worked very specifically with the parents in terms of Kathleen's eating pattern. Kathleen was put on a behavioral contract which required specific eating habits and a minimum body weight. The siblings and parents were instructed to discontinue lengthy and emotional discussions of Kathleen's eating pattern. Rather, Kathleen was expected to maintain an agreed upon weight, to eat on a scheduled basis, and to do only certain exercises at certain times. Teachers from her school were also informed of the contract and asked to assist. Thus, because of Kathleen's relative youth, a more directive and behavioral approach was successful in helping her maintain her weight.

A third criterion in the selection of family therapy is the severity and symptomatology of the illness. These variables are considerably more difficult to evaluate since they require a more detailed assessment over a longer period of time. However, some general rules can be applied. If the anorexic or bulimic patient exhibits severe symptoms (e.g., the anorexic with extremely low body weight, or the bulimic with a very high frequency of bingeing or vomiting), then a more restrictive and structured treatment is required. This usually takes the form of hospitalization, especially with the anorexic who may require intravenous feeding. Neither family therapy nor any other outpatient treatment can impose the necessary control over the patient's environment to counteract the effects of such severe symptoms. More often than not, the family members are themselves experiencing impairment in general functioning and are in such a state of crisis that they welcome the reprieve occasioned by the hospitalization. Inpatient treatment is often the "last resort" treatment for the anorexic and is implemented if the anorexic expresses dangerously low body weight, especially if she also shows cognitive distortions, extreme social withdrawal, suicidal ideation, and/or blunted affect. Family therapy is ineffective if the patient is too physically ill to become engaged in the therapeutic process. Also, family members, concerned with the patient's physical well-being, are considerably less invested in "psychological" contributants to the disorder. However, family therapy is often very effective immediately following the hospitalization of the anorexic (Russell, 1981). By then, the severity of the symptoms has attenuated and family therapy serves a fourfold function: (1) to provide structure and guidance in maintaining the anorexic's weight by way of behavioral contracting, (2) to help the family adjust more constructively to the patient's return, (3) to structure interactional patterns in such a way as to prevent the emergence of the same patterns of interaction that contributed to the eating disorder in the first place, and (4) to provide the family and the patient with continuity of treatment.

This state of affairs is seldom the case with the bulimic. Severe bulimia doesn't precipitate the dramatic physical and cognitive deterioration noted in severe anorexia. Bulimics often "hide" their symptoms from their families and can do so successfully since there is no obvious physical product of their illness such as the low body weight of the anorexic. However, when severe stages of the disorder are reached, even the most clever and cautious bulimic is often "discovered." Frequently, parents will call a therapist when they are aware that one of their children is bulimic. The parents are fraught with confusion and guilt, and feel unable to confront their child with their knowledge. Occasionally, the bulimic patient will inform the parents on his/her own accord, but most often the parents become aware of large amounts of missing food or excessive expenditures in grocery stores. One frequent reaction of a bulimic to a parental confrontation of this sort is anger and denial. Often, the therapist can engage the entire family in treatment to allow the family and the bulimic an avenue for confronting and accepting the bulimia. In many cases, the bulimic is referred to group therapy, and future contacts with the family therapist are in the guise of adjunct, supportive therapy.

Family Characteristics

A second set of criteria in the assessment of a family is various familial characteristics. The first and most practical criterion is availability of the family members. Are the members living in the same house as the patient? If so, they should be included in the therapy regardless of how little they may interact with the patient. If they do not reside in the home (e.g., a married older sibling), do they live nearby, so that convergence at the therapist's door is a possibility? While you as the therapist may decide that family therapy is clearly the "treatment of choice," you are unlikely to progress if family members are unavailable (e.g., living in another city).

Related to this consideration is a more nebulous one, namely, motivation of the family members to become involved in treatment and to see the identified patient get better. Client resistance is a well-known phenomenon to most seasoned clinicians, but this problem becomes more salient when "treatment compliance" depends on several people rather than on one individual. Usually, if the parents are well motivated, the rest of the family will follow suit. If the parents demand that all the children attend the sessions, family therapy can be quite successful even if the children vary in their degree of investment in the therapeutic process. In fact, it is often the most ostensibly resistant family member that provides the most impetus for change once therapy has commenced. One family, treated over a period of approximately six months, consisted of a 14-year-old anorexic male, his 11-year-old sister, and his 7-year-old brother. The parents had no difficulty convincing the two males in the family to participate in treatment, but they received persistent and adamant refusals from their daughter. Eventually, the parents demanded that she participate in the family sessions since the therapist had informed them that she wanted to see all family members. Once there, the therapist expected her to be tight-lipped and uncooperative. Instead, she became the "spokesperson" for the family, expressing both emotionally and verbally the sources of contention and conflict in the family. She later stated that she was afraid to participate in therapy because she perceived it as an opportunity to "say all these awful things" about her family and knew she would be unable to resist saying them. What this young, insightful girl didn't realize was that her honest portrayal of her family's discontent opened the door for positive changes to occur.

Typically, the families of anorexics are compliant with the therapist's recommendations for treatment and will rarely refuse initial requests for family therapy (Minuchin et al., 1979). In fact, more often than not, the parents will initiate the request to be seen as a family.

A second consideration in using family therapy is the degree of contact the client has with various family members. In general, as mentioned earlier, if the family member resides in the same home as the patient, he/she should be included in treatment. Generally, the anorexic patient has few overt conflicts with her family so it is often difficult to discern which family members are germane to the treatment until several sessions have occurred. This suggestion of including all family members living in the home with the patient extends to the bulimic as well. In this case, conflict is usually more obvious since bulimics tend to be more verbal and more behaviorally rebellious (e.g., shoplifting; Green and Rau, 1977; Pyle, Mitchell, and Eckert, 1981).

Treatment

I liken the family therapist to a person climbing aboard a small boat filled with several people. All the people are complaining about one another; some dislike the rough waters; others are unhappy with how the boat is being handled. Occasionally, a seemingly happy and positive interaction occurs. Although they all complain, none is willing to make any changes for fear of tipping over. Their need to keep the boat afloat overrides their wish to have things exactly their way. They have all agreed to allow a new person, the therapist, on board, and the boat has made its way to shore. As the therapist joins the group, she senses the tension among the group members and begins to hypothesize about the various relationships. Who's in charge of guiding the boat? What jobs have been assigned to the various members?

The manner in which the therapist begins to initiate changes in this small group depends on the constellation of the family, the dynamics of interaction, the lines of authority and the degree to which they are enforced, the separate relationships among the members (especially the husband and wife), and the particular theoretical framework of the therapist.

As noted earlier, many theorists involved in family therapy make use of the "systems" approach described by Minuchin (1974). He postulates that the illness is a manifestation of deep family conflict: the anorexic is caught in the midst of dysfunctional family interactions and expresses the family discord through her eating disorder. Consonant with the "systems" model, Minuchin refers to various "subsystems" within a family, namely the spouse subsystem (husband and wife), the parental subsystem (mother and father), and the sibling subsystem. Minuchin looks for the "boundaries" between these subsystems. Boundaries refer to the lines of communication among the various members of the family and can range from overly rigid (e.g., the extremely detached, authoritative father) to diffuse (e.g., the lenient mother who tries to be her daughter's "best friend"). Either overly rigid or overly diffuse boundaries have been noted in families of anorexics (Garner, Garfinkel, and Bemis, 1982).

Minuchin also categorizes families along a dimension of "detached" to "enmeshed." The former refers to the family in which little communication occurs, especially emotional expression. Such families have very defined lines of authority, and the family is perceived by its members to be uninvolved emotionally and often unsupportive. The enmeshed family is one in which few boundaries exists, and those that do are quite diffuse. Here, each member is acutely aware and involved in another member's emotional status. Parents do not enforce their role as parents, and often the children are involved in making such parental decisions as curfew and assignment of household duties. Minuchin sees both types of families as dysfunctional, with each type producing characteristic deviance in its members.

With regard to the anorexic (Minuchin makes no statements about the family dynamics of the bulimic, and his family therapy is described solely for the anorexic), Minuchin hypothesizes that the anorexic is involved in an enmeshed family. More specifically, he postulates that "triangulation" occurs — a dysfunctional pattern of interaction in which the child is placed between the spouses. The child receives all the negative messages meant for the other spouse, which places the child in the position of trying to handle the burden of parental discord. The parents "detour" their conflicts into this child rather than confront them openly and honestly. The result is the emergence of psychosomatic (in this case, anorexic) symptoms. These symptoms serve to "keep the family together" by forcing the members of the family to address the severity of the symptoms. The anorexic symptoms temporarily stabilize the family because the parents now have an alternative (and far more pressing!) problem to focus on, rather than their marital discord. The goal of treatment, then, is to disengage this child from her position in the family and to "free" her of the maladaptive functions she serves.

This is a simplified formulation of Minuchin's theory, and certainly the beginning therapist can expect to see wide deviations from this notion when confronting an anorexic and her family. However, by examining the manner in which interactions occur, the degree of intactness of the lines of communication, and the extent to which each member fulfills certain functions in the family, the therapist can begin to make changes in the family and to evaluate the effect of such changes on overall family functioning. Minuchin and other structured family therapists postulate that the therapist must "disrupt" the typical patterns of interaction in a family through such therapeutic manuevers as "joining," in which a therapist takes the side of one member and frequently forces a conflict to emerge in the session. By disrupting the typical patterns of interaction, new, more adaptive forms of interaction can emerge. At that point, the therapist's role becomes one of maintaining these positive changes.

Before describing an actual case, a discussion of the second major theoretical framework, the behavioral approach, will be presented. In actuality, there are very few behaviorists who have addressed the issue of family therapy (Patterson, 1971; Wahler, 1976), and in fact, there is no single behavioral formulation for family therapy with eating-disordered patients. However, behavioral theories have led to empirically validated treatment strategies in a wide range of behavioral disorders, and many individualized treatments have been recommended for anorexics and bulimics (Bhanji and Thompson, 1974; Blinder, Freeman, and Stunkard, 1970; Cairns and Altman, 1979; Hersen and Detre, 1980; Ollendick, 1979; Rosen, 1980).

Behavioral interventions involve the use of behavioral contingencies; these refer to the establishment of a relationship between the occurrence of a particular behavior (or set of behaviors) and an outcome. A contingency is an "if . . . then" relationship between two events. The patient is required to maintain a certain body weight or eat a certain amount of food; in exchange, she receives certain rewards (e.g., money, privileges). These contingencies can be agreed upon by the patient herself or by the parents, depending on the age and motivational level of the patient. Patterson (1970) has made considerable use of such contracting in his work with families of delinquents.

Many families of anorexics could potentially profit from some inclusion of behavioral techniques in family treatment. Although there are no behaviorally based family approaches, many individualized treatment strategies can be used successfully with families. Also, as noted earlier, the use of multidimensional treatments (Garner, Garfinkel, and Bemis, 1982; Piazza, Piazza, and Rollins, 1980; Russell, 1981) includes behavioral interventions. The flexible therapist can implement many strategies in the course of treatment.

Case Histories

The application of family therapy techniques can be illustrated by some actual cases. Two families will be presented in which some success was evidenced through the course of family therapy. Only certain aspects of the therapy will be described for the sake of brevity.

Mark M. Mark is a 15-year-old anorexic male in the severe stages of the disorder. When first meeting with his parents, the therapist was informed that Mark was 30 percent below his average weight; at 5 feet 7 inches he weighed approximately 80 pounds. Mark's parents contacted a large mental health clinic and discussed their need to pursue family therapy. The father was a successful businessman in the area, and his wife was a part-time elementary education teacher. They had four children: Mark, age 15 (the identified patient); Susan, age 13; David, age 9; and Peter, age 6. In general, they were a fairly happy family. The children had all been doing well in school, they all had good peer relations, and the parents reported satisfaction in their jobs and with their marriage. One year prior to this first contact, the oldest son, Mark — a compliant, rather quiet and introspective boy — decided to try out for his high school basketball team. He began a rather restrictive diet and a rigorous weight-lifting program. At first, the diet was unsuccessful in that he did not lose any weight and reported having considerable difficulty staying off sweets. His parents and siblings noted no significant personality changes in Mark, though his mother stated that he became moderately irritable. Within the three months following the start of the diet, Mark began to show pronounced weight loss, significant (though gradual) social withdrawal, and extreme irritability toward his family. He became a "pea pusher," according to his mother, who stated that he would "push the food around on his plate, trying to look like he was eating, without putting anything in his mouth." He was examined physically and informed that he suffered from no physical disorder. The physician finally recommended family therapy. The possibility of hospitalization was discussed, and it was decided that first the family would get involved in family therapy. If the weight dropped below a certain point (determined by the physician), Mark would be hospitalized. This "threat" of hospitalization can often work in the therapist's favor as it increases the motivation of all family members to comply with treatment.

The first tactic of the therapist in this case is to get an overall idea of what makes this family tick. Are the parents happy with each other? (You can pick this up after a few sessions of watching them interact with each other.) How do the siblings get along? What about Mark — what kind of person is he? Some therapists recommend personality testing with the identified patient (e.g., MMPI, anxiety or depression scales). The use of personality testing depends on the framework of the particular clinician. In Mark's case, no such testing was done as it was not a standard procedure of the center to have such testing completed. In this case, Mark (similar to the characteristic description of the anorexic) was an ostensibly compliant son, highly perfectionistic about his work and usually worried about his grades, fairly passive in relationships (more the follower than the leader among his peers), and a somewhat anxious boy who seemed to be sick more often than his siblings. Interpersonally, Mark liked a person either very much or not at all; he reacted to people with strong emotion, either positive or negative. He interacted with his parents fairly well until the anorexia became more severe. Then he appeared to ignore them and met their demands to eat with quiet noncompliance.

After two sessions, the therapist usually gets a sense of the family and can begin to make definitive interventions. The first approach the therapist took with this family (among many possibilities) was to behaviorally regulate Mark's eating patterns within the home. He was required to eat meals with the family (after we role played meals at home during our sessions), and the family was instructed to decrease the frequency of conversations involving food. Mark carried around a notebook in which he recorded his intake as well as the times of day at which he ate. This notebook was discussed only with the therapist and the dietitian to whom the family had been referred. Parenthetically, family therapy alone with an anorexic in this stage of the disorder is absolutely inappropriate. A medical professional must be involved to monitor the physical side effects of the illness and to set a minimum weight, below which the patient must be hospitalized. If the family does proceed with therapy at this state of the illness, then a certified dietitian should be involved to help the patient structure his nutritional intake.

Thus, the first stratagem involved behavioral contracting which included some provision of extra privileges if Mark met his goals for adequate eating. It was lucky that Mark was an individual for whom some privileges were rewarding. Many times, the anorexic reports no potential reinforcers and is unwilling to contract for anything! In such cases, aversive control techniques are required to gain control over the patient's eating behavior. These would include the withdrawal of positive events or the presentation of an aversive event (e.g., hospitalization) if the required changes in eating do not occur. With regard to Mark, this was not necessary. He agreed to a behavioral contract based on receipt of certain privileges.

As therapy progressed, relationships within the family became the focus of interaction. Although Mark's parents described themselves as maritally happy, it appeared that their communication with one another was often circuitous and indirect. Mark's mother, busy and successful in her outside activities, was committed to the notion that her husband handle the discipline in the family. As the years went by, she became somewhat intimidated by him, and found herself less and less able to confront him when she disagreed with his parental decisions. Consequently, her disagreement with his decisions took the form of subtle undermining of his authority by being extremely lenient with the children in his absence. In many ways, she gave up her rights as a parent and tried to interact with her children as an equal. The resulting inconsistent parental discipline became most salient with Mark since he was the oldest. Thus, one goal of therapy was to strengthen the parental boundary. By "joining" (Minuchin, 1974) the mother during the session, the therapist encouraged her to confront the father more directly, to voice her disagreements more openly, and to resolve them with her husband. This approach is called a "united front." Parents are instructed to discuss the issues between themselves, make a final decision, and then apply the rule to the children. This is a powerful technique and often goes a long way toward reducing tension in a home and improving the overall quality of relationships, especially between the parents.

Through the use of behavioral contracting and various structured family therapy interventions (only a few of which were discussed above), Mark gradually gained weight, though very slowly. He never required hospitalization, and follow-up nine months after family therapy had been discontinued revealed that he was maintaining his weight.

Susan R. Susan is 20 years of age and has been bulimic for the past three years. At a weight of 121 pounds and a height of 5 feet 6 inches, she is regarded by most people as attractive and slim. She binges approximately twice a day in the privacy of her dormitory room (during the week) and in her parent's home (in her bedroom) on weekends. She consumes approximately 3500 calories per binge within a 30-minute period. Binge foods include cakes, cookies, ice cream, and "junk foods" (potato chips, Fritos). Usually within 20 minutes following the binge, she self-induces vomiting by pushing her index finger down her troat. She then feels drowsy, and occasionally naps and wakes in a depressed, guilt-ridden mood. She berates herself for her "sick habit" but feels powerless to change. She reports that any type of stress can precipitate a binge, especially academic pressures. She describes herself as popular and has a steady boyfriend who knows nothing of her problem.

Susan's family consists of her middle-aged parents (her father is an accountant, and her mother works part-time outside of the home). She has an older sister, age 23; twin sisters, age 16; and two brothers, ages 14 and 11. Susan goes to college in her parents' hometown and goes home on the weekends even though she lives in the dormitory. She describes her family as close but not emotionally supportive. Her parents disapprove of her boyfriend and complain that she "travels in a fast crowd."

Susan reports that her bulimia began during her freshman year in college. While a senior in high school, she was moderately overweight (144 pounds) and began dating a freshman from the local college. Being athletically inclined, he teased her about her weight and encouraged her to exercise. Susan soon began to lose weight and described this period of time as happy for her. However, when she began college herself, she found the academic work grueling. Her weight fluctuated, and she began to steadily increase her weight over the freshman year. Afraid of losing her boyfriend, she learned to "get the best of both worlds" by overeating her favorite foods and self-inducing vomiting. Over time, however, the binges increased in frequency and severity, and they began to "take over" her life.

Susan's mother, after reading an article on bulimia and recognizing many of the symptoms confronted Susan. Two weeks later, the family appeared for family therapy.

The approach with this family was mainly a behavioral one. Susan and her family met for five sessions, after which Susan became a member of a local eating-disorders group. Family therapy focused on informing the family members of the disorder and allowing them the opportunity to ventilate the considerable emotional dismay they experienced. Susan, quite distraught by her father's reaction that the disorder was a "disgusting habit," was able eventually to express her anger at him for "never even caring enough to notice what I was doing." The most dysfunctional dyad was Susan and her father. Susan felt that he disfavored her among all the children because "I was never a big brain like you." The father, a detached and emotionally aloof man was initially resistant to address his daughter's reactions on an emotional level. He would respond to her with a rational and logical answer. However, as the therapy progressed, he became more emotionally expressive, exhibiting his anger at Susan for her choice of boyfriends and, in effect, confirming his love for her by explaining how much her rebellious behaviors hurt him. An interesting aspect of this family was the degree of solidarity of the siblings. All the children shared various complaints about their parents and highly reinforced each other's comments. The overall effect of the therapy was to provide this relatively emotionally bound and caring family with an opportunity to express their feelings.

The behavioral aspect of the therapy was an agreement between the parents and Susan about her eating behavior while in the home. Probably the most important goal of adjunct family therapy with bulimics is to help the significant others in the bulimic's life to set limits on their own responsibility toward the bulimic's binges. In other words, should the parents (or spouse, etc.) have to continue filling the cupboard and refrigerator after the bulimic binges? Should the significant other refuse to observe the bulimic while bingeing? One general rule of thumb is that the bulimic should be wholly responsible for the expense and other problems of his/her binges. Loved ones should be clear and very specific about what aspects of the binges they will tolerate. In Susan's case, she was required to *immediately* replace all foods eaten during a binge; she was required to eat her meals with her family when at home; further, she was not allowed to discuss her binges with family members or to ever binge in their presence. In addition, Susan contracted to eliminate all naps during the day. The elimination of naps served the twofold purpose of "normalizing" her daily routine (most "normal" eaters don't need to nap after they eat) and of making the immediate consequence of a binge less reinforcing.

Conclusion

This section has been aimed at introducing therapist referring agents, as well as patients and/or their families, to the application of family therapy techniques with families of anorexics and bulimics. One issue not discussed is that of case closure. When is the family finished with the therapy? My particular bias toward the need for careful treatment-outcome studies is reflected in this issue. Therapists owe their clients information and feedback about the progress and eventual length of treatment. Unfortunately, at this point in our knowledge, this decision is typically a subjective one, based on a myriad of variable idiosyncratic to the particular clinician. The stage of experimental inquiry is simply not conclusive yet, and we are limited to our clinical experiences in what we can present. What is needed is a much more thorough data base on which to judge treatment effectiveness and gauge a particular treatment. Methodologically sound clinical-outcome studies would provide such a data base. At this point in time, it is incumbent upon the therapist to remain up-to-date on the available literature and to provide some objective measures of treatment effectiveness. With family therapy, the problems of evaluation of treatment are multiplied since family therapy, among all forms of outpatient treatment, is one of the most poorly researched.

In most cases, it is up to the clinician to suggest eventual treatment closure. Families will consistently report a subjective alleviation of distress or tension in the home, and this fact will evidence itself in the course of the therapy sessions. Actual changes in communication patterns are noticeable to the clinician, and she can look for durable positive changes in these interactional patterns. Also, it is not always appropriate to use the patient's overall weight as a barometer of success with the anorexic family. Very often, the family therapy "frees" the client of some of the variables maintaining his/her eating disorder, but if the anorexia is well under way, other extrafamilial variables have become active in the client's repertoire and must be altered using different techniques such as individual therapy (behavioral contracting) and group therapy.

*　　*　　*

GROUP THERAPY

Group therapy is finding its way into many professional programs for anorexia nervosa and bulimia. Although controversial, it has been a helpful therapeutic approach for many reasons. First, it allows people with the disorder to learn from each other not only what is helpful, but also what the hazards are in working toward recovery. Additionally, group members are able to give each other support, understanding, and encouragement which can help to alleviate some of the loneliness and isolation often felt by persons with these disorders. Participation in a group allows one person to reach out to another, thus taking the focus off self for a time. With all members sharing the common experience of these disorders, group can be an environment in which there is more honesty, since the conning and lying that usually accompany these disorders can generally be identified and attended to by other group members. Members develop their own subculture, forming new values beneficial to their recovery and discarding harmful values (which are often promoted in our culture).

There can be some drawbacks to the "processing" when anorexics and bulimics are in group.* For one thing, sufferers are often "people pleasers" and are likely to be unable to say what they really mean. So unless tended to, group can become a situation where everyone is very "nice" to everyone else and no one really deals with feelings. Also, since the identity of the group members is often fragile, they have a tendency to take on and experience one another's problems, unless this trend also is specifically tended to. In addition, the therapist needs to be alert to the tendency of some clients to adopt methods of weight loss utulized by other group members.

Philosophy

The philosophy of the group leader(s) will determine to a great extent how the group will be experienced. The group leader(s) may be very nondirective, thereby forcing all of the responsibility for processing on the group members. This can be helpful in allowing more expression from the members, but it does not allow the leader(s) to give professional insight or to educate if there are questions. The more directive approach allows for professional insight and education, but can cut down on processing by members who will always look toward the leader(s) for answers/responses instead of looking inward and questioning self. A happy medium can be found between the two extremes and usually can produce a balance in the processing.

Another issue regarding the philosophy of the leader(s) is whether or not to discuss process. For example, if a member has serious

---

*"In interactional psychotherapy "process" refers to the relationship implications of interpersonal transactions. A therapist who is process-oriented concerns himself not solely with the verbal content of the patient's utterance, but with the "how" and the "why" of the utterance, especially insofar as the "how" and "why" illuminate some aspects of the patient's relationship to others with whom he is interacting" (Yalom, 1975, p 122).

thoughts of suicide and shares them with the group, we teach the group how to respond supportively to this situation. Hearing the person out, helping to problem solve, and giving feedback on reactions to the disclosure are important skills for the members to develop. Some group leaders will openly discuss the process and in fact educate the group in group skills; other leaders will use more indirect methods. Our philosophy is that process should be identified and specifically taught.

Pre-group Screening

Pre-group screening involves an interview with a potential group member before she makes her final decision about entering group. It is also helpful for the group leader(s) in determining who would most likely benefit from the group.

In addition to these benefits, there are a variety of reasons why pre-group screening is helpful:

1. It gives the leader(s) an opportunity to fully explain the dynamics of the group. Its focus, rules, makeup, and philosophy are all important issues that should be explained to the potential member.

2. We have found it also important to explore the expections of the person wishing to enter group. Does she view it as an instant cure? Does she feel the group should be responsible for her recovery? If so, she will quickly be disillusioned and angry because the group has failed her. If the expectations are too irrational and the person seems unable to accept responsibility for her recovery, she will have a more difficult time in group. Such people are often among the early dropouts in group.

3. The pre-group interview also allows the group leader(s) to screen out inappropriate people from the group. Some individuals are too ill to be helped by group. They may need individual counseling or hospitalization before group experience can be helpful. The individual who does not feel that she has a problem may be very resistant in group. Also, if a person is not group oriented and does not want to share the attention of the leader(s) with other members, that individual will be very uncomfortable in group, and probably quite disruptive.

4. During the interview, any questions the individual may have can be answered, and this will allow the person to make a more

knowledgeable choice regarding group membership. Group is not for everyone, but it can be very helpful if the person is suited to, and ready for, the group experience. Pre-group screening allows for a better chance of a good match-up.

5. The expectations of the group leader(s) can be clarified for the client during the pre-group screening.

Structure

The structure of groups can vary a great deal. On the following pages we have included some of the many issues involved in the development of a group.

Size. Group therapy groups usually range in size from 5 to 12 members. If group has less than 5 members, the processing changes and the verbalization can become nonproductive; if more than 12, it becomes difficult to handle the group and still allow time for all the members who wish to participate. Furthermore, the quieter members will have a tendency to withdraw if the group is too large, and this has a great effect on group processing, since other group members wonder what they are thinking.

Focus of Group. The focus of the group can be:

1. Education
2. Developing healthy eating patterns
3. Dealing the the underlying thoughts and feelings which trigger the focus on food
4. A combination of the above three

Examples of some of the many types of eating-disorder groups can be found in Appendix F.

Some things to consider when making the focus decision are:

1. Time (amount of)
2. Needs of members
3. Professional background of group leader(s)

If education is chosen as a focus, some possible topic areas are:

1. Assertiveness skills
2. Rational versus irrational thinking
3. Interpersonal relationship work
4. Health issues
5. Feminist issues related to eating disorders
6. Information and research regarding eating disorders
7. Stress management
8. Nutrition
9. Self-identity

We have found it very important in group work to define the focus carefully. In our initial work with eating-disordered groups, we tried to do too much — tried to be all things to all people — and this only led to confusion on the part of group members. We found ourselves unable to cover any one thing in depth. If we taught assertiveness skills, the eating plan work and the group therapy areas lost time and emphasis. If the emphasis was on eating plans, the other areas would suffer. We never seemed to be able to carry through long enough in one area without other areas suffering. Group members would then feel as if they were not getting what they had expected from group. With only a two-hour format per week, this reaction is understandable.

Today, we have a group which primarily concentrates on the underlying thoughts and emotions that result in the focus on food and trigger the binges or the starving behaviors. The group works toward identification of these thoughts and feelings, along with the development of different, more productive coping skills. These new coping skills are developed in many aspects of the person's life. For example, concerning problems in relationships with persons of the opposite sex, we stress honesty with self. What are the real feelings involved? How do these feelings affect the situation? What are one's rights as an individual? What other options does one have in this situation? Another area that is dealt with in this group format is rational versus irrational thinking. Very similar irrational thought patterns appear among anorexic and bulimic persons. Helping them to identify these irrational thoughts, to learn how to refute these thoughts, and finally to replace them with more productive thoughts, works well in group (see "Identifying Anorexic and Bulimic Thoughts" earlier in this chapter).

We stress the importance of developing new coping skills (as described earlier in individual therapy techniques). Persons must have something to replace their usually very long-standing habits and thoughts before they ask themselves to give up maladaptive food-related behaviors.

Open/Closed Group. We define the closed group as one in which the membership is controlled and new members are allowed in only when the leader(s) and/or the members give permission. This type of group also very often has pre-group screening. People are not allowed to come and go freely, in and out of the group. Because confidentiality is such an important aspect of the group, a closed group gives a greater feeling of security; furthermore, it ensures the appropriate size of the group for productive processing. In a group whose main objective is therapy, the group is usually closed. A group in which the main objective is education can be open or closed, depending upon the philosophy of the leader(s).

Format. The format of groups can vary greatly. We will not deal with all possible formats here, but rather will present some basic guidelines we have used.

1. Open with something positive that has happened to each person during the past week by going around the group and having each person share. This is a good ice breaker, getting everyone involved at the beginning of group, and it also provides a direction of positive thought which counters the multitude of negative thoughts that can occur.

2. Open with a problem which each member is presently working on that week.

3. Open with discussion of the individual group member's goal for the week. Did she accomplish it? What will her goal be for next week? The goals are *not* generally food related (usually feelings, thoughts, etc.).

4. Open with asking for time. This can be done at the beginning of each group. The objective of this rule is to find out how many members have concerns to bring to group and thereby to allow time for each member. Once the number of members wanting time is known, one of the members can begin by sharing her concern. Everyone is cognizant of how many members have requested time for

that session, and group members become very aware of the importance of allowing enough time for each member who has asked for time. Some defining is often necessary with this rule in order to answer the question, For what reasons do I ask for time? Some members may feel that their concerns are never big enough or important enough if this question is not defined. An added benefit of asking for time is that it encourages assertiveness in the individual member.

Identity Work. Often we find that group members complain that they feel so "awful" at the end of group. They indicate that they like group and feel it helps them, but that afterwards they feel worse than when they had arrived. On questioning further, we discover that during group, as each person talks about a problem, many of the members have great difficulty distinguishing between their own feelings and the feelings of the person speaking. For example, if a group member experienced increased bingeing, other members begin to feel that they also want to binge, or if a person expresses thoughts of suicide, some group members start to feel suicidal also.

In order to help solve this problem, we developed an activity at the end of group called "separating away." In this activity, we ask each member to mentally separate her identity from the identity of other members, especially members to whom she has reacted in that group session. So, for example, if one group member has talked about her high anxiety over school work, another member who identifies closely with this would mentally separate herself from the first group member's problem by identifying her own uniqueness and her separateness from the other person. Members need to understand and acknowledge that these are feelings experienced by other group members. If a similar situation occurs in their own life, they can own that problem and work with it. This is different from experiencing another's problem.

We stress that the way group members can best be supportive of another person is to individuate from them, because only then will they be able to reach out and help each other. If they do not individuate, they will be too burdened with their own feelings to reach out to another member. The "separating away" or mental imagery can be handled in several ways. We always ask each member to close her eyes and be silent; then one of us will give instructions. The following examples have been found helpful in the separation:

1. Mentally separate your identity from each individual group member by going around the group in your mind and identifying the differences between you and each of the other members.

2. As you get in touch with your feelings, identify which group members have had a negative emotional impact on you during this meeting. Then identify in your mind your uniqueness and the differences between you and the other members.

3. Think about your uniqueness. Identify things about yourself that make you different from other members. Feel your strengths and your individuality.

4. When we are finished "separating away," we go through muscle relaxation and deep breathing exercises, teaching the members to spot muscle tension and learn to relax each tense area.

5. After the relaxation period, we open our eyes and ask someone in the group for a positive thought to leave with the group. We do this in order to finish on a positive, uplifting note, which seems to set a tone for the group members as they leave group. Members will share a feeling of closeness with the group, a meaningful saying that they have heard, or a feeling of strength and hope for the future.

Length and Frequency of Group Sessions. The length and frequency of the groups can vary greatly. Our groups are held once a week for two hours. We have found that a meeting time of less than one and one-half hours really limits the amount of processing. If the group runs over two hours, the members seem to suffer fatigue and the group tends to become nonproductive. We feel that the group should meet at least once a week because anything further apart might cause a loss of continuity. Group could be held more than once a week, but this is often not possible given the time constraints of most professionals. However, in some areas specific programs are available for anorexics and bulimics which are very concentrated and meet daily for a specified number of weeks (see Appendix D for a description of an intensive program). After participating in the concentrated programs, members often are advised to become part of a weekly group.

Makeup of Group. There is ongoing discussion among professionals regarding the makeup of groups. A key question that arises is whether the anorexics and bulimics should be separated. Is it all right to mix the two diagnostic syndromes? We have experienced mixed groups in which members were anorexic and bulimic, and groups in which members were only bulimic, and we have found both to be workable. Separation of the restricting, nonpurging anorexics from the binge-vomiters, when feasible, can be helpful. Then conversations and problems are fairly similar for all members.

Another factor to consider in group membership is the age range of the members. Again, there is much discussion among professionals regarding this factor. It may he helpful if the groups are separated into adolescents and adults when possible, to allow more continuity. However, many groups are doing very well in which all ages are included within one group, and in fact this can be advantageous, adding a richness of experience to the group.

It can be a difficult experience for one group member to be very different from everyone else in the group — for example, if there is only one male in the group, if one person if very thin, or if one person is excessively overweight. These different members may experience feelings of isolation or nonacceptance. These situations are not necessarily a problem, but awareness of these potential problems is necessary so that if they do occur, the situation can be dealt with in the group.

Group Leader(s). Will your group have one or two leaders? Should the leader(s) be male or female? Does it matter? These are questions of philosophy and opinion. We will share our ideas, keeping in mind that there are many other opinons. We believe it is important to have two leaders for the group. Here are our reasons:

1. There is less pressure with two leaders because the emotional strain can be shared.
2. Since each person is unique and no two people lead a group in exactly the same way, the group can benefit from the two approaches.
3. Two heads are better than one, especially when there are so many dynamics occurring in the group processing.
4. With two leaders, discussion of how the group is progressing and of concerns regarding individual members is possible. The leaders can discuss the situations that arise in group and plan strategy for future meetings.

We have experienced groups with only female leaders, and groups with male and female leaders. Both worked very well. We recommend at least one woman leader in order to allow modeling of the female role as leader. The important consideration is not the gender of the therapist. The important considerations are the therapist's ability to work in a group situation and the group leaders' ability to work with each other. Conflict between leaders can be highly detrimental to the group, because group members then often feel the need to take sides, and the group can become divided and nonproductive.

Rules

Rules are necessary, but they will vary from group to group. Rules can be set by the leader(s) or the members or in a combined effort. The following are some of the ground rules we have used.

Attendance. A person missing in the group meeting affects all of those present, especially if no one knows why the person is absent. If a person misses frequently, this can affect the continuity of the group, and resentment toward that person can build. Missing group can also be an indication of avoidance. A common reason for members' absences is guilt. If they aren't doing well and don't want others to know it (which is not unusual), the tendency is to avoid the group meeting. Seldom does a group member who is feeling good about her progress inexplicably miss group sessions. You may set attendance rules such as "the third miss (excused or unexcused) and you're out." This will work for a group with a set commitment time, but in an open-ended group would require the allowable absences to be set within a time frame. For example, only one miss per month, or only four in six months is a definite rule. A rule such as two misses and you're out is untenable, if one is a member for two years, this becomes very restrictive.

Another suggestion for attendance rules is to stress the importance of members' contacting another person in the group if they plan to miss a session. There is concern within the group when no one knows why someone has missed, because the absence typically means that the person is having a difficult time and cannot face the group. Whatever the rules, it remains important to deal directly with the attendance issue so that all concerned have an understanding of it.

Confidentiality. The rules of confidentiality are vital to group members because of the great need for secrecy which members generally feel. They will not want outsiders to know they are in the group, and they may need very structured rules in order to feel security within the group. A rule we use that may be helpful as a guideline is "You may tell anyone you choose that you are a member of the group, but you do not have the right to identify any other member in the group or to share any of the information that is discussed during group sessions." Once the confidentiality rules are set, they need to be reviewed occasionally to reassure the members and offset their fears of someone finding out that the person is in group.

Commitment–Open Ended. The structure of the group will vary from setting to setting. On the college campus, the quarter and semester systems offer a natural length of time for the group to run. Members may leave and new members may join at the beginning of each new quarter or semester. In the community, the group may run a set number of weeks or months, or it may be open ended with new members taken in as members leave the group.

Visitors. Will visitors be allowed in the group? Be it friends of members or other professionals, this topic needs to be attended to. Nonprofessional visitors are questionable. While other individuals may be greatly interested, the primary question must be of what benefit their presence could be to the group. Professional visitors can be helpful if they present information of which the group is in need. However, we recommend that the presentation occupy only part of the group time. When completed, the group should have time to process the information and react to it. We further recommend that this be infrequent.

Silence. Should a person be forced to speak in group? Does one have the right not to share information if she so chooses? These are philosophical questions, but we have listed them in this section because they are often developed as rules. Group input again is critical in developing this rule.

If a rule exists that members share only when they so choose, situations will arise in which some members use the rule as a means to avoid working on a problem. However, if members are forced to share information when they are not emotionally ready, they may experience a loss of trust in the group. We use the following rule: when a member is ready, then she will choose to share. This puts the responsibility on the individual member. Furthermore, group often includes some rather shy members who need to experience group for quite a while before they are ready to share. This rule allows them time to develop group skills and confidence.

Outside Activities of Group Members. An extremely important aspect of the group structure involves the outside activities of group members.   Does a group member have any responsibility to the other members outside of group? We have found that as members call each other and are supportive outside of group, cohesiveness and trust develop inside the group. Members get to know each other as friends and supporters, and the trust is often built on this. Members can be required to call each other every week or to work in pairs outside of group on their eating plans; also, members may sponsor new members and help them to feel at home with group.

There are some problems involved with outside activities. One problem is that it is very difficult to get members to reach out and support each other or to ask someone else for help. Once the call is made, they usually report "talking for a long time," but getting this to happen is diffcult. The members have a great concern over intruding into someone's life. "What if I call and they are busy?" "If she is having a good day and I call and tell her I'm having trouble, I will ruin her day." These concerns are very real and need to be dealt with. Sometimes setting specific ground rules can be helpful, such as asking the person if she is busy or can talk. If the answer is yes, talk; if it is no, set a time and call back. Another difficulty is that if members visit with each other and complain about others in the group, or about dissatisfaction with rules or leaders, this promotes the indirect communication pattern that is so common with eating-disordered people. Nothing is ever resolved because the target of the criticism is never told of the dissatisfaction. If this happens, the leader(s) must deal directly with the problem, and must model the skill of confronting issues and working toward resolution together.

Evaluation of Group Member's Progress

It is important to evaluate the group in order to find out if it is helping at least some of the members and, if so, which ones. We presently use the Eating Disorders Inventory (EDI) as an evaluative tool at the beginning and end of each 12-week period of group in order to determine if change is occurring. This instrument was developed by David M. Garner, Janet Polivy, and Marian P. Olmsted, at the Clarke Institute of Psychiatry and the University of Toronto.

REFERENCES

Individual Therapy

Alberti, R. E. and Emmons, M. L. *Stand Up, Speak Out, and Talk Back.* New York: Pocket Books, 1975.
Andersen, A. Psychiatric aspects of bulimia. *Directions in Psychiatry* Lesson 14:1–7. 1981.
Baer, J. *How to Be an Assertive (Not Aggressive) Woman in Life, in Love, and on the Job.* New York: New American Library, 1976.
Banaszynski, J. Bulimia/self-destructing victims use food for naught. *Minneapolis Tribune* (July 5, 1981).
Beck, A. T. *Cognitive Therapy and the Emotional Disorders.* New York: International Universities Press, 1976.
Bemis, K. M. Current approaches to the etiology and treatment of anorexia nervosa. *Psychological Bulletin* 85:593–617 (1978).
Bennett, W. and Gurin, J. Do diets really work? *Science* 82:42–50 (March 1982).
Bensen, H. *The Relaxation Response.* New York: William Morrow, 1975.
Boskind-Lodahl, M. Cinderella's stepsisters: a feminist perspective on anorexia nervosa and bulimia. *Journal of Women in Culture and Society* 2(2):342–356 (1976).
Boskind-Lodahl, M. and Sirlin, J. The gorging-purging syndrome. *Psychology Today* 50, 52, 82, 85 (March 1977).
Bruch, H. Perceptual and conceptual disturbances in anorexia nervosa. *Psychosomatic Medicine* 24(2):187–194 (1962).
Bruch, H. *Eating Disorders.* New York: Basic Books, 1973.
Bruch, H. Perils of behavior modification in treatment of anorexia nervosa. *Journal of the American Medical Association* 230:1419–1422 (1974).

Bruch, H. *The Golden Cage: The Enigma of Anorexia Nervosa.* Cambridge, Mass.: Harvard University Press, 1978.

Burns, D. The perfectionist's script for self-defeat. *Psychology Today* 34–52 (November 1980).

Chernin, K. How women's diets reflect fear of power. *New York Times Magazine* 38 (October 11, 1981).

Crisp, A. H. *Anorexia Nervosa: Let Me Be.* New York: Grune and Stratton, 1980.

Exchange Lists for Meal Planning. New York: American Diabetes Association.

Food for Thought. Center City, Min.: Hazelden Educational Services. 1980.

Garner, D. M., Garfinkel, P. E., and Bemis, K. M. A multidimensional psychotherapy for anorexia nervosa. *International Journal of Eating Disorders* 1: 3–46 (Winter 1982).

Goleman, D. Make-or-break resolutions. *Psychology Today* (January 1982).

Hedblom, J. E., Hubbard, F. A., and Andersen, A. A. Anorexia nervosa: a multidisciplinary treatment program for patient and family. *Social Work in Health Care* 7(1):67–86 (1981).

Kelley, C. *Assertion Training: A Facilitator's Guide.* LaJolla, Calif.: University Associates, 1979.

Keys, A., Brozek, J., Henschel, A., Mickelsen, O., and Taylor, H. L. *The Biology of Human Starvation.* Vols, 1 and 2. Minneapolis: University of Minnesota Press 1950.

Lange, A. and Jakubowski, P. *Responsible Assertive Behavior: Cognitive/Behavioral Procedures for Trainers.* Champaign, Ill.: Research Press, 1976.

Lucas, A. R. Bulimia and vomiting syndrome. *Contemporary Nutrition* 6(4): (1981(a).

Lucas, A. R. Toward the understanding of anorexia nervosa as a disease entity. *Mayo Clinic Proceedings* 56:254–264 (1981). (b)

Lucas, A. R. When friends or parents ask about "pigging out." *Journal of the American Medical Association* 247(1):82 (1982).

Lucas, A. R., Duncan, J. W., and Piens, V. The treatment of anorexia nervoxa. *American Journal of Psychiatry* 133(9):1034–1038 (1976).

Marlatt, G. A. and Gordon, J. R. Determinants of relapse: implications of the maintenance of behaviors. In *Behavioral Medicine: Changing Health Life Styles* (Davidson, P. O. and Davidson, S. M., eds.). New York: Brunner Mazel, 1980.

Minuchin, S., Baker, L., Rosman, B., Liebman, R., Milman, L., and Todd, T. A conceptual model of psychosomatic illness in children. *Arch. Gen. Psychiatry* 32:1031–1038 (August 1975).

Minuchin, S., Rosman, B., and Baker, L. *Psychosomatic Families: Anorexia Nervosa in Context.* Cambridge, Mass.: Harvard University Press, 1978.

North, B. and Connell, M. (Eds.). *It's a Weighty Problem.* Fargo, N.D.: College of Home Economics, North Dakota State University 1981.

Orbach, S. *Fat Is a Feminist Issue.* New York: Berkeley Publishing Corp., 1978.

Palmer, R. L. *Anorexia Nervosa: A Guide for Sufferers and Their Families.* New York: Penguin Books, 1980.

Phelps, S. and Austin, N. *The Assertive Woman.* San Luis Obispo, Calif.: Impact, 1975.

Rosen, J. Bulimia nervosa: treatment with exposure and response prevention. *Behavior Therapy* **13**:117–124 (1982).

Russell, G. Bulimia nervosa: an ominous variant of anorexia nervosa. *Psychological Medicine* **9**:429–448 (1979).

Steele, S. *How Much Is Too Much: Healthy Habits or Destructive Addictions.* Englewood Cliffs, N.J.: Prentice-Hall, 1981.

Stuart, R. *How to Manage Binge Eating.* Weight Watchers. 1970.

Thoma, H. On the psychotherapy of patients with anorexia nervosa. *Bulletin of the Menninger Clinic* **41**(5):437–452 (1977).

Yalom, I. D. *The Theory and Practice of Group Psychotherapy.* New York: Basic Books, 1975. (2nd Edition.)

Family Therapy

Anderson, A. Anorexia nervosa: diagnosis and treatment. *Psychiatry Update Series,* Princeton, N.J.: New Jersey Biomedia, 1979.

Barcai, A. Family therapy in the treatment of anorexia nervosa. *American Journal of Psychiatry* **128**:286–290 (1971).

Bemis, K. Current approaches to the etiology and treatment of anorexia nervosa. *Psychological Bulletin* **85**(3):593–617 (1978).

Bhanji, S. and Thompson, J. Operant conditioning in the treatment of anorexia nervosa: a review and retrospective study of 11 cases. *British Journal of Psychiatry,* **124**:166–172 (1974).

Blinder, B. J., Freeman, D. M., and Stunkard, A. J. Behavioral therapy of anorexia nervosa: effectiveness of activity as a reinforcer of weight gain. *American Journal of Psychiatry* **126**:1093–1098 (1970).

Blitzer, J. R., Rollins, N., and Blackwell, A. Children who starve themselves. *Psychosomatic Medicine* **23**:369–383 (1961).

Bowen, M. Theory in the practice of psychotherapy. In *Family Therapy: Theory and Practice* (Guerin, P., Ed.). New York: Gardner Press, 1976.

Bruch, H. *Eating Disorders: Obesity, Anorexia, and the Person Within.* New York: Basic Books, 1973.

Caille, P., Abrahamsen, P., Girolami, C., and Sorbye, B. A systems theory approach to a case of anorexia nervosa. *Family Press* **16**:455–456 (1977).

Cairns, G. F. and Altman, K. Behavioral treatment of cancer related anorexia. *Journal of Behavior Therapy and Experimental Psychiatry* **10**(4):353–356 (1979).

Casper, R. C., Eckert, E. D., and Halmi, K. A. Bulimia: its incidence and clinical importance in patients with anorexia nervosa. *Archives of General Psychiatry* **37**:1030–1035 (1980).

Conrad, D. E. A starving family – an interactional view of anorexia nervosa. *Bulletin of the Menninger Clinic* **41**:487–495 (1977).

Crisp, A. H., Harding, B., and McGuinness, B. Anorexia nervosa: psychoneurotic characteristics of parents: relationship to prognosis. *Journal of Psychosomatic Research* **18**:167–173 (1974).

Garner, D. M., Garfinkel, P. E., and Bemis, K. M. A multidimensional psychotherapy for anorexia nervosa. *International Journal of Eating Disorders* 1: 3–46 (1982).

Goodsitt, A. Anorexia nervosa. *British Journal of Medical Psychology* 42: 109–118 (1969).

Goodsitt, A. Narcissistic disturbances in anorexia nervosa. In *Adolescent Psychiatry* (Feinstein, S. C. and Giovacchin, P., Eds.), Vol. 5: Developmental and Clinical Studies. New York: Jason Aronson, 1977.

Green, R. S. and Rau, J. H. The use of diphenydantoin in compulsive eating disorders: further studies. In *Anorexia Nervosa* (Vigersky, R. A., Ed.). New York: Raven Press, 1977.

Haley, J. *Changing Families.* New York: Grune and Stratton, 1971.

Halmi, K. A. and Loney, J. Familial alcoholism in anorexia nervosa. *British Journal of Psychiatry* 123:53–54 (1973).

Hersen, M. and Detre, T. The behavioral psychotherapy of anorexia nervosa. In *Specialized Techniques in Individual Psychotherapy* (Karasu, T. B. and Bellack, I., Eds.). New York: Bruner-Mazel, 1980.

Hsu, L. K. G. Outcome of anorexia nervosa: a review of the literature. *Archives of General Psychiatry* 37:1041–1046 (1980).

Kalucy, R. S., Crisp, A. H., and Harding, B. A study of 56 families with anorexia nervosa. *British Journal of Medical Psychiatry* 50(4):381–395 (1977).

Liebman, R., Minuchin, S., and Baker, L. An integrated treatment program for anorexia nervosa. *American Journal of Psychiatry* 131:432–436 (1974).

Minuchin, S. *Families and Family Therapy.* Cambridge, Mass.: Harvard University Press, 1974.

Minuchin, S., Baker. L., Rosman, B. L., Liebman, R., Milman, L., and Todd, T. C. A conceptual model of psychosomatic illness in children. *Archives of General Psychiatry* 32:1031–1038 (1975).

Minuchin, S., Rosman, B. L., and Baker, L. *Psychosomatic Families: Anorexia Nervosa in Context.* Cambridge, Mass.: Harvard University Press, 1979.

Ollendick, T. H. Behavioral treatment of anorexia nervosa: a five year study. *Behavioral Modification* 3(1):124–135 (1979).

Patterson, G. R. *Families: Applications of Social Learning to Family Life.* Champaign, Ill.: Research Press Co. 1971.

Piazza, E., Piazza, N., and Rollins, N. Anorexia nervosa: controversial aspects of therapy. *Comprehensive Psychiatry* 21(3):177–189 (1980).

Pyle, R. L., Mitchell, J. E., and Eckert, E. D. A report of 34 cases. *Journal of Clinical Psychiatry* 42:60–64 (1981).

Rosen, L. W. Modification of secretive or ritualized eating behavior in anorexia nervosa. *Journal of Behavior Therapy and Experimental Psychiatry* 11:101–104 (June 1980).

Russell, G. Bulimia nervosa: an ominous variant of anorexia nervosa. *Psychological Medicine* 9:429–448 (1979).

Russell, G. The current treatment of anorexia nervosa. *British Journal of Psychiatry* 138:164–166 (February 1981).

Schneider, S. Anorexia nervosa: the "subtle" condition. *Family Therapy* 8(1): 49–58 (1981).

Schwartz, D. M. and Thompson, M. G. Do anorectics get well? Current research and future needs. *American Journal of Psychiatry* 138(3):319–323 (1981).

Selvini-Palazzoli, M. *Self-starvation. From the Intrapsychic to the Transpersonal Approach to Anorexia Nervosa*. London: Chaucer, 1974.

Sours, J. A. The anorexia nervosa syndrome. *International Journal of Psychoanalysis* 55:567–576 (1974).

Teyber, E. Structured family relations: a review. *Family Therapy* 8(1):39–48 (1981).

Wahler, R. G. Deviant child behavior within the family: developmental speculations and behavior change strategies. In *Handbook of Behavior Modification and Behavior Therapy* (Leitenbert, H., Ed.). Englewood Cliffs, N.J.: Prentice-Hall, 1976.

Wells, K. and Forehand, R. Childhood behavior problems in the home. In *Handbook of Clinical Behavior Therapy* (Turner, S. M., Calhous, K. S., and Adams, H. E., Eds.). New York: John Wiley & Sons, 1981.

Whipple, S. B. and Manning, D. E. Anorexia nervosa: commitment to a multifaceted treatment program. *Psychother. Psychosom.* 30:161–169 (1978).

Winoker, A., March, V., and Mendels, J. Primary affective disorder in relatives of patients with anorexia nervosa. *American Journal of Psychiatry* 137(6): 695–698 (1980).

Wulliemier, F. Anorexia nervosa: gauging treatment effectiveness. *Psychosomatics* 19(8):497–499 (1978).

4
Additional Aids for Recovery

There are two important areas of help to the sufferer which are not covered in Chapter 3. We do not believe they are therapy approaches even though the experience can be therapeutic. Diet counseling and self-help groups can be useful aids in the recovery of a person with an eating disorder.

DIET COUNSELING

Some counselors are fortunate enough to have the services of a registered dietitian available at their work site. Other counselors may find that in their community there are dietitians interested in, and available for, diet counseling with the anorexic or bulimic individual. This section has been included because we have found that with some clients, the collaborative help of a registered dietitian can be beneficial in working toward their recovery.

As we have stated before, our belief is that recovery can occur only when the underlying psychological problems have been dealt with and solved. However, along with these problems, the person with anorexia nervosa or bulimia has also developed inappropriate eating habits or patterns. For some individuals, diet counseling has helped change destructive eating patterns into productive ones. The dietitian not only knows a great deal more about nutrition than we do, but also may have some creative ideas which will help the person stay on the new eating plan. Also, hearing the information from someone other than the counselor, especially someone known to be knowledgeable about nutrition, can have more of an impact.

You may ask, "Why would my clients need the use of a dietitian when they already know more about nutrition than I ever will?" We agree that most anorexic and bulimic individuals are very well read on the topic of nutrition, but they lack the skill of applying that information where they themselves are concerned. We even know of registered dietitians with these disorders who have found diet counseling to be quite beneficial.

One warning here: we believe that diet counseling services should never be used *instead* of psychological counseling. Diet counseling should always be in conjunction with psychological counseling, otherwise little progress will occur. If a new psychological foundation has not been developed, the person may have changed the eating behavior, but the psychological problems remain. The behavior change is then usually only temporary since new coping skills have not been developed; the same thoughts and emotions remain to trigger the anorexic and bulimic behaviors. We have worked with clients who successfully changed their eating patterns but then discovered that if they wanted to continue the progress toward recovery, they had to deal with the roots of the problem — their thoughts and feelings.

We believe it important to refer our clients only to individuals who are qualified to do dietary counseling. The background and training of the individual should be investigated. In order to become a registered dietitian, the individual must have a degree from an accredited dietetics program, complete an accredited internship, and pass the registration examination for dietetics. There can at times be confusion about the difference between a registered dietitian and a nutritionist. The registered dietitian has the above-mentioned requirements; a nutritionist can have a variety of backgrounds, but usually will not have the in-depth training in dietary counseling that the dietitian has.

Another requirement for the individual doing the diet counseling should be that he or she has a basic understanding of anorexia nervosa and bulimia; otherwise, these psychological disorders may be viewed as merely overeating or lack of self-discipline and will-power. One of the authors overheard two dietitians discussing a third dietitian who was bulimic. They had a difficult time understanding how a person with a degree in dietetics could become bulimic. The comment "She really should know better than to become bulimic" demonstrated their ignorance regarding this problem. These individuals would not be appropriate referral sources until their understanding of the disorder was more adequate and sympathetic.

Since the need for confidentiality is especially great with these clients, one last requirement is that the dietitian have an awareness of the importance of confidentiality to the anorexic or bulimic.

When a referral is made to the dietitian, it is important that the client or the counselor indicates that the person has either anorexia nervosa or bulimia. We know of instances where the client did not indicate the real problem but said that she "wanted to lose weight" or "had a problem with overeating." This partial information will not allow the dietitian to work adequately with the client.

We recommend private individual visits with the dietitian for two reasons. First, because of the needed confidentiality, private visits are best. This can be a painfully embarrassing disclosure to even one other person. It is unrealistic to expect the client to address the problem initially in the presence of others. Second, the specific dietary needs vary greatly from individual to individual. No one set plan will fit all clients. This is one of the reasons that working with a dietitian can be so helpful. Dietitians can develop an individually tailored plan to help the client. For example, some clients will need to work with a very structured plan which allows no leeway and must be followed as closely as possible. Other clients will find that an overly structured diet will only trigger their compulsive tendencies and thereby render the plan unworkable for them. These individuals must develop a more flexible approach with different ground rules.

We know of a situation in which an individual who was bulimic decided to cut out refined sugar in her diet because some other group members were doing so. She found the rigidity of this plan detrimental to her, and she had to develop a more flexible plan which included a piece of hard candy after each meal. However, some of the other group members still maintained the no-refined-sugar plan and found it workable. The dietitian can tailor a plan to fit the needs of the individual.

There are, of course, many different approaches to diet counseling. We recommend any approach which is honest and direct, and stays within the parameters of the dietetics field — that of nutritional counseling only. Psychological counseling should be done by the mental health professional.

The question often arises, What is the relationship between the counselor and the dietitian? First of all, it is extremely important that each of these professionals has at least a fundamental understanding of, and respect for, the other's work, thus facilitating a team effort which will benefit the client. Secondly, periodic consultations should take place to discuss, at least briefly, clients they have in common. If either of the professionals has questions or concerns regarding the other's approach, open communication is absolutely necessary. This can be especially critical in the light of the tendency of some eating-disordered clients to pit one professional against another, whether this be counselor and dietitian, counselor and psychiatrist, or whoever.

The following clinical study was written by Barbara North, a Registered Dietitian. We have included it in the book to give the reader a general idea of one study. It is not meant as a guide for dietitians since each case is unique and must be dealt with on an individual basis.

Clinical Study

Barbara North, R.D.
Food and Nutrition Department
College of Home Economics
North Dakota State University
Fargo, North Dakota

History. Connie is a 22-year-old college female with bulimia. She is a senior, majoring in pharmacy at a small midwestern university. She takes a heavy course work load each quarter so she can graduate in four years.

The disorder developed four years ago when she was a high school senior. Two years prior to the development of bulimia, she had lost weight which was related to her involvement in dance. She is a perfectionist who was also successful in high school as a member of the dance team. Connie is a most attractive young woman.

Connie's diet consists of fruit juices, salads, vegetable soups, pancakes, toast, pizza, lasagna, ice cream, little milk, and carbonated beverages. She avoids meat. When bingeing she increases her total intake of all foods, especially greasy (fatty) foods.

Because of Connie's difficulties, she vomits on the average of three times per day when bingeing. She consumes at those times approximately 5000 calories per day. When she is not bingeing her daily calorie intake is 1200 calories. Her weight (100–105 pounds) is in the ideal or desirable body weight (IBW/DBW) range for her height (5 feet 1 inch). Her nutrient intakes are adequate to meet the Recommended Daily Allowances (RDA) for her age and sex.

Nutritional Management and Treatment Plan. Connie first visited the dietitian at the campus health center in October 1981. She was very nervous and upset. During the interview, she wept periodically. The goals of treatment were outlined. Connie was to eat regular meals as well as to include foods that supplied adequate nutrients. She was to deal with gorging herself and then vomiting by ingesting foods on a regular basis and making decisions for substitutions that would not cause her to be anxious.

A structured nutritional care plan was devised jointly by Connie and the dietitian. The diet was designed so that she would be able to select foods from the serving line at one of the dining centers on campus where she had a seven-day contract. It was agreed that she would eat three times each day and would think about foods she could eat and those she felt she couldn't eat, so that during the weekly follow-up appointments she could become clear on these things herself. Connie increased her physical activity by running the stairs in the dormitory and adjusted the running activity to maintain her weight. She did this in order to compensate for the calories she was required to eat by the diet plan.

She continued to keep weekly or biweekly follow-up appointments with the dietitian until the end of spring quarter at which time she graduated. She showed progress by the end of the fourth month. At that time, there was a setback. According to Connie, the regression was attributable to final exams. During the spring term, she continued to progress. According to Connie, she did not binge and purge more than once a month. Even though the prognosis is guarded, it seems conceivable that for this young woman it could be from fair to good.

* * *

SELF-HELP GROUPS

Self-help groups, by definition, are groups which allow the individual to help herself conquer a problem. The organization may be open to anyone or may have specific requirements for membership. Some groups are nonprofit, and some are profit-making corporations which require certain fees for membership.

Should all anorexics and bulimics be part of a self-help group to further aid their recovery? We feel that this ought to be an individual decision on the part of the client. We have found that many of these groups can be helpful, but only if the individual deems them important in her recovery.

Stanton Steele (1981) in his book *How Much Is Too Much?* identifies some reasons why self- help groups can be useful. Such groups

1. limit a person's serious contacts to those who share his problems and his approach to dealing with them;
2. teach a way of thinking that eliminates doubt and alternate conceptions;
3. provide a group identity and emotional support;
4. require regular attendance at meetings and strict conformity to rules;
5. pervade the person's life and protect and cushion the individual. (p. 59)*

It is important for the individual to view the group in a realistic light. If a person experiences the group with total dependency, she may not take on individual responsibility for her recovery. Also, if something then goes wrong, the individual can blame the group and sidestep her own responsibility. The person's view of the group as a *tool* for recovery is a necessary part of self-help group membership.

Specific information on various self-help groups can be found in Chapter 4. We will not describe these groups at this point. There is, however, one issue which needs to be discussed. Every once in a while a client will come back from her initial visit to an Overeaters Anonymous (OA) meeting and say, "I don't like it because they talk religion at the meetings." The talk described is in regard to a higher power, and for many people this can mean a specific religion. Also, each group differs in how the higher power is emphasized.

First of all, we ask the client to give OA several chances before closing the door on this organization. Second, this is an opportune

*Reprinted with permission from *How Much is too Much,* by Stanton Peele, © 1981 by Prentice-Hall, Inc. Published by Prentice-Hall, Inc., Englewood Cliffs, N.J.

time to discuss with the client her own spirituality. We view the individual as having a spiritual part along with the mental, emotional, and social components of her personality. This spiritual part need not be "religious." However, we believe that spirituality does have to be developed in whatever approach or belief system the individual desires. This component needs to grow and flourish for the individual's total recovery.

OA also deals directly with this issue:

> "Is OA a religious organization?" Overeaters Anonymous has no religious requirement, affiliation or orientation. The twelve step program of recovery is considered "spiritual" because it deals with inner change. OA has members of many different religious beliefs as well as some atheists and agnostics. (*About OA*, pamphlet)*

We strongly recommend the use of self-help groups as a part or an aid in the individual client's recovery.

The following are first-person accounts of how eating-disordered clients viewed their membership in Weight Watchers (WW) and OA.

Personal Reflection: Group Experience — Weight Watchers

I have been a "lifetime" member of Weight Watchers (WW) for over a year now. Within the past seven years I have joined, dropped out, and rejoined the organization numerous times. I feel somewhat deceptive and awkward being a member since, technically, I do not fit into the category of individuals that WW was originally founded to cater to — namely, people with a basic food focus, not individuals with a particular disease such as bulimia.

The three areas of the WW program I use are: the eating plan, the scheduled weigh-ins, and the literature provided about behavior modification. The fourth area, group meetings, is not beneficial and seems to work against my recovery. The meetings are headed by a WW lecturer, and the format is as follows: introducing new members, announcing how much weight was lost by each present member, presentation of a certain topic by the lecturer, discussion of the past and upcoming weeks. During the one-hour meetings, the conversation centers around specific foods ("legal" and "illegal"), calories, weight, recipes, restaurants, etc. Of course this is what WW is all

---

*From *About OA*. © 1979 by Overeaters Anonymous, Inc. Reprinted by permission of Overeaters Anonymous, Inc.

about, and the members view these areas as things to take in stride as they concentrate on losing weight or maintaining their achieved goal weight. I found that certain words such as "binge" had a different connotation for the "average" WW member (i.e., to overeat, whereas I use it to mean gorging insanely). Overall, the typical WW member views the entire realm of food differently from the way a bulimic person does. The meetings worked against me because the focus was always on food (something I try to avoid thinking about). After almost every meeting, I would inevitably have a full-fledged binge.

Members of the WW staff were helpful to a certain extent: they were empathetic and gave moral support during the weigh-ins and group meetings. In my case, though, I never ceased to amaze them. In the past, when my weight fluctuated drastically I ended up feeling isolated, freakish, and wondering what in the world was wrong with me, especially at the weekly weigh-ins. It goes without saying that the staff was totally bewildered by my abnormal weight gains and losses because I chose not to let them know I had bulimia.

Indirectly, WW is one of my "support" groups. Membership gives me a sense of working toward a goal — establishment of sensible eating habits and normalization of one's weight. It is good that I joined WW because the monthly weigh-ins keep me from backsliding, and also serve to remind me where I was and how much progress I've made since I first joined. I need the program to keep the feeling of being in control, since it provides structure and requires self-discipline and faithfulness in order to remain "legal" (abstinent).

Even though the WW *group* aspect does not work for me, I still highly recommend the WW program to individuals with bulimia. A member must experiment to find out which parts of the program work for her and mold these findings to fit her own unique situation.

Personal Reflection: Group Experience — Overeaters Anonymous

Meeting Structure. Readings are given from the book *Alcoholics Anonymous,* substituting words like "food" for "alcohol," and "compulsive overeater" for "alcoholic." These readings give an explanation of our program and a description of the compulsive overeater. After the readings, the leader tells his or her personal story of recovery, describing what he or she was like before Overeaters

Anonymous (OA), what happened as a result of OA, and what he or she is like now. After this, we break for coffee, and newcomers can ask questions or check out literature which outlines food plans and tells about OA. There is also other inspiring literature which has been written by OA members. After coffee, we get together for a time when those who need to may share what is on their mind. It is during this time that the fellowship of OA is clearly seen as members share their experience, strength, and hope with each other. There is no requirement to say anything. Many OA members have gone to several meetings, especially in the beginning, and simply listened. The first part of the meeting lasts one hour; then comes break and sharing, which is an additional half hour. So, if a meeting opens at 7:30, it always closes by 9:00.

What It Feels Like to Be a Member. Usually, it feels good to be a member because I know that I am not alone and that there are many other "normal" people who have the same compulsion, problem, or disease (whatever one wants to call it) that I do. I know that they understand me and therefore can help me, and that I can do the same for them. Being a member of OA offers *hope,* and that's why I would recommend it to another person.

Feelings Going into the First Meeting. Before going to my first meeting, I was excited because I knew of OA from my sister and she was pretty positive about it. Having already lost a fair amount of weight, I went into this meeting with the attitude that I was going to help *them.* Little did I realize how much I needed the help. At my first meeting, I felt sort of uncomfortable and thought, "I'm not one of these people." However, I went back and those uncomfortable feelings slipped away.

What Specifically Aided in Recovery. It's not really one thing, but a combination of things, that help in recovery. The knowledge that I can take life one day at a time is a major factor; it is one of our slogans. Of course the knowledge alone isn't enough. The fellowship and the people that we call on the telephone give us the strength to actually put the slogan into practice. The reason this "one day at a time" is so valuable is that when looking at the food aspect of our disease, we tend to think, "I can never last that long without this particular food," or "I could never diet that long." The slogan "one day at a time" shows us that it's not "that long" — only 24 hours. This slogan is also valuable to many compulsive overeaters because we are perfectionists, so when we screw up on our food plan, we feel guilty and are tempted to think negatively and just forget about losing weight because we think we can't do it. I have always been the type to write off a diet after one failure. Through OA I've learned to get back on the right track the next day and *forget the failures* of yesterday, only remembering them for the purpose of what I can learn from them. I've learned that I can abstain from eating compulsively *just for today.* Another thing that has directly helped me is the use of the telephone. In OA we can call each other and get those thoughts or feelings out that make us want to eat. In this way, we are using people instead of food for solace. Many times when I've wanted to eat compulsively, just the knowledge that I would have to be honest with myself and tell someone about it afterwards has stopped the binge. If I don't like one food plan or way of eating, I can be open-minded enough to try something else. I think what has helped me most is learning that compulsive eating is a progressive disease. We strive for progress in recovery, not for perfection. On the other hand, I believe that if one does not attempt to recover, one will become progressively worse. Because of this, I choose to stick to OA. So you see, it's not just one thing, but a combination of things, that specifically aids in recovery.

Individual Work. One can put in as much or as little time as one wants to, according to the time one has. OA works, but one has to work the program as well. I think that the more time people put into the program, the more successful their recovery is. The major portion of the time I put into OA is spent on the telephone. We make calls to others when we need help, and we make calls to other members in the group to encourage them. This (calling others) is called service and is done to get one out of *self.* Maybe I'm not doing too well or am feeling sorry for myself one day. Well, the faster I help someone else, the faster I can forget my own problem, or at least get it into the right perspective. Service is what keeps OA going. After one has reached goal weight, service becomes the main part of the program. We have a slogan that says, "To extend the hand and the heart of OA to those who still suffer: for this I am responsible." Reading OA literature and writing down my feelings are other activities that I participate in outside of meetings. However, there is no specific amount of time that I *must* devote to these activities daily. There is a little morning meditation book that I read daily, but it takes a mere five minutes.

How the Group Was Helpful in Working toward Recovery. The group has been helpful because of the wonderful fellowship it provides. It is made up of so many different people from different backgrounds, and because of this, there is always *someone* I can relate to. Members of the group share their experience, strength, and hope, and you suddenly realize you are not alone. It's a great realization.

REFERENCES

Exchange Lists for Meal Planning. American Diabetes Association and American Dietetics Association, 1976.
Food for Thought. Center City, Mn.: Hazelden Educational Services, 1980.
North, B. B., and Connel, M. (Eds.), *It's a Weighty Problem.* Fargo, N.D.: College of Home Economics, North Dakota State University, 1981.
Steele, S. *How Much Is Too Much.* Englewood Cliffs, N.J.: Prentice-Hall, 1981.
Alcoholics Anonymous. Alcoholics Anonymous World Service, Inc. New York, 1976.
About OA. Overeaters Anonymous, World Service Office. Torrance, California, 1979 (pamphlet).

5
Information Distribution

There is a need to distribute information about anorexia nervosa and bulimia for two reasons: (1) to educate and (2) to advertise services which are available. We have divided this chapter into two sections — one dealing with the college/university campus and the other with the community. The information distribution section for junior high and high school has been included in Chapter 6.

Most often in our audience — be it reader, viewer, or listener — there will be an anorexic, a bulimic, or a person close to a sufferer. It is important that information be presented in an appropriately positive manner. If too bleak a picture is painted, this can be overly discouraging for the sufferer or person close to the sufferer. The individual may become disillusioned and decide not to seek help because the situation seems so hopeless. On the other hand, painting an inappropriately rosy picture of recovery may create expectations in the individual which constitute an impossibility.

COLLEGE/UNIVERSITY CAMPUS

In this section we will identify the information distribution resources and indicate ways of using them.

Student Newspaper

Student newspapers are a wonderful communication line to students. The papers are usually read by most students and by many faculty and staff. In order to get articles printed, one should contact either the editor, a reporter or, if many of the articles come out of a news writing class, the journalism instructor.

The education aspect of the article is important. Try to have the writer include such information as: (1) definitions of anorexia nervosa and bulimia, (2) symptoms of each disorder, (3) prevalence on college/university campuses, (4) types of professional help available, and (5) reasons why it is important to seek professional help. Articles should also include people or agencies that a student can contact for more information or professional help. Also, the appropriate telephone numbers should be given.

Because anorexics and bulimics are so very concerned about keeping their problem secret, it is helpful to have any article explain confidentiality. An added bonus, resulting in a more interesting article, would be an anonymous interview with a student who is encountering the problem.

Some last recommendations are that you proofread the articles before they are printed to ensure that the information is accurate and easily understood. Also, the want-ad section of the student newspaper can be useful in publicizing a support group or other services which are available. Other sources of information distribution can be alumni and faculty newspapers. However, since these papers are not read as often by the student, the target population here would be alumni and faculty members.

Campus Radio and Television

Often, campus radio and television stations have informational programs and interview or talk shows. These are excellent vehicles for reaching students and faculty. If the show is live, it can be an aid to allow the audience to telephone in questions and reactions. Also, if a support group or a referral service is being developed, including a short, 30-second announcement can be helpful.

Classroom and Residence Hall Presentations

There may be classes in psychology, sociology, health, dietetics, child development, family relations, education, women's studies, and so forth in which the instructor is willing to have someone speak to the class. If not, one may be able to give the instructor information to present in his or her classes.

Presentations in the residence halls create a slightly different challenge for the speaker. Are the presentations mandatory for the residents? Usually not. Often, concerns are expressed by the residents for individuals who, it has been discovered, have a problem with anorexia nervosa or bulimia. Questions frequently involve what one student can do to help another student. Should I confront the person when I really think she has the disorder? What if she denies it or gets mad at me? These and other questions are covered in Chapter 10.

If a student is becoming noticeably thin, not eating properly, obviously vomiting, leaving milk cartons or paper bags of vomit around, or using the utility sinks in the custodial areas to vomit, residents and staff can get upset. The speaker's perspective on the situation will be important for the residents and the sufferers involved.

These presentations can be counted on to spark a number of questions and a lively discussion because eating disorders are such an intriguing topic on campus.

Book and Article Checkout System

Once word gets out that a therapist is an interested professional, he/she will be contacted by students, staff, and faculty who experience eating-disorder problems. The therapist will also be contacted by friends, siblings, spouses, parents, instructors, etc., who suspect that a person close to them has the problem. If the therapist believes his/her role is to educate, then a book and article checkout is advisable. We recommend that the materials selected be educationally sound, easily understood, and not written for sensationalism. The articles can be put into folders. Practitioners may develop general information packets or packets for specific populations such as parents and family members, victims of anorexia nervosa, victims of bulimia, and professionals. These folders should continue to be updated as more accurate, well-written articles become available.

One additional recommendation: if funding permits, these folders may be given out for individuals to keep. If funding does not permit this, we recommend that the checkout card be confidential so that the person cannot see who else has checked out the information.

Many other ways of distributing information exist on campus — such as inservice seminars for faculty and staff, telephone information systems, health center fact sheets, and newsletters from the food service. Evaluate the specific campus and choose its best network for messages. Creativity can take one further than the basic information listed here.

COMMUNITY

Information distribution in the community can be viewed as quite exciting, no matter what the size of the community may be. However, the size and structure of the community will determine what methods of distribution are most effective. Keep in mind that your goals are to educate the community about anorexia nervosa and bulimia, to distribute information on the services available, and to publicize upcoming activities and presentations.

Newspapers and Community Newsletters

Newspapers and newsletters are excellent methods of information distribution. The size of one's community will often determine the type of newspaper and newsletter coverage. Articles on the various services available, the therapy approaches that professionals are using, and local research on these disorders, as well as interviews with persons presently recovering from the disorders, are usually well received in most communities. Always request that some knowledgeable person be allowed to proofread the article before its publication, and make sure that the article includes a person or agency that the reader can contact for more information.

Also, notices of group meetings, speakers, and workshops can be printed in the activities section of the paper.

Radio and Television

Radio and television offer a special challenge in developing methods of information distribution. Local public service programs and health programs are often productive places to start and excellent ways to reach the community. An interview program format allows a range of areas to be covered. If possible, questions from listeners or viewers can add to the interest of the program. Reporters and program planners are usually eager for volunteers and ideas for programs.

Also, 30-second community service spots can be useful in spotlighting services available in one's community.

Presentations to Community Groups

Many groups in the community continually look for presenters for their meetings. Service clubs, homemakers' organizations, church groups, and women's groups are some of the types of organizations which one can approach. One of the difficulties in dealing with a community group is the varying degrees of exposure that people in the audience will have to the topic. Some persons will be familiar with it and have a family member experiencing one of the disorders, while others may have little or no previous exposure. It is helpful for the audience if one distributes a nontechnical reading list along with the names and telephone numbers of individuals, organizations, and agencies to contact for further information.

Professional Meetings

By professional meetings we mean those attended by mental health professionals and medical persons. These meetings can involve either general presentations or specific program development, or research presentations. The preparation of material for these groups is more exacting than for other groups since one's audience, for the most part, will have some knowledge of the topic beforehand. Also, since opinions on therapy and research vary among professionals, the presenter must be able to support any statements and welcome different points of view. It is often beneficial for the audience if a discussion of some of the differing viewpoints can be held toward the end of the presentation, to allow members of the audience to form their own opinions of which approaches to therapy or research would be best for their situations. This is also a method for learning other ways of viewing and treating the disorders.

6
Junior High and High School

JANET M. PRATT, M.S.Ed.
*School Counselor
Agassiz Junior High School
South Senior High School
Fargo, North Dakota*

The School Counselor and Eating Disorders

It has been stated earlier in the book that the richest area in which to direct our efforts in dealing with eating disorders may be that of prevention. The school counselor can indeed have an impact here, both directly and indirectly. First of all, the counselor deals directly with students who are developing disorders or who have already been diagnosed. Since the counselor is in the school setting when many of these disorders begin, he or she is in a position to recognize early symptoms and start the referral process. Equally important, however, is the counselor's indirect effect on the school in the area of prevention. Guidance programs for students and informational programs for the whole school community can be a positive influence in raising awareness, enhancing self-concept, and easing some of the problems of growing up that adolescents encounter.

The relationship of psychological and emotional needs to eating disorders (such as anorexia nervosa and bulimia) has been explained earlier in this book. Since the school plays a large part in the growing-up process of young people, the staff members need to know about this relationship and, wherever possible, meet the needs of the adolescents within their school. The counselor can be a vital force in creating a climate within the school in which the staff is aware of the existence of the problem of eating disorders and knowledgeable enough to deal with it. The counselor can be a leader in this task in general ways:

1. By having a broad, general knowledge of the disorders and being able to recognize the symptoms
2. By having good communication with staff, administrators, and parents so that guidance and educational programs can be established
3. By knowing the professionals in the community who can treat suspected disorders
4. By understanding the treatment process and some of the practical aspects such as cost and time commitment
5. By adopting and coordinating a developmental guidance program in the school, which recognizes the needs of adolescents, nurtures a healthy self-concept, and deals with the problems involved with growth toward independence

This chapter will deal with some basic ways in which the school counselor can accomplish these tasks.

Power and Control: Strong Adolescent Needs

During the junior high and high school years, the need for power and control (independence) seems to assert itself strongly, sometimes, for parents and teachers, to a frustrating degree. Perhaps most conflicts in home and schools during the transitional years are due to a struggle for power and control. It is important for parents and educators to keep this in mind and to realize that the *main* business of life for the adolescents themselves during these school years is, as they see it, not the three Rs, but taking charge of their lives or assuming *control.*

That this is important is illustrated clearly in a television advertisement which shows a grown woman saying to her parent through clenched teeth, "*Please,* Mother, I can do it myself!" Perhaps the reason we find this humorous is a strong sense of identification with the frustration the woman feels.

Similarly, when an adolescent perceives his or her life to be continually managed and supervised by others, he or she may begin to search for means of experiencing the pleasures of autonomy. The need to "grow up," to become self-reliant, and to feel adequate, capable, and worthy of respect is so strong that the young person may reach out in some socially unacceptable way to fulfill this need. One manner in which this can manifest itself may be an eating disorder.

The female adolescent, for example, underestimating or not realizing her own strengths and abilities, will search for ways to make herself more acceptable, to feel better, to find approval. She reaches out for "beauty" (often equated in our society with thinness) in an attempt to overcome her own feelings of inadequacy. She may resort to her own body shape and eating habits as the *one* thing in her life (as she sees it) that she can control without receiving negative reaction or interference. At the onset, at least, she will probably encounter no opposition or criticism. In fact, as she begins to lose weight, she may enjoy approval and support from peers, adults, and society in general.

The school counselor can surely be of help in this area. First, he or she can find ways to remind parents and educators of the adolescent's strong need for power and control. Focusing on this need can raise understanding and help in some conflict resolution. Second, the counselor can point out some of the ways in which the adolescent may try to cope if this important development need is not met. Parents and educators also need to know that these unhealthy methods of coping most often emerge during adolescence and that the chances for successful treatment are best if they are discovered early.

Expanding Existing Programs

A source of frustration for the counselor can be that it appears, at first glance, that he or she actually does very little in dealing with eating disorders. Working in the area of prevention can be a job that receives little recognition, and the success of such programs is very difficult to measure. While the counselor is promoting school programs that deal with self-concept and awareness, he or she is also doing individual counseling, working with teachers on challenging some unhealthy societal values, teaching nutrition, encouraging sex role equality in the school, working with students in course selection and career goals, and educating parents about healthy family interaction. With programs of this scope and nature, one is likely to lose sight of the fact that the counselor is already helping to prevent eating disorders. He or she must keep in mind that many programs which presently exist in the school may indeed go a long way toward prevention, even though many of them never mention anorexia nervosa or bulimia. The positive, indirect effect that these programs have on the student body in avoiding the development of eating disorders should not be minimized.

There are, however, some things the counselor can do to improve the effectiveness of existing programs and make them more *directly* responsive to the problems of eating disorders. For example, many schools offer programs for *parents* that deal with parent/child communications (e.g., *Systematic Training for Effective Parenting,* or *Parent Effectiveness Training*). Since most families have probably experienced some conflict about food or eating habits, a program of this type could provide an opening for information about eating disorders and how to deal with them. Many therapists believe that family dynamics play an important role in the onset of anorexia or bulimia, and the counselor can help parents to understand these dynamics.

Another possibility for expanding a program (this time for the education of *teachers* about eating disorders) would be to add some information and a list of symptoms to the back-to-school in-service training or workshops which most schools hold in the fall of the year. Anorexia nervosa and bulimia are certainly health problems which deserve attention along with other health concerns that the counselor shares with teachers and staff.

If a list of suggestions such as the one included in this chapter is used during in-service training for teachers, it must be presented with care and with some words of caution about its use. Although many of these symptoms may be found in the anorexic or bulimic young person, it is also possible for one or more of them to be observed in the "normal" developmental process of an adolescent. This point must be made clearly so that the list of symptoms will be used with sensitivity and discretion. Teachers and counselors need to be aware that it is not their place to make a diagnosis; rather, they should be sensitive to signs so that proper referrals can be made if several of these symptoms are observed (see Table 6-1).

Counselors can also work with teachers in their particular subject areas: some language arts and social studies teachers, for example, present units on propaganda and advertising. It would be relevant to have the students take a special look at the persuasiveness of the media in promoting the value of thinness in our society while they are studying the psychological and cultural aspects of advertising in

TABLE 6-1. List for Counselors and Teachers.

Symptoms of eating disorders which may be observed in the school setting:

1. Noticeable weight loss or extreme thinness
2. Finding excuses to skip lunch period
3. Unusual eating behaviors; ritualistic eating habits
4. Unusual concern about school performance: earned grades are never "good enough"
5. Oversensitivity to criticism
6. Unusual concern over change in routine; not flexible or adaptable
7. Tendency to perfectionism
8. Closed communication; usually very proper, polite; may appear tense or too animated
9. Unusual concern about appearance; very neat, "not a hair out of place"
10. Withdrawal from friends and activities; an unusual commitment or immersion in an activity (e.g., music or dance) to the exclusion of other activities
11. Amenorrhea (absence of the menstrual cycle)
12. Unusual, compulsive behaviors, particularly having to do with food
13. Mood swings
14. Very controlled behavior, able to hide feelings
15. Conversation largely about food and weight
16. Intolerance of others to a large extent
17. Low self-esteem (this may not be initially apparent)

general. Teachers can have a very powerful impact on young people in getting them to look at and question these values. Most teachers are very open to working the counselor into the classroom schedule for such a unit, and welcome the information and support that the counselor can provide.

Gathering Information on Eating Disorders

The counselor, of course, needs to have a good understanding of eating disorders to help raise the awareness of the staff and parents, and to be able to recognize the symptoms of anorexia and bulimia in the early stages. Gathering and reading all the information that is currently available can be a time-consuming job, but there are agencies and other sources that will ease this process for the counselor.

Public libraries and college campuses are good places to start. There is a growing amount of current literature being published in both lay magazines and professional journals. Counseling centers on college campuses and community health centers may also have materials which they will loan or donate. Counselors can begin by reading and compiling literature, and by watching for announcements of lectures and workshops concerning the disorders. From this basic learning and collection of materials, the counselor can put together a basic information packet that is appropriate for the age level at his or her school. If the counselor works at an elementary level school, it may be necessary to put together two basic literature packets, one for students and one for teachers and parents. This would probably be a good idea at the secondary level as well.

The counselor will soon discover that reading and gathering knowledge on eating disorders is no small job. The literature is currently varied, and often contradictory. Many different theories and treatments are being explored, and at this time, some of the research is questionable. It takes a great deal of time to assimilate and sort out the different approaches. It will quickly become apparent to the counselor that there are no final and simple answers about anorexia nervosa or bulimia, and that keeping abreast of current literature is difficult.

To ease this problem, it is a good idea to sit down and talk with the school librarian. The librarian (or instructional materials' director) can be extremely valuable in the counselor's attempt to raise awareness of eating disorders in the school. He or she can help to compile an up-to-date bibliography of what is on hand currently as well as a priority list of future orders. The school can be put on the mailing list of such organizations as National Association of Anorexia Nervosa and Associated Disorders, Inc. (ANAD) which will supply information periodically and offer suggestions for starting self-help groups in the area. The librarian can channel magazines and catalogues which contain relevant information, to the counselor or to other appropriate departments. For example, the September 1981 issue of *Co-Ed* (a widely used publication in junior and senior high schools) contains an article entitled "Anorexia Nervosa: When a Diet Can Lead to Death." The teacher or counselor made aware of this article could work it into a classroom unit.

The librarian can also be alert for audiovisual materials on nutrition, exercise, fashion, and style. These could be used as springboards for the counselor to share information on eating disorders with students. Body image, fashion, and health are high interest subjects often used in home economics and physical education classes; in many cases, the teacher would be receptive to working with the counselor on expanding the unit to include information about eating disorders.

Besides the area of general information, the librarian will, from time to time, be aware of individual students who are looking for information on eating disorders. In cases like this, confidentiality can be an important issue. The counselor will need to make sure that the librarian understands the concept of confidentiality. Perhaps a confidential card file can be arranged for the loan of these materials.

Sharing Information

Communicating with Staff and Parents. An important first step for the counselor in preparing his or her program of prevention is to share with the principal the findings and plans for helping students with eating disorders. The principal may have some suggestion about how he or she would like information to be shared with the staff and the parents of the student body.

The principal, for example, might ask the counselor to present the information at an in-service workshop or to the PTA council. PTAs are most often very receptive to an idea for a program which is school related and of current interest. The counselor could take the lead in putting together a program on eating disorders for a PTA meeting. The following is a sample of such a program devised through the home economics and physical education departments with the help of the counselor.

Program Title: "Thin Is In — Or Is It?"

Introduction (principal)

Purpose of the Program — An Overview
- A look at the health and habits of our children at home and at school
- Fads and fashions: the values that mold them
- Our concerns as teachers and parents

Style (home economics teacher — slide presentation)
- What our students are learning from the media (examples of advertising)
- What they are learning and making in school
- Style — a need for individuality

Physical Fitness (physical education teacher)
- What does "physical fitness" really mean?
- Goals and aims of the school's physical education program

Body Image (counselor)
- What does body image have to do with self-concept?
- Some information about eating disorders
- What can we, as parents and teachers, do to help prevent eating disorders?

If the counselor knows the parents of a child who has been diagnosed as anorexic and whose family has taken part in the recovery of the child, these parents may be willing to share their experience with such a parent/teacher group. It is not unusual for a family that has had the benefits of therapy and come through the trauma a stronger and healthier unit, to be glad to share this experience with others.

I have had the pleasure of speaking with parents in this situation and have found the family's insights and gratitude at having worked through their dilemma to be inspiring. When one mother was asked what she wished, looking back, that the school or school counselor had done to help in the process, she replied, "I wish they [the school] would have encouraged her [my daughter] to keep involved [in school activities]." She also added that at the time she began to realize that there was something seriously wrong with her daughter, she "didn't even think about going to the school for support. I went all over the city looking for someone who *knew* something about it [dieting and severe weight loss]." She reported that when she did finally find some professionals who began treating her daughter, not one of them (at first) seemed to understand the *parents'* need for help and understanding, or appeared to want to listen to their concerns and frustrations. The implications here for the counselor and the school could not be clearer.

One simple, yet effective, way for the counselor to be of help to parents at the first contact is to have available a current issue of the newsletter from American Anorexia Nervosa Aid Society (133 Cedar Lane, Teaneck, N.J. 07066). This publication offers such help as a list of dos and don'ts for parents of anorexic children (see Table 6-2).

A school with a counseling staff that is known to the community to be knowledgeable, caring, and supportive would not be ignored by parents in their first attempts to seek out help.

Communicating with Students. A useful tool for disseminating information to students and stimulating interest about eating disorders is bibliotherapy. It is a very effective method of raising awareness and spotting potential problems. For example, the librarian could be asked by the counselor to suggest current fiction on the subject that is available for various age levels. One such book is *The Best Little Girl in the World* by S. Levenkron. The counselor might then arrange with the English teachers for some class time to review the

TABLE 6-2. How to Handle the Anorexic Child in the Family.*

DON'T

1. *Do not urge your child to eat or watch her eat or discuss food intake* or weight with her. Leave the room if necessary. Your involvement with her eating is her tool for manipulating parents. Take this tool out of her hands.
2. *Do not allow yourself to feel guilty.* Most parents ask: "What have I done wrong?" There are no perfect parents. You have done the best you could. Once you have checked out her physical condition with a physician and made it possible for her to begin counseling, getting well is her responsibility. It is her problem, not yours.
3. *Do not neglect your marriage partner or other children.* Focusing on the sick child can perpetuate her illness and destroy the family. The anorexic must be made aware by your actions and attitudes that she is important to you, but no more important than every other member of the family. Do not commiserate: this only confirms the child in her illness. She knows you love her.
4. *Do not be afraid to have the child separated from you* (either at school or in separate housing), if it becomes obvious that her continued presence is undermining the emotional health of the family. The final separation is death; don't allow her to intimidate the family with threats of suicide.
5. *Do not* put down the child by comparing her to her more "successful" siblings or friends. Her self-esteem is a reflection of your esteem for her. Do not ask questions such as, "How are you feeling?" or "How is your social life?" She already feels inadequate and questions only aggravate the feeling.

DO

1. *Love your child as you should love yourself.* Love makes anyone feel worthwhile.
2. *Trust your child to find her own values, ideals and standards,* rather than insisting on yours. In any case, all ideals are just that – only ideals. In practice we fall short too; our own behavior is adulterated with self-serving rewards.
3. *Do everything to encourage her initiative, independence, and autonomy.* Be aware though, that anorexics tend to be perfectionists so that they are never satisfied with themselves. Perfectionism justifies their dissatisfaction with themselves.
4. *Be aware of the long-term nature of the illness.* Anorexics do get better; many get completely well, very few die. But families must face months and sometimes years of treatment and anxiety. There are no counselors or psychiatrists with the same answer to every case. A support group such as a parents' self-help group may make a significant difference to your family's survival; it helps you to *deal with yourself* in relation to your anorexic child. But you must make the child understand that *your* life is as important as hers.

*From the January-February 1981 *Newsletter*, American Anorexia Nervosa Aid Society, 133 Cedar Lane, Teaneck, N.J. 07066.

book that is selected and discuss it with the classes. The counselor should choose a book that is popular with the students and one with which they can easily identify. The book, along with a current article in a teen magazine, could provide excellent material to stir interest and raise awareness. Bibliotherapy is a nonthreatening way to help students recognize their own problems. Perhaps it may even encourage any students who have personal concerns about the illness to see the counselor privately.

Another way for the counselor to communicate with students about eating disorders is to be a part of a nutrition unit in a home economics class. The counselor could offer to deal with the psychological aspects of food. The following discussion outline was used by a counselor in seventh grade home economics classes.

Fat? Skinny? or Just Right?

Part I. My favorite food is _____
My favorite food group is_____
My favorite meal is_____
Why do I look forward to that meal especially?_____

What messages have I heard from my parents about food and eating?_____

Family food rituals (traditions): _____

Do I eat only when I'm hungry?_____
If not, what are some of the other reasons?

_____   _____
_____   _____
_____   _____

Does anyone is my family have a weight problem?_____

Part II If you could change your figure, what would you change? _____

On a scale of ont to ten, indicate your degree of satisfaction about your body image.
1 2 3 4 5 6 7 8 9 10
What do you think is the ideal weight for your height (the weight at which you feel most healthy, energetic, happy, etc.)?
Think of some ways that advertising gets us to think that thin is beautiful?

Part III Concept of BODYMIND – a delicate balance:
Can you read your body's messages? _____
Can you tell the difference between
hurt and angry? _____
tired and hungry? _____
bored and hungry? _____
restless and hungry? _____
Identify your "comfort foods." _____

_____   _____

How do we get in trouble with food? _____

At this point the counselor placed a simple diagram on the board depicting a mobile in balance — the parts of the mobile being the three words *physical, emotional,* and *intellectual.* She then went on to explain briefly the basic function of the pituitary gland and the hormones activated at puberty. The counselor stressed the importance of adequate nutrition to maintain the body's delicate balance.

Knowing Community Referral Sources

While gathering information about eating disorders, the school counselor will very likely become aware of the professionals in the community who are known to work with anorexics and bulimics. With a little "detective" work, the counselor will discover those agencies and individuals who are becoming known in the community as having experience in working with eating disorders. Psychologists, psychiatrists, general practitioners, counselors, and social workers all may appear on the list as possible therapists. Some of them may conduct groups, while others may work solely with individuals. It is important for the counselor to find out the different approaches to, and methods of, therapy that are being used by the various therapists since method and style may affect the success rate for different individuals. If, for example, the counselor is working with a junior high age girl whom he or she wishes to refer, it would probably be best to suggest an agency which the counselor knows uses family therapy as a part of the treatment.

The school counselor should also be able to offer some general information to the family about financial responsibility, probable time commitment, and the location of the office of the agency or therapist. These details can do a lot to help the family over the first anxiety-provoking steps of reaching out for help. The counselor who has become a trusted and familiar figure to the student suffering from an eating disorder, can certainly help ease the tension by offering this kind of information even though these details may seem relatively unimportant in the light of the illness with which they are dealing.

The initial steps of the treatment process can also constitute a time when the other family members (parents especially) begin to feel alienated from the daughter (or son) who has the eating disorder and from the treatment process itself. They do not know what is expected of them. At this time, the counselor can assist the parents in finding a support group and, if none exists in the community, may help them in organizing one with such guidelines as those suggested by Anorexia Nervosa and Associated Disorders (ANAD).

The counselor should attempt at this time to set up some procedure by which the communication channels between the client and the school (counselor) can be kept open. It is easy for this relationship to break down from lack of contact after the referral has been made. However, it is also clear that the counselor could be an important link for the client as treatment proceeds. The school is the environment in which the client will have the most opportunities to be independent, and will be able to test her self-reliance and try out her skills at forming better interpersonal relationships. It is in school that the student will be in charge of herself to the greatest degree, and a trust relationship with the school counselor at this time could be of real benefit to her.

If the client has been hospitalized, it would be ideal to hold a meeting with the parents, teachers, and therapist before her return. There must be mutual understanding of the problem and consistent support for the client when she returns.

The school counselor may very often be in a tricky position at this juncture: even though he or she can be a real support for the client and provide a place for her to go at times to share her concerns, disappointments, and successes, the counselor may feel that he or she has become "an enemy" of the patient. The counselor may sense that by talking with teachers, parents, and therapists, he or she is being viewed by the client as "one of them" and the trust relationship that once existed has been damaged. This is probably most apt to happen to the counselor in the elementary or middle school where parental concern and responsibility are more apparent and the counselor may be viewed by the girl as part of the authority structure of the school. This is a problem that exists for school counselors with many of their cases, not just eating disorders, and must be weighed and dealt with individually.

If this problem is handled sensitively, the counselor can, in most cases, be of help to the entire family. He or she can do this by making very clear to the client at the outset that their conversations are confidential and that the client will always be told if other communications with parents, teachers, or therapists are necessary. Openness and honesty with all parties concerning this issue will usually avoid any serious problems in this area.

If this hazard is successfully avoided, the counselor can become very significant to the anorexic at this point in her recovery. As the patient moves outward from her family toward independence, the counselor can be the person to encourage and support her as she transfers dependence from her family to herself. The counselor can help in this transition, and the process will be easier if the counselor has made it clear to the parents what his or her relationship will be with their child.

School Programs for Students: An Important Prevention Step

A great deal of the counselor's work in most schools focuses on the importance of healthy self-concept. Body shape is an integral part of the self-concept, and it is not surprising that adolescents experience some less than positive feelings concerning their physical image. So many body changes are occurring that many young people (perhaps most of them) struggle with great uncertainty about what *is* or is not happening to their bodies and what is still *going* to happen. While they are dealing with these doubts and concerns, they hear the message in our society that "thinner is better." The next logical step (in the minds of some discontented adolescents) is to try to take control over this part of their lives — to do something about it.

Unfortunately, for some young people there are few areas in their lives where they enjoy a feeling of autonomy. For some adolescents, one of the only areas over which they perceive some control is in what they eat and what they look like. As stated earlier, experiencing a sense of power or control over their lives is a strong developmental need for adolescents. Add to this the fact that physical appearance can bring a great deal of positive attention from family and friends, and there exists powerful motivation. These are tempting payoffs for adolescents with low self-esteem. So they try to take control, to effect some change in their appearance. The focus of their lives becomes fixed on food and what it will do to them.

These points have been made again to emphasize the importance of self-concept programs in the school and to show their relationship to prevention programs for eating disorders. Such programs do not have to deal primarily with nutritional information, diet, and exercise. The school counselor needs to keep this in mind since it is often easy to lose sight of the importance of his or her work when some staff, administrators, and sometimes the community may look askance at the affective part of the school curriculum as not being relevant to basic education.

Chemical dependency is a case in point. Chemical dependency did not decrease when the schools added drug information to their curricula. However, after this was recognized as a feelings disease, and after it was accepted that chemically dependent students have difficulties with self-esteem and in relating to others, the schools changed their focus to these factors, and the programs have become more preventive in nature.

Similarly, students with eating disorders seem to have problems with self-acceptance, feelings of inadequacy, emotional dependency, and relating to others. Figure 6-1 shows graphically how these two disorders can be compared and where the school can intervene with prevention programs. Two examples of programs which schools can adopt to try to deal with some of these developmental issues will be described briefly here.

Operation Aware is a program based on the precept "Be yourself." It promotes the idea that the best way for adolescents to grow and develop in their world is (1) to know themselves, their values, and their standards; (2) to recognize problems when they occur and know where to go with them; (3) to recognize in themselves and others attempts to run from problems or to take them out on others; and (4) to recognize peer or group pressure when it occurs. The program is aimed at 10 and 11 year olds, the main thrust occurring in the first year of middle school or junior high school. The idea behind this program is that these are the years when adolescents begin

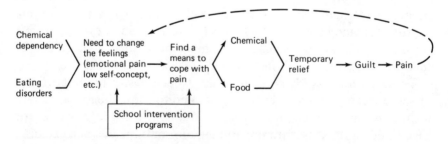

Figure 6-1 Similarities between chemical dependency and eating disorders. (Adopted from Vernon Johnson's *I'll Quit Tomorrow*, Harper and Row, 1980.)

to view themselves as grown-up and more in control of their lives. The students who have an unusual fear of this transition may be the ones who will reach for maladaptive ways of coping, such as chemical dependency or eating disorders. The main idea of the program is taught by presentation of several simple concepts through discussion and vicarious participation through films, field trips, and role playing. The program is taught by trained school staff members, with the school counselor acting as a consultant and/or coordinator.

Another program which facilitates the counselor's job in preventive work is the advisory system. This system can be particularly helpful with referral procedures. It places the staff member outside the role of teacher with a small group of students and into the role of advisor. This makes it far more likely for nonacademic problems to come to the counselor's attention. It is especially useful in spotting eating disorders, which usually begin unobtrusively in quiet, well-behaved children. These students are often conscientious and sometimes perfectionist, and are not likely to cause any obvious problems in the classroom. A well-informed advisor can be very helpful here in recognizing these students.

The advisory system is based on the idea that each student should be provided with one caring adult outside of the regular classroom, whose job it is to watch his or her students' progress and social adjustment. The advisor sees the students daily, and he or she watches the students' academic progress, their attendance, and their ability to get along with others. The advisor is kept informed by other teachers of classroom difficulties and attitude problems. It is intended that the advisory system create stronger ties among the advisor, the advisee, and the advisee's parents.

In a school in which the advisory system is strongly supported by the staff, the referral system (for potential or existing problems) is an effective one. The advisor, being in close touch with his or her advisees, is apt to spot problems or symptoms which otherwise may go unnoticed in the busy classroom. This is especially true of the "good" child who is quiet and well behaved, characteristics often found in the child with an eating disorder.

Referrals can be made by the advisor to the counselor who then can begin the process of meeting with the student, conferring with the parents, and gathering information from other staff members.

Symptoms in the School Setting

One can see, after reading the list of symptoms of eating disorders which appear in Table 6-1, that no *one* behavior can safely be viewed as a symptom of an eating disorder. Even when several symptoms from the list are apparent, the counselor must be very cautious about drawing hasty conclusions. The following is a case history which will demonstrate how one student was referred for help.

A Case History

Jane was a sixth grader who was beginning her first year at a large middle school (grades 6,7, and 8). Jane's parents had been divorced two years earlier, and she lived with her older sister and her mother who worked in a professional position. She had been in two elementary schools before this which were structured with self-contained classrooms. The middle school she had just enetered is a large school (about 1000 students), and it is departmentalized. That is, the students have a homeroom teacher for attendance purposes and then go from room to room for a seven-period day; hence, they have seven different teachers throughout the day.

Jane was referred to the counselor by her history teacher in the fall of the year. The teacher reported that each day for two weeks, Jane had asked to leave history class to go to the nurse, saying she had a stomachache. The history teacher assumed at first that it was just a case of nerves and hunger since the history class met at noon (the "lunch run" period); also, it was still very early in the year when sixth graders often have some trouble adjusting to the new school and schedule. However, the history teacher became concerned when Jane continued this routine for several days and, consequently, referred her to the counselor.

In checking with the nurse, the counselor discovered that Jane would complain of a stomachache and a sore throat, and would pace the floor very fast when she came into the office. She would say she "needed" to call her mother. When she did so, she would talk for several minutes. There was an audible change in her voice tone as she talked with her mother, from a normal tone to a high, childish voice with a whining quality.

The counselor called Jane in the day after the referral, during the first period, and found her to be a bright, conversational, very well-groomed child. She was small for her age and probably on the low side of normal weight. Jane spoke animatedly about her family and her teachers at the school she had attended the previous year, saying she really wished she could go back there. She said, at this time, that she didn't like the cafeteria food (a rather common complaint with students) and that was why she left history class. She was afraid she might throw up, especially since physical education followed lunch period.

The counselor arranged for Jane to spend a few days with her during Jane's physical education class so that they could get to know each other. These sessions continued for a few days, but Jane continued to leave history class to call her mother. She was very distraught at these times, pacing and shaking her long, dark hair from side to side in a rhythmic way. Her face was flushed and her mouth so dry she could scarcely talk. She would insist on calling her mother.

During the counseling sessions, the counselor allowed Jane to take the lead. Jane would talk freely about her family and how lucky her older sister was, saying, "Everything came so easy for her." She dwelt on things she would like to buy (mostly clothes) and things she would like to own some day. During one session, the counselor asked Jane what she liked best about herself, and Jane replied, "That I'm skinny." The Piers-Harris Self-Concept Scale revealed that Jane was most concerned about her popularity with peers. Her anxiety level was high, according to the scale, and her perception of her behavior was her highest subscore, indicating that she perceived herself to be a very well-behaved, "good" girl. Jane would also explain to the counselor — in detail — the exact amount of food she had eaten in the cafeteria. She seemed very proud to have consumed two or three bites. This led the counselor to suspect that eating was also an issue at home. Jane said that she did not sleep well at night, often awakening with bad dreams. When this happened she would have to sleep with her mother.

During the time that the counselor was seeing her, Jane began to resist going to other classes and to her homeroom first thing in the morning. The counselor conferred frequently with Jane's mother at this time, since the problem seemed to be escalating. The counselor expressed her concern about a possible eating disorder. She suggested some informative literature on the subject and recommended some outside referral sources. The mother was very receptive to reading about anorexia but reluctant to seek outside help. However, she did make an appointment with a psychologist who saw Jane one time only. Jane refused to say a word during the session, and her mother then reported to the counselor that she couldn't pay that kind of money to have Jane go and just sit there.

This seemed to be a turning point. The mother's frustration and exasperation precipitated some new rules at home which she consistently enforced, and the counselor, with the help of other staff, began some gentle but firm insistence that Jane attend all her classes. There were some attempts by Jane to manipulate the staff and her mother into excusing her from a class, but firm, friendly insistence by the staff usually won out. On the few occasions when this method did not work, Jane was allowed to sit alone at a desk outside the counselor's office, and although she was not treated in an unfriendly manner, she was not given special attention. Within three weeks, Jane was attending classes regularly and had been selected by her homeroon teacher to be the student whose job it was to welcome new students to the school, show them around the building, and introduce them to teachers. Two months later, Jane was exhibiting increasingly assertive behavior in class, and appeared more relaxed and happy both at home and at school. The mother reported that her daughter was eating a little better though her food selection was very limited. The mother said she felt better after having read the literature on eating disorders and was more sure of herself in dealing with her daughter.

As one can see in this case history, there were several signals that pointed to an eating disorder. The case, however, was never formally diagnosed. This perhaps is not important. What is important is that Jane's problems were seen by an aware staff and parent as potential signs of a dangerous and complex illness, and were dealt with accordingly. Early referral in this case may have checked some problems that could have developed into a deep-seated, long-lasting eating disorder. It is impossible to know. On the other hand, it can be said that Jane did exhibit some symptoms which may have been "red flags" of anorexia nervosa. A sensitive, aware teacher recognized a problem, referred it to the counselor, and helped to deal with it. The counselor was then able to work with both the student and, in this case, an open-minded, caring parent. She provided some information and suggested referral sources for the parent to seek help outside the school for her daughter. At the time of this writing, Jane is being monitored and doing very well. She shows very few signs of repeating her attempts to withdraw from the challenging task of growing up.

The mother, too, is watching, but with less confusion and alarm than before. She is now more knowledgeable concerning eating disorders and is well aware that her daughter's symptoms had indicated a possible anorexic condition. She can now observe her daughter's normal adolescent struggles in growing up and be more sensitive in helping her through this difficult period. It is hoped that she will recognize any maladaptive behaviors which may recur and that she can support her daughter in turning them around if they do occur.

It is a delicate and challenging task for a parent — knowing when to let go. The adolescent appears at times to need independence, parental support, and protection simultaneously. No wonder that parents need support groups to help them through this puzzling job of rearing a teenager. Parents often say, "I don't know which behaviors are normal and which are signs of trouble," and "When do I need help and where do I get it if I think I do?"

The school counselor (particularly in schools that deal with minor children) can certainly be a significant person in easing this confusion that parents often experience. The neighborhood or community which has a counselor in the school or college who can fill the role of support person, consultant, and liaison is indeed fortunate.

Summary

The school counselor can be an effective agent in the process of dealing with eating disorders in the following ways. First, as a support person, the counselor can:

1. be an intelligent listener, aware of eating disorders: the symptoms, the treatment, and the recovery;
2. give appropriate feedback to clients and their parents;
3. be able to suggest options;
4. provide encouragement and support to clients and their families;
5. help to organize support groups.

Second, as a consultant and liaison, the counselor can:

1. be knowledgeable by keeping up with current studies about eating disorders;
2. provide information and make it easily accessible to clients, their families, and staff;
3. educate parents and staff with in-service workshop and presentations to parent groups;
4. be aware of community resources and professional help.

Finally, but perhaps of greatest importance, the school counselor can have an impact on eating disorders in the area of prevention. Guidance programs aimed at seeing to the normal developmental needs of clients can have broad implications in deterring eating disorders. Such programs, dedicated to the promotion of healthy self-concept and sound interpersonal relationships, can have far-reaching effects. Although it will probably not be specifically stated that one of the goals of such a program is to prevent eating disorders, this may in fact be the case. For, although it is difficult (if not impossible) to measure what does *not* occur as a result of a particular program, it must be remembered that the psychological needs for approval and control, which were mentioned earlier in the book as precipitating factors in the onset of eating disorders, will not be as extreme in the individual with a healthy self-concept and sound interpersonal relationships. The school counselor needs to remember this from time to time when he or she is feeling ineffective or inadequate in direct attempts at dealing with the illness. The aware counselor can then rest assured that his or her developmental guidance program does, in fact, play an important part in the prevention of eating disorders.

REFERENCES

Anorexia Nervosa and Associated Disorders, Suite 2020, 550 Frontage Rd., Northfield, Ill. 60093

Dinkmeyer, D., and McKay, G. *Systematic Training for Effective Parenting.* Circle Pines, Mn.: American Guidance Service, 1976.

Gordon, T. *Parent Effectiveness Training.* New York: Peter H. Wyden, 1970.

Johnson, V. *I'll Quit Tomorrow.* New York: Harper and Row, 1980.

Levenkron, S. *The Best Little Girl in the World.* Chicago, Ill.: Contemporary Books, 1978.

Newsletter. Teaneck, N.J.: American Anorexia Nervosa Aid Society, January-February 1981.

Operation Aware, Inc., College of St. Scholastica. 2410 Morris Thomas Road, Duluth, Minn. 55811.

Pearlstein, R. When a diet can lead to death. Co-Ed. September 1981.

7
College and University Campuses

Since we are both employed in university counseling centers, this chapter is very near and dear to our hearts. Because of the years we spent struggling and groping for answers, and trying to develop services, we decided to write down our discoveries. Our hope is that these perspectives on anorexia nervosa and bulimia on our campuses will be of help to other college counselors.

Our approach has been to keep as up to date as possible on therapeutic approaches, applicable research, and the latest ideas of leaders in this field. Even though there are so many unknowns with respect to eating disorders, we feel a responsibility to use the ideas which seem most workable and most theoretically sound. In doing so, we try to remain flexible enough to discard what is not working, while being open to new theories and methodologies and, above all, listening to what our clients can teach us.

The Role of the College Counselor

The role a counselor takes on in working with anorexic and bulimic students, instructors, and staff is determined by many variables. The size of one's college or university and the size of one's counseling center staff will vary greatly from person to person. Your center may have a large staff and offer extensive, specialized services, or your center may consist of one person who is not only in charge of all the student counseling, but also in charge of training resident hall staff, operating a career center, teaching study skills classes, and so on. Therefore, our purpose in this chapter will be to share some of our ideas. Your part will be to take the information and adapt it to your own campus situation, whatever that may be.

If your training has been in the student personnel area, you may feel that your role will be primarily to educate students about the problems associated with these disorders and to make referrals for therapy to other professionals, either on campus or in the community. We address referral later in this chapter and also in Chapter 8. Now we come to the critical point: what role you take as a professional will be decided by you. Good luck, and don't underestimate your capabilities in the role of change agent. You can change the environment of the campus from one in which these disorders are hidden, misunderstood, and perhaps even inadvertently fostered, to one in which the disorders can be openly discussed and more easily identified, and preventative interventions may be employed. The counseling center can be a place where any person encountering the problem can receive professional help either by the counselor directly or by referral to another agency.

Coordination of Services

The task of coordinating campus services for individuals with anorexia nervosa and bulimia generally falls on the shoulders of either the counseling center staff or the health center staff. If attention is not given to this coordination and to the development of a unified program, different departments will each go their own way resulting in duplications, possible misunderstandings, and student confusion.

Furthermore, once a program has been established, ongoing communication between the involved departments is vital. For example, if a student has been referred by a counselor to the health center, it is important for the counselor to know if the student followed through on the referral. Simple interdepartmental notices can be utilized for this purpose (see Appendix H for a sample copy). If tests were run, the counselor needs to know the results of those tests. For instance, it is not unusual for eating-disordered students to downplay the amount of exercise or purging that occurs. If the health center staff is not aware of the situation, a low potassium reading may simply result in potassium pills being dispensed. However, if the person is continually vomiting, this will be to no avail. The potassium cannot be replenished if the pills are not retained.

Another typical problem may occur if a student goes to see a dietitian who is unaware of the student's disorder. The student may be told that she needs to eat up to 1000 or more additional calories per day. This information, given to an anorexic or bulimic, can have disastrous effects and cause the student to panic. Immediately increasing calories too quickly will seem not only impossible but terrifying, and there is a strong likelihood that the student will not return.

Another familiar situation occurs when residence hall floor members try to tempt the thin anorexic student to eat by using high caloric, high sugar goodies; this results in the anorexic becoming more obstinate and positive that these students only want to make her fat. To avoid working at cross-purposes with one another and to maximize treatment, communication on a regular basis is necessary for all individuals involved.

In the following sections, we identify various campus services and indicate some of the ways these services can be coordinated.

Health Center Services

Most college health centers have a physician(s) (either full- or part-time) and a nursing staff. Some centers also have the services of a dietitian, medical technologist, and a pharmacist. Often, an eating-disordered student's first contact with a professional will be through the health center. This might occur for the following reasons:

1. The student has experienced loss of menstruation which precipitates having a checkup by the physician.
2. The student may want to lose weight and will set up an appointment with the dietitian for a reducing plan.
3. The student is referred to the physician by a staff or faculty person because of the student's great weight loss.
4. The student may be experiencing depression, high levels of anxiety, and/or difficulty sleeping, and will request medication from the physician.
5. The student may experience other physiological problems as a result of the vomiting and/or laxative abuse, and will contact the physician, fearful of the damage her body may be undergoing.

If the health center staff is aware of the warning signs, they can be instrumental in diagnosing the problem while it is still in an early stage. Also, for some students, the health center might be a less threatening place to approach initially. Some students who refuse to go to the counseling center will go to the health center. In order for the health center to make an appropriate referral, it will need information from you regarding the services available both on campus and in the community.

Housing and Residence Hall Staff

If your counseling center is located on a campus with campus housing, this section applies to you. If your school has residence halls, the coordination of counseling center services with those of the residence halls is a very important link in the service chain. We believe that it is essential to develop eating-disorder education programs not only for the residence hall staff but also for the residents. Also, assistance must be provided in developing some general guidelines to be followed when an eating disorder is suspected. It is important to inform students and staff directly about the services that are available to them and about how to obtain these services. For example, what should a head resident do if a student is obviously losing too much weight? What should a custodian do if he/she finds that someone is vomiting in their utility sink or depositing bags of vomit in the waste containers? What should a student resident assistant do if floor members bring up a concern over someone who is displaying anorexic or bulimic behavior symptoms? What should a student do if her food is constantly disappearing and she doesn't know what to say to the roommate who is taking it?

These specific situations naturally will differ on each campus, as will the solutions that you develop to fit your particular campus. Our recommendation here is to inform the housing staff specifically what steps they can take. These steps may be:

1. To inform the counseling center generally and let one of the counselors deal with the situation
2. To inform a specific contact person who is working with anorexic and bulimic students either on campus or in the community
3. To inform a previously specified person within the housing staff (often the head resident) so that person will make the decision as to the proper referral
4. To inform the health center staff and have them determine the appropriate steps to be taken

One situation which occurred on one of our campuses began when a head resident called the counselor and indicated her concern over a student who was becoming thinner and thinner. The student refused to go to the counseling center or to the health center, and many other residents were reporting the small amount of food that the student seemed to be eating. What should the head resident do? The counselor offered to visit the student in the dorm. Would the student agree to this? Yes, if the head resident could be present.

The counselor met with the student and the head resident. The student was defensive, distant, and unwilling to acknowledge that there was a problem. The counselor informed the student of the reasons she was concerned about her, some of the possible consequences of not eating, and the services available to her both on campus and in the community. Also, the student was given some articles to read which specifically dealt with anorexia nervosa. The student was told that if her condition got more serious, if she lost more weight or started passing out, intervention would occur because of the seriousness of the situation. This student, after a few weeks, chose to receive services off campus and began her recovery work in a community mental health center.

Another situation began with a call to the counselor by a student resident assistant. Several residents of her floor were concerned about a student who was throwing up frequently. They felt she could not possibly always have "the flu." What could the resident assistant do? The counselor shared some possible dialogues that could occur, such as: "I am very concerned about you Joan. I'm aware that you often throw up after eating and I'm wondering if you might have a problem with bulimia. I care about you and am concerned about what you may be experiencing." In this specific situation, the resident assistant invited the student to go with her to the counseling center and visit with a counselor who was working with bulimic students. The student agreed, and the meeting was informative and productive. A few weeks later, the student decided to join the eating-disorder group on campus and to visit with a dietitian. She is presently working hard toward recovery. We encourage counselors to be direct and open when inquiring about eating behaviors. To do this, the counselor must be somewhat knowledgeable about eating disorders. This approach gives the student freedom to admit the behavior rather than defend or hide it.

Frequently, fellow students or staff members encountering the situation in the residence hall will wish to discuss it with a professional before they approach the person identified as having the problem. We recommend that they contact a counselor at the counseling center and, either over the phone or in a visit to the center, discuss the options that they have in communicating their concern to the individual with the suspected eating disorder.

Food Services

Sometimes the campus food service will have a dietitian or nutritionist on the staff to help develop diets for students with special needs, such as the diabetic, the dieter, the vegetarian, the athlete, and so on. Contact with this person can be helpful in many ways. First of all, some anorexic and bulimic students may desire special diets, and the dietitian or nutritionist may be a referral source. Secondly, once a student is working toward recovery from one of these disorders, she may need special consideration in foods available for her meals. For example, if it is difficult for her to eat fried chicken, can tuna fish be provided by special request? Since most food service menus are planned far in advance, and are usually posted and available to students at least one week ahead of time, prior planning by the student is possible. The food service can be very helpful by suggesting alternative foods that provide the necessary nutrients and informing the students how to receive these foods. Since this is a situation in which the student is asking for special consideration, it is a good opportunity for her to work on her assertiveness skills.

Faculty

The size of your campus will determine how much personal contact you can have with the faculty. The more personal contact occurs, the easier referrals will be. Unless the counselor has a method of reaching each instructor individually, instructors will usually gain knowledge of these disorders through student and staff publications and memos (see Chapter 5). We have had faculty contact us when concern has been aroused through some kind of self-report by the student. For example, in a nutrition class, students may be asked to chart their food intake. Through this project, the instructor may become aware of some unusual eating behaviors. Also, members of the faculty have contacted us when a student has chosen to do a report on anorexia nervosa and/or bulimia and in the report has indicated she is experiencing these very behaviors.

The faculty is an important part of the campus network services. The more information faculty members receive, the more helpful they can be in their referral and support roles.

Conclusion

Although community referral sources will be covered in Chapter 8, we want to note here also the importance of developing a strong network of services both on and off campus. Keeping close ties with community services is vital. Psychiatrists, mental health professionals, social service agencies, and self-help and therapy groups can enhance the services you provide and allow for a more complete therapeutic fulfillment of the needs of the anorexic and the bulimic student.

8
Community Resources

The goal of this chapter is to explore the use of services in the community, such as referrals to (1) a mental health center, private or public agency; (2) a psychiatrist; or (3) a hospital situation.

As a professional in any setting, it is important for each one of us to develop a referral network. (By referral network, we mean the lines of contact with other professionals and agencies which have been previously developed and are ready for use when information or referral is needed.) Then if a situation arises in which services other than our own are needed, we have this network to facilitate the referral. This kind of network is important when working with anorexic and bulimic individuals. Referral to the mental health center, to a psychiatrist — or even hospitalization — is often necessary.

The type of network developed is determined by certain variables: (1) your background and training, (2) your work setting, and (3) the community in which you work (rural or metropolitan). The network can be developed in many ways, such as telephone and letter inquiry of services, personal visits with the professionals or to the agencies or hospitals, contacts made at professional meetings and conventions, and so forth.

Mental Health Centers, Private and Public Agencies

You may hear of a specific treatment program for anorexics and/or bulimics or of a particular professional in one of the agencies who is doing special work in this area. It would be important to develop communication with such an individual or agency and find out if that treatment program could help your client. Also, you should inquire about the referral procedures and the cost involved for treatment services.

Once the decision has been made for the referral, an appointment for an intake (initial interview) is set up. This interview will determine if the referral is appropriate for the services the agency provides and, if so, to which professional or program your client will be assigned. The information you give to the professional or agency before the intake about why the referral is being made, which individual or program you are making the referral to, and other specific matters, will help expedite the intake. A release of information form must be signed by the client before this information can be given to the agency (see example in Figure 8-1).

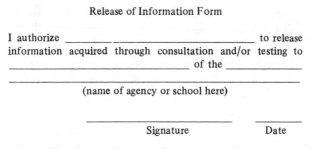

Figure 8-1. Release of information form.

Once the treatment has been assigned to your client, your role changes. Your client is now in a treatment program in another agency or center. How your role changes depends on several variables: your relationship with your client, the type of services she will receive from the agency or center, and your responsibility for following the progress of your client. Clients often need further support during treatment. Directives from the assigned professionals can be helpful to you as you define your new role.

Here are some examples of how your role can vary. Sue was referred to a local mental health agency because she showed symptoms of clinical depression and started to have some thoughts of suicide. She had been working with a counselor on her bulimia for approximately two months and was making some slow but constructive progress. The referral involved intake by a psychiatric nurse and a visit with a psychiatrist at the mental health center. Their evaluation determined that antidepressant medication might be helpful for the depression. With communication between the counselor and the psychiatric nurse, it was decided that Sue would continue her weekly visit with her counselor to work on the bulimia and would visit the mental health center monthly for medication checks. Because the release of information sheet was signed by Sue, additional information by either the agency or the counselor could be given.

A very different situation was involved with Tim's referral. Tim was a bulimic who was not responding to weekly individual and group treatment, and was feeling very hopeless about the likelihood of progress toward recovery. The counselor made a referral for him to an intensive treatment program for bulimia. This program lasted for four weeks and involved Tim's living in another community 100 miles away. The referral information was sent to the agency, and Tim's acceptance into the program came after his intake interview. The agency recommended that after Tim completed the four weeks in its program, he should continue group and individual work with his former counselor. The counselor was designated as the primary therapist again for Tim after the four weeks in the intensive program.

If you are questioning your role, you may ask the agency or designated professional how you might be helpful. Since you are the referral source, you may have some responsibility in checking on your client's progress. It will also be very important for you to check to see if your client has carried through on your referral, since this can be a critical juncture for losing contact with the client. If it is a referral source that you are relatively unfamiliar with, you may, as a learning tool for yourself, want to keep in touch with the professional who is working directly with the client.

You may need to obtain information from the agency before the referral. Some of the possible questions might be:

1. What kinds of services are available?
2. What qualifications, training, and experience does the professional have in the areas of anorexia nervosa and bulimia?
3. What are the intake procedures?
4. What will the charges for services be?
5. Are insurance coverage and sliding-scale billing possible?
6. How is an appointment made?
7. What is the usual length of treatment?
8. What is the role of the referring professional during and after treatment?
9. Are any personality or psychological tests administered? If so, which ones?

The answer to question (8), the role of the referring professional, is especially important for you to know. After treatment, will you be working with the client again and, if so, in what capacity? Also if the answer to question (9) is that psychological tests are given, you may spare your client additional costs if you are qualified and have the facilities to administer these tests yourself. For example, college counseling centers usually provide these services to students at little or no charge, and the results of the testing could be sent to the referral agency or center.

Often the hardest part of making a referral is knowing *when* to refer. If in doubt, visit with the agency or other professionals and then make your decision after all of the variables involved with that particular client have been considered.

Psychiatric Referrals

As a counselor or therapist, you will frequently be in need of the services of a psychiatrist for your anorexic or bulimic clients. These services may be for:

1. Diagnostic and evaluative work
2. Medication
3. Psychotherapy
4. Hospitalization

Whatever the referral is for, it is helpful to have established a professional contact with a psychiatrist(s) you can rely on, who works with anorexic or bulimic individuals.

The following questions and answers may facilitate your referrals to psychiatrists.

1. *How can I find a psychiatrist who works with eating disorders?*

Psychiatrists can be found in a variety of settings such as private practice, professional corporations, mental health centers, private and public agencies, Veterans Administration hospitals, and college and university campuses. One possible way to find out which psychiatrists in your area are working with eating-disordered clients, is to contact a college or university counseling center or campus health center. Since all campuses are encountering problems of anorexia and bulimia, they are likely to have psychiatric referral services. Another contact is the family doctor or general practitioner who may have suggestions regarding which psychiatrists to get in touch with. Every state has at least one district branch office of the American Psychiatric Association which can help you with referral information. Referral information is also available from several national associations for eating disorders (see Chapter 9).

2. *How do I make the referral?*

A release of information form (see Figure 8-1) will be necessary if you are going to visit with the psychiatrist in person, by telephone, or by letter. We recommend that you (not your client) make the initial referral contact, unless the client or the client's family is insistent on making it themselves. If you set up the appointment, you know that it has been accomplished, and then your only concern is that the client gets there!

A letter of referral to the psychiatrist will be greatly appreciated. In this letter, include:

(a) Your diagnosis of the individual
(b) The scope of the problem
(c) Special circumstances in the client's life (an example would be if the client's mother is dying of cancer, etc.)
(d) Your concerns
(e) Any recommendations for treatment

3. *When should I refer a client with anorexia nervosa or bulimia to a psychiatrist?*

There will never be total agreement among professionals in answering this question. Your good common sense will be your best guide. If you aren't sure or are worried, it is worth a call to the psychiatrist, or to another professional, to review the case and then make your decision.

If your client is experiencing weight loss, tiredness, listlessness, or abdominal pain, and hasn't had a medical checkup, we highly recommend one. There can be many other problems which have similar symptoms, and only a medical checkup can give you the accurate information. You can refer your client to a general practitioner or internest, or to a psychiatrist who can then make a referral if he or she feels other medical attention is necessary.

When the client is overwhelmed by feelings of helplessness and hopelessness, and is near the point of loss of functioning, possibly with thoughts of suicide, it is often time to make a referral to a psychiatrist. Also, if your client uses amphetamines at all, we recommend an automatic referral because amphetamines pose a particular danger for the anorexic or the bulimic. The overuse of diuretics, diet pills, or laxatives can be fatal, and a difficult judgment must be made here by the professional whether to refer the client to a psychiatrist or not. If the client is just beginning to use these products, it is important to keep tabs, as much as possible, on their usage. No general guidelines exist in this area and the professional must take into consideration all aspects of the case.

If you are seeing a client with a continuous depression that lasts ten days to two weeks, this depression may or may not be the result of starvation and should be evaluated since some kind of medication or even hospitalization may be appropriate. The depression is often accompanied by suicidal ideation, and this must be attended to right away.

Depression and Suicide

Everyone gets depressed, "down in the dumps," or has the "blues" sometime in her life. There also are feelings of depression which occur only with concerns regarding the eating disorder. Such depression, especially in bulimics, shifts rapidly, and the person experiences frequent highs and lows. However, the depression we are talking about is the serious depression which involves an obvious mood shift — feelings of emptiness, helplessness, and social isolation; sleep and appetite changes; loss of concentration; and sometimes suicidal ideation.

The lifetime prevalence for this depression ranges from 8 to 20 percent for the general population (Porkorney, 1981, p. 1). In the anorexic and bulimic population, its incidence seems to be even greater. We include information on depression because you will be dealing with it in many of your clients.

Depression must be attended to for many reasons. (1) It is extremely debilitating to the person experiencing it. (2) The depressed person may require medication and certain types of psychotherapy. (3) The person may become suicidal and even need hospitalization for treatment of the depression.

Interestingly, we often see the onset of depression at the time when clients start to deal with the eating disorder. In fact, depression is a normal and expected part of recovery — a grief reaction to the loss of the eating-disorder behavior. Clients begin to face their problem, taking a look at their relationships and their imperfections. This may be an extremely difficult time for them. Since many of their present coping skills are inadequate, they get into quite a stressful state. They begin to experience some of the emotions they have previously avoided by "eating" or "starving" them, but once they begin to experience these emotions, they become overwhelmed. What should they do? How can they deal with their anger toward their parents? How do they adjust their nonassertive behaviors with their peers? How do they accept their imperfections? For whatever reason, depression seems to appear or to become more intense at these times.

It is important to determine the severity of the depression the individual is experiencing because a psychiatric referral may be the next step. Antidepressants do help most individuals who have serious depression. Also, if the person is seriously considering suicide, the psychiatrist may decide that hospitalization is necessary. We do not recommend the sole use of antidepressant medication. We believe psychotherapy or counseling is important in conjunction with the medication.

If you are concerned that your client may be suicidal, some very important questions should be asked in order to determine the seriousness of the problem. These questions are as follows:

1. Have you experienced a recent change in appetite lately? (The depressed person very often experiences a loss or increase of appetite. The professional must be careful here because bulimics frequently mask this symptom.)

2. What losses or problems have you experienced in the last year? (Sometimes it may seem to the person as if there are no reasons to feel depressed, but in looking back, it may

have been a very stressful year.)

3. Have you recently experienced a loss in weight? If so, how many pounds in what period of time? (Here again, caution is advised in working with eating-disordered clients because the weight loss may be due to the eating disorder.)

4. Has your functioning at school or at work changed? (Usually the person becomes less productive and feels extremely nonproductive.)

5. Is there a history of depression or alcoholism in your family? (Very often a history of depression can be found in other relatives. Alcohol use often can be a way or trying to solve depression — thus the question on alcoholism.)

6. Are you thinking about suicide, about killing yourself? If the person answers yes, then the following questions should be asked:

    (a) Have you a plan of how you would do it? (If the answer is yes, the person is indicating a serious suicidal situation because she has determined a method already. If the answer is no, the person is indicating that her suicidal plans are as yet not clearly defined in her own mind.)

    (b) Can you implement your plan? (For example, if the person's plan is to use pills, do they have them in their possession or can they get them?)

    (c) Have you ever attempted suicide before? (If the answer is yes, the situation is more serious because there is already a prior suicidal pattern.)

    (d) Has there been any suicide in your family?

    (e) How close are you to putting your suicide plan into action?

For the inexperienced clinician, these may be hard questions to ask. Don't be concerned that you are giving the depressed individual the idea of suicide. Anyone who is depressed enough for you to be concerned about has had the thought already. As responsible professionals we need to determine what the thoughts have been.

Once you know the answers to these questions, you can then determine your next step. If the situation seems extremely serious, the emergency room of a hospital may be the step to take with your client. If it is not an extreme emergency, but still serious, we recommend contact with a psychiatrist to determine if medication and hospitalization are necessary. If the person does not seem to be in immediate danger, we recommend that a contract be developed with her regarding her staying alive — having her promise to call or contact someone if the suicidal thoughts become stronger. Make sure she carries certain telephone numbers with her at all times:

1. Your number
2. An agency number
3. A crisis line number
4. A suicide prevention line number
5. Numbers of family and/or friends

The higher the trust level and the stronger the relationship between the counselor and the client, the better chance there is of the client keeping the contract. Such clients will truly believe that they should no longer live: you can be a help in convincing them that these feelings stem from the depression and that they will not always feel this way. It is imperative that the client accepts the concept of "help" and is willing to allow you to help her.

Hospitalization

Hospitalization of the anorexic or bulimic client can occur for many different reasons and in many different ways. We believe that hospitalization for these problems should be via the informed psychiatrist. These are complex psychological problems which should be treated by a psychiatrist on the psychiatric floor and not by another physician on the medical floors. The main psychological issues usually are not addressed on the medical floors.

There are many ways that your client can be hospitalized. (1) You might contact a psychiatrist, and he or she will facilitate the admission into the hospital. (2) You may contact a mental health center or agency, and its personnel will often expedite the hospitalization through their channels. (3) In an emergency situation especially, you may bring the client into the emergency room of a hospital, and have the mental health professionals and psychiatrist on call make the admission into the hospital. If you are aware of the hospital services in your community, choose the hospital with the most appropriate program for your eating-disordered client.

Once hospitalization has occurred, your role becomes one of support for the client and, if necessary, the client's family during her hospital stay.

When is hospitalization necessary for individuals with anorexia nervosa or bulimia? As discussed in Chapter 3, each client has a different medical history, and there is no uniform set of rules that determines when a person will be hospitalized. Some situations in which hospitalization may be necessary for the anorexic or bulimic client are:

1. Extreme weight loss
2. Depression
3. Suicidal thoughts
4. Alcohol and drug dependency
5. Inability to cope with life stress
6. Physical side effects such as dehydration, electrolyte imbalance, etc.

Hospitalization for inability to cope with life stress, situation (5) usually occurs when the individual is experiencing feelings of helplessness, feelings that her life is out of control, and real feelings of panic. An added danger at this time is the suicidal ideation which often goes along with these feelings.

Conclusion

The use of community agencies and professionals will be an important aspect of your work with your clients. Since each community is different, as are the makeup and philosophy of its mental health professionals, your decision will be based on this information. Good luck in your referrals; your good judgment must always be the final word.

REFERENCE

Porkorney, A. D. DSM-III and affective disorders. *Directions in Psychiatry* Lesson 8 (1981).

9
Additional Sources of
Information and Support

In addition to professional help, there are many other resources which afflicted individuals, their families, and their friends may find of assistance. Unfortunately, no centralized listing of these resources exists. The first part of this chapter will provide specific information regarding these additional sources of support. This can be duplicated, along with your own additions, and distributed to interested parties.* Keep in mind that while these organizations were developed primarily for victims and those close to them, they can be of value to the professional helper as well. The second part of this chapter specifies resources primarily intended for the professional engaged in treating or researching eating disorders.

SELF-HELP RESOURCES

OVEREATERS ANONYMOUS
World Service Office
2190 190th Street
Torrance, California 90504

Overeaters Anonymous, patterned after Alcoholics Anonymous, is an organization dedicated to the compulsive overeater. While OA is not designed for the bulimic person, the fact that bulimics are compulsive eaters certainly qualifies them for membership. The sole requirement for OA membership is simply a desire to stop eating compulsively. Although discussion is generally restricted to compulsive overeating, while purging is not addressed, there are many OA members who engage in both bingeing and purging behaviors. In some locations, notably metropolitan areas, it is possible to find Overeaters Anonymous groups made up primarily of individuals with bulimia.

---

*Since most of these organizations are nonprofit and operate on a shoestring budget, a self-addressed and stamped envelope should be included in your correspondence.

A good number of people attribute their success in overcoming the problem of bulimia, at least partially, to membership in Overeaters Anonymous. However, the level of awareness and understanding of bulimia can vary from group to group, and we suggest checking this out before referring anyone to OA.

Bulimia, as we discussed previously, is often accompanied by chemical abuse. In these instances, Alcoholics Anonymous and Narcotics Anonymous can also be helpful. Local listings can be found for all three of these groups in the telephone directory and community newspapers. A packet of information designed specifically for the professional is available from Overeaters Anonymous.

* * * *

NATIONAL ANOREXIC AID SOCIETY, INC.
P.O. Box 29461
Columbus, Ohio 43229
Director: Patricia Howe Tilton

NAAS identifies itself as a "support and educational organization for individuals suffering with anorexia and/or bulimia and for their families." NAAS has established support groups in a number of states and has developed a national medical referral program. Four quarterly newsletters are included in the nominal membership fee.

* * * *

ANOREXIA NERVOSA AND RELATED EATING DISORDERS, INC.
P. O. Box 5102
Eugene, Oregon 97405
Phone: 503/344-1144
President: Dr. Gene Rubel

ANRED is an organization dedicated to alleviating the problems of eating disorders. It provides information and support to any person concerned about food-related problems. ANRED's services include 24-hour hotline (503/344-1144), self-help groups for sufferers and their families, therapy groups, educational programs, a speakers' bureau, a monthly newsletter, and a national referral network. ANRED will also cooperate with research projects and be of assistance in any other way they can.

AMERICAN ANOREXIA NERVOSA ASSOCIATION, INC.
133 Cedar Lane
Teaneck, New Jersey 07666
201/836-1800; weekdays 10:00 A.M. – 2:00 P.M. EST
President: John A. Atchely, M.D.

The aim of AANA is to provide services and programs for anyone involved with anorexia nervosa and/or bulimia and to aid in the education, research, cure, and prevention of these illnesses. The services offered include information, referrals, counseling, self-help groups, a speakers' bureau, and research. General meetings are held five times per year (free), during which professional presentations or communication workshops are held. A newsletter is likewise published five times per year. The self-help group for anorexics and bulimics meets once a month, as does the group for parents spouses, and siblings. These groups are jointly led by recovered anorexics, parents of recovered anorexics, and mental health professionals. The organization will assist in setting up chapters in other areas. Arrangements can be made for personal correspondence or telephone contact with recovered anorexics. A book by and for family members is also currently in progress.

* * * *

NATIONAL ASSOCIATION OF ANOREXIA NERVOSA
AND ASSOCIATED DISORDERS, INC.
Box 271
Highland Park, Illinois 60035
312/831-3438
President: Vivian Meehan

ANAD was the first national educational and self-help organization dedicated to alleviating the problems of eating disorders. This organization provides a telephone hotline (312/831–3438), national referral information, self-help groups, early detection and prevention programs, educational programs, assistance with research projects, and a thick packet of information to anyone who writes or calls, ANAD also will assist, in very concrete ways, with the formation of new chapters and self-help groups throughout the country, and it provides a number of continuing services even after the group has been established.

* * * *

THE ANOREXIA NERVOSA AID SOCIETY OF MASSACHUSETTS, INC.
Box 213
Lincoln Center, Massachusetts 01773

ANAS provides information referral and a monthly newsletter. Plans are in progress for installation of a telephone answering machine. This group does not involve the membership in research projects.

ANAS played a considerable role in the development of a comprehensive outpatient treatment clinic in the New England area. This evaluation and treatment clinic is offered through Massachusetts General Hospital's Department of Psychiatry; it offers evaluations of medical and psychiatric status, nutritional history and dietary patterns, and social and family situations. Treatment programs are individualized, and consultation with various specialists is available as needed.

* * * *

THE CENTER FOR THE STUDY OF ANOREXIA AND BULIMIA
Institute for Contemporary Psychotherapy
1 West 91st Street
New York, New York 10024
212/595-3449

The Center for the Study of Anorexia and Bulimia is composed of five divisions: treatment, New York Anorexia Aid, prevention, training, and research. The treatment division offers direct therapy on a sliding-scale basis to the afflicted individual and/or her family. New York Anorexia Aid provides support groups throughout the metropolitan area. The prevention division distributes information and promotes early detection of eating disorders. General information pamphlets on anorexia and bulimia are available upon request. Discussion groups, workshops, and other special projects are undertaken. The prevention, training, and research divisions will be discussed further under "Resources for Professionals," later in this chapter.

* * * *

ANOREXIC AID
The Priory Centre
11 Priory Road
High Wycombe, Bucks
England

Anorexic Aid is the only self-help organization in the United Kingdom and functions as a network of groups. It is the British counterpart of the American self-help organizations previously described. A quarterly newsletter is published, and a bibliography provided, upon request.

* * * *

FEEDING OURSELVES
30 Bartlett Avenue
Arlington, Massachusetts 02174
617/661-3727
Director: Emily Fox Kales

Feeding Ourselves offers a comprehensive ten-week program which focuses on weight management, body image, and eating problems related to obesity and bulimia.

The program aims at exploring the whys of overeating, relearning how to eat, and confronting the meaning of "fat" and "thin" in each individual's life.

A small group format is utilized, with individual counseling available as needed. Movement and relaxation techniques are incorporated into the program. Advanced and ongoing support groups are also available. Other services include weekend workshops; consulting and in-service training for mental health agencies, hospitals, and nutrition and weight control clinics; educational programs and speakers; management and employee programs for industry and nonprofit institutions. Fees are assessed. Self-help materials are available for purchase.

* * * *

DIETERS COUNSELING SERVICE, INC.
227 East 57th Street
New York, New York 10022
212/421-1220
Director: Leslie Jane Maynard

Dieters Counseling Service provides extensive referral information regarding both medical facilities and support groups for individuals afflicted with eating disorders and their families. The organization also provides a bibliography.

****

HOSPITALS AND UNIVERSITIES

Some hospitals and universities have developed eating-disorder clinics: University of California – Los Angeles, University of Minnesota, Mayo Clinic, Micheal Reese Medical Center at the University of Chicago, University of Cincinnati, Massachusetts General Hospital, University of Toronto, Canada, and Johns Hopkins Hospital, to name a few.

RESOURCES FOR THE PROFESSIONAL

We would highly encourage the professional helper to make contact with some of the aforementioned organizations for two reasons: first, for one's own knowledge and information; and second, in order to become part of their referral bank. There are areas of the country for which few or no referral resources are known. If you provide services to people with eating disorders, it is important to forward this information to these primary referral organizations.

In addition to these resources, there is a newcomer on the scene which is directed specifically toward the professional and is clinical in nature:

THE INTERNATIONAL JOURNAL OF EATING DISORDERS
Van Nostrand Reinhold
Professional Journals and Periodicals Division
7625 Empire Drive
Florence, Kentucky 41042
606/525-6600

The birth of this publication was one of the more exciting happenings of 1981 in the field of eating disorders. This is a multidisciplinary journal committed to publishing basic research, reviews, and theoretical manuscripts related to the area of eating disorders. Each issue contains a comprehensive bibliography of new literature and reviews of major published works in this field. Announcements of relevant conferences and professional meetings can also be found in this journal. The publication is available in microfiche as well. To subscribe, write to the above address. Papers are welcomed for review and should be addressed to the editor: Craig Johnson, Ph.D., Michael Reese Medical Center, Psychosomatic and Psychiatric Institute, Chicago, Illinois 60616. Instructions and guidelines for submission of material are available upon request.

We might add that one of the senior advisors to the editor is the noted Hilde Bruch, M.D., of Baylor College of Medicine.

* * * *

BOOKS

We have provided a bibliography of books and articles for further reading at the end of each chapter. While all of these are recommended, we feel compelled to bring special notice to those by Hilde Bruch, R. L. Palmer, Arthur Crisp, and Mara Palazzoli.

* * * *

THE CENTER FOR THE STUDY OF
ANOREXIA AND BULIMIA

The Center for the Study of Anorexia and Bulimia and several of its five divisions were described in the first section of this chapter. Here we will discuss those divisions which are oriented toward the professional. The prevention division has introduced an early detection and prevention (of eating disorders) program into the New York public school system. This is, to the best of our knowledge, the first venture of this kind and magnitude. This organization would seem to be an excellent resource for anyone interested in similar prevention efforts.

The training division offers to mental health professionals specialized programs for the treatment of eating disorders. A national conference is also being planned.

The research division is gathering data on patients in the treatment division for use in research studies in the areas of demography, etiology, and treatment.

* * * *

FEEDING OURSELVES
AND
DIETERS COUNSELING SERVICE, INC.

Feeding Ourselves and Dieters Counseling Service were cited in the previous section. In addition to the services they provide to victims of eating disorders, they also provide in-service workshops to mental health professionals.

* * * *

JOURNAL ARTICLES

The array of professional journals that have or may carry articles on eating disorders is staggering. Probably the simplest way to approach the world of journals is with a bibliography in hand. Such bibliographies can be obtained from other journal articles, books on the subject, self-help and referral organizations, colleagues, and even clients.

The U.S. Department of Health and Human Services has published a comprehensive literature survey for anorexia nervosa. This contains references to the literature and abstracts for the years 1978–1980. This document (#HE20.8134:1) can be obtained from your local or regional United States document depository (usually the public library or a library affiliated with a university).

* * * *

HOSPITALS AND UNIVERSITY MEDICAL SCHOOLS

The nearest metropolitan area hospitals and medical schools may have programs and/or identified specialists for treating eating disorders. A physician or psychiatrist in your local community may be aware of such treatment programs and be able to provide a specific reference. If he or she is not aware of any programs, that does not necessarily mean that none exist! Remember, this is a resource not only for the referral of clients/patients, but also for yourself. You might be able to set up in your community a workshop utilizing these specialists as speakers. Then again, an on-site visit to the hospital or clinic program for eating disorders might be arranged along with an opportunity for consultation and discussion with the people working with the program.

* * * *

WORKSHOPS

Information on workshops can be obtained from the *International Journal of Eating Disorders* as well as from some of the organizations listed in the beginning of this chapter. National and state conferences of the medical, dietetic, and counseling professions may also occasionally include a session or two on anorexia nervosa and/or bulimia. Suggestions to your own professional organization specifying this topic as one of interest may be helpful in bringing about such presentations.

* * * *

The listings in this chapter should not be considered exhaustive; rather, these are the well-established organizations and resources of which we are aware. More than likely, by the time this book is published, other organizations will have come into being. You might use the above-mentioned resources to check the current situation for your own locale. Your local mental health association may also be able to provide an update for your region.

10
Hints for Significant Others

As you begin to treat eating-disordered individuals, you will find yourself invariably dealing not only with the family, but also with concerned friends, teachers, roommates, residence hall directors, and so forth. Living with an individual who has anorexia or bulimia is no easy task, and these other people in the sufferer's life also need support. The support required can range from providing simple information about the disorder, to therapy — the latter being the case most often with parents, spouse, or boyfriend/girlfriend.

These significant others are likely to be quite concerned about the afflicted individual and worried about doing or saying the "wrong thing." The anorexic especially arouses great concern in others because of her frailty and vulnerable appearance. Certainly no one wants to be in any way responsible for her demise by inadvertently "pushing her over the brink." Moreover, these individuals would like to be of help in some way, to be a positive force in the victim's life. "But how?" they will ask. "What should I do?"

Complicating the matter further may be additional problems which have arisen within the relationship due to the presence of the eating disorder itself. For example, a residence hall director may want to be supportive of the afflicted student, yet must also deal with an irate maintenance staff that is tired of cleaning up the aftermath of vomiting episodes. Roommates may be unsure of how to handle the problem of missing food. Most likely they cannot afford, and do not want, to support their friend's "food habit." Yet they may also be wary of a confrontation. There is a fear that they may not handle this properly and that the victim will not be able to withstand it. Then again, there may simply be unconfirmed suspicions about the possibility of a classmate being anorexic or bulimic and uncertainty as to how to approach the situation.

This chapter will address these kinds of concerns. In it we will share some of the questions that have routinely been put to us and our suggested answers which have been born out of digging through the literature and from experience. For the most part, though, we did not really find many answers in the literature and had to improvise as we went along. Therefore, our advice and ideas are not based upon scientific research; rather, this is a report of what has worked for us and our colleagues. You will undoubtedly — and it is our hope that you will — come up with additional answers of your own.

We warn you, though, that none of the answers is simple or cut and dried. Further, since we, as therapists, do not have to live in the situation, our answers may not be as helpful as those of others who have had that experience, such as parents. The American Anorexia Nervosa Association (AANA) is in the process of compiling a book written *by* parents *for* parents of eating-disordered individuals. When this book becomes available, it will undoubtedly prove an extremely useful resource. Although we cannot give specific reference information at this time, requests can be sent directly to AANA (see Chapter 8 for address).

It can be difficult even for the professional helper to determine the best approach at times, and we make a point of being open about this with the parties who come to us for help. This is less a matter of being the "expert" with all the answers and more a process of collaboration: we recommend pooling information, both about the disorder in general and the individual in particular (excluding of course anything that could be considered confidential), before deciding upon a specific course of action.

On many occasions, especially when we first began to encounter eating disorders, we wondered how others in our roles dealt with certain situations and wished there had been some experienced person we could call and ask, "What do *you* do when...?" It is because of our own head scratching that we have come to write this chapter.

Family

Palmer (1980) suggests in his book *Anorexia Nervosa* that the anorexic and her family be especially deliberate and organized in their approach to eating in order to "put eating in its place" and to add a measure of control to eating situations. Palmer's suggestions include keeping definite mealtimes; recording food intakes and calories, with both upper and lower limits set; and setting agreed-upon rules for discussion of food, eating, and weight so that there is an opportunity for such discussions but also a limit to them. Otherwise such discussions can (1) consume all conversation and all the family's energy, and (2) allow the victim to remain focused on food. Obviously it is important not to ignore the problem, but it is also important not to let the problem become all-enveloping.

The anorexic is tremendously fearful of losing control over eating. The fear is that should she begin to eat, she might not be able to stop. This is not a totally inappropriate fear since she is in an extremely deprived state and some individuals do in fact go on to develop a problem with binge-eating. For this reason, it is extremely important to reassure the victim of the disorder that this is not going to be allowed to happen. We want a responsible eater in the end. Attempts should not be made to overfeed the individual or entice her to eat by, for example, fixing her favorite foods. Nor should efforts be made to cajole the person into eating at times other than mealtimes. It is very important not to encourage or condone either overeating or inappropriate eating. Palmer suggests not going along with new food fads and emphasizes providing a "run of the mill" diet. Comfort and reassurance should be given regarding the fear of eating too much, and the person can be encouraged to eat at mealtimes but, as stated before, not between meals.* Additionally, controls can be set for weighing herself and cooking for others.

Palmer explains that the table will remain a battleground as long as struggles and conflicts exist over weight and eating. He emphasizes the importance of the individual's seeing the problem and conflict as her own, as must her family. He acknowledges that this can be very difficult, but if the parents are able to step out of their role as "feeders" and instead take on the role of "controllers" — that is, lending control to the eating situation — the battle is then allowed to be experienced as the victim's internal battle (versus an external one with other people). Now this may well prove an impossible task for the family. The eating may have become too entangled with other issues. Furthermore, the victim is their own child (or spouse, or sibling), and the fear, frustration, and anger may simply be too difficult to control. This is another advantage of hospitalization: it is much simpler for those who are not intimately associated with the victim to deal with her. These outsiders are also more likely to be accepted

---

*An exception to this would be the planned snack often employed as part of a treatment plan.

as helpers and allies. Parenthetically, it is amazing how little fuss might be made in the hospital when control of the food is taken away. Sometimes relief is experienced. At other times, a decision is simply held in reserve to cooperate now, get out of the hospital, and then lose the weight again.

Parents should do everything possible to encourage independence and decision making on the part of their eating-disordered child. Emotional support is clearly necessary during this time, but it should not be confused with inappropriately "rescuing" the afflicted child. We also suggest that parents seek support for themselves, either through professional help or through a self-help organization for family members.

Parents feel helpless in the face of the child's refusal to eat. Even if they should be able to convince her to eat, it is still possible for her to throw up or use laxatives. Extreme fastidiousness and other compulsions can also be difficult to live with. Days filled with tantrums, hysterical sobbing, and hostility can take a serious toll on the entire family.

The presence of an eating-disordered child can put strains on the marriage as well. Both parents do not always agree about how to deal with the situation. It is easy for the child to become a wedge between them. It is imperative that parents work out a united approach and stick with it.

Parents need to be encouraged to go out and have fun; to work as a team that the child can enter into if she wants to, but can also choose to remain apart from. The child needs patience, kindness, and firmness. The responsibility for eating and weight should be placed between the child and the therapist. The parents can be encouraged to call the therapist whenever they are unsure of how to proceed in a situation or when problems erupt.

Families who must live with bulimia face some different problems. Should they hide food? Should they rule the kitchen out of bounds? Perhaps a padlock should be installed on the refrigerator?

While bulimia is not as apparent as anorexia and generally does not elicit quite as dramatic a response, it nevertheless can cause real turmoil within a family (not to mention a financial drain).

Palmer's suggestions are also relevant to parents of a child with bulimia. However, victims of bulimia tend to be older adolescents or young adults, and their living situation may be quite different. The child may have a schedule that makes it difficult to eat together, or she may only be home during vacations from college. In this situation, the afflicted individual needs to be responsible for her own eating behavior.

Some ways in which older teenage clients have worked things out in the family have been:

1. to have a separate food allowance and to do their own grocery shopping or prepare a shopping list for whoever does the family shopping;
2. to have their own cupboards, keeping their food separate from the rest of the family's; or
3. to prepare their own food and eat on their own schedule.

College students working toward recovery typically have an extremely difficult time maintaining appropriate eating when they go home for weekends or vacation periods. This is a time of particular stress to be sure. Even in those instances when they are looking forward to seeing their families, "home" generally remains a stressful environment for a variety of reasons. However, in addition to this, students report two major food-related difficulties: haphazard meals and ready availability of foods.* We have found it helpful to have students discuss the particular difficulties with their families prior to going home and to develop a plan for dealing with them. An example of the plan one student developed follows.

Jean was in her third year of college. She had a brother who was a year older and a sister still in high school. Her family lived in the country, and both parents worked outside the home. Jean reported several difficulties associated with being home over vacation periods. First, her brother worked during these times as did her parents. Her sister was heavily involved in high school activities and was seldom home either. Consequently, Jean was home alone all day without transportation. Because of the family's different schedules, the evening meal was usually quite late, much later than the time Jean would normally have eaten. Her mother enjoyed baking and always had a variety of goodies around. You can imagine the difficulty which this situation presented.

---

*Several clients have reported that the onset of bulimia occurred shortly after the family ceased the eating of regular meals together because of conflicting schedules.

Jean's family was none too happy with these visits home either. They would come home and find all the food gone. The groceries for the entire month disappeared in several days, and no goodies were left for anyone else. This situation led to arguments, particularly between the brother and sister but often involving the entire family. Furthermore, the bathroom smelled of vomit, which was a particular source of irritation to Jean's mother. She cleaned it daily, using an old toothbrush to get into all the crevices, but to no avail.

The contract Jean and her parents developed with the help of the counselor was that Jean's mother would refrain from baking or buying sweets while Jean was home on vacation. Jean would also drive her mother to work so that she could have transportation and an opportunity to visit friends in town during the day. The family had an extra small refrigerator for their bar, and it was decided that this would be Jean's refrigerator during her visits home. All of her food would be kept in this refrigerator. Because she had difficulty waiting so long to eat supper, she was to decide upon her own eating schedule and prepare her own food. Any excess food she took from the family was to be replaced at her own expense and effort. Cleaning the bathroom also became her job. In this way, Jean assumed greater responsibility for her own behavior, and her mother ceased providing undue temptation. Access to the car provided for more freedom and a greater variety of options for dealing with spare time. Both Jean and her parents reported a much calmer and more pleasant vacation experience.

Another situation that we are frequently faced with is the frantic telephone call from a parent saying, "My daughter is out in the kitchen bingeing. Should I just go ahead and let her binge?" If the parents do not want the child bingeing in their home, they have the right to define what eating will be allowed. One ground rule that parents have found helpful is that whatever bingeing is done will be done outside the home and not on the family's food.

It may be helpful for the parents to explain to their child that they do not want to reinforce this behavior. By overlooking its occurrence, parents are indirectly giving their approval. Therefore, the decision of whether or not to binge will remain the individual's. Where the binges take place and whose food is consumed, however, can be defined by the parents. This is another situation in which a family discussion and contracting can be helpful.

Parents must take responsibility for meeting their own needs even in the face of their child's illness. They must continue to live their own lives and take time for their other children as well. Parents should also encourage the eating-disordered child to develop relationships with others outside of the family, particularly with peers.

Roommates

Living with an eating-disordered individual can be quite a challenge even if the people are not related. Not all roommates can handle this, and in these instances, a room change is desirable. However, in the majority of cases this is not necessary, and roommates are eager to do whatever they can to help the victim in her recovery. Frequently what happens, though, is that the anorexic or bulimic begins to feel "watched" and resentful. The roommates should be encouraged to talk about this openly.

The support of roommates and friends can certainly be helpful in the recovery process. A student at one of our universities set up a meal plan with a friend who ate normally — someone whom she respected and admired, a positive model. The two made out their food plans in the morning, then exercised, and ate together, Gradually, over a period of months the eating-disordered individual became more and more independent, for instance, eating one and then two of the three meals without her friend. This friend played a most supportive role in her eventual recovery. However, concerned roommates or friends need to be reminded not to "own" the victim's problem, that is, not to take it on as their own. Furthermore, roommates should be encouraged to deal directly with any problems that arise.

Friends

The more socially isolated anorexic is very lonely and sees herself as basically unlikable; yet as lonely as she is, overtures on the part of others may be constantly rebuffed. This behavior seems related to the belief that others couldn't possibly like the "real" her; thus they will not be allowed to get close at all. This can be a most trying ordeal for friends and others who are trying to be supportive yet are consistently met with the cold shoulder. It can be helpful to keep in mind that regardless of how antagonistic the anorexic individual may act, there is a great need for friendship and support. Also, persistence will usually pay off in the end.

Even with anorexic students who are not obvious social isolates, we hear a similar refrain. Complaints are voiced that so-called friends do not like their inner person, only the outward acceptable facade — the facade that the anorexic often loathes, resents, and feels entrapped by on the one hand, yet clings to and fears giving up on the other lest people be driven further away. "Afterall," her thinking goes, "no one likes a girl who isn't nice and smiling all the time, one who gets angry or depressed." One student had a smile so fixed that when she cried it was with a smile — not a nervous, embarrassed smile, but a *bright, shiny* smile plastered upon her face, with tears spilling all around. This was so sudden and incongruous that it took the observer several seconds to realize that the drops of water were in fact tears.

How Can Teachers Help Support the Recovery Process?

Eating-disordered individuals are typically very demanding of themselves and have a tendency to take a heavy load of difficult classes. The teacher or advisor can encourage taking fewer classes, balancing difficult classes with less difficult ones, and so forth, to ease the load.

At the college level, the interruption of schooling is generally the biggest hurdle to voluntary hospitalization. Schoolwork is an obsession for many sufferers, and they are rigid in their belief that they cannot interrupt it. There is also the fear of falling behind. Moreover, the student may be near the end of the term, having already completed much of the work, but be unable to receive credit for it unless the term is finished. If the student is enrolled in college or a private high school, money becomes another issue. "Waste" of money is difficult for many people, but it can be a particularly sensitive area to the generally frugal anorexic student. Parents may also have a concern about the financial aspect. If the school and instructors are flexible and cooperate with the hospitalization (for example, by allowing more time to finish the courses begun and paid for), a great deal of the stress and resistance to treatment can be alleviated. Usually hospital personnel are willing to administer tests or cooperate with the fulfillment of academic requirements. Some hospitals, especially if they are major treatment centers, have education components and personnel associated with the treatment program.

Teachers can make a point to be available for consultation, at least by telephone. At the college level, some instructors have arranged for lectures to be tape recorded, mailed tests, made arrangements for independent study projects, or given "incompletes" or "in-progress" grades with the agreement that the work will be made up when the individual is able. If the student is not hospitalized, teachers should be available to discuss difficulty with schoolwork. They can encourage the student *not* to take course work so seriously. Contrary to usual practice, in working with eating-disordered students it is important to acknowledge the importance of *not* overdoing assignments.

The student may need to miss class for doctor's appointments or therapy sessions. Understanding and cooperation with this can go a long way. It is important to realize that treatment will involve emotional turmoil and that this turmoil can add to the difficulty of completing schoolwork. On the other hand, care needs to be taken so that rules are not bent excessively, since part of the problem with anorexia is that the illness often ends up controlling everyone and lending a "specialness" to the victim.

Avoid comments on external appearances, particularly weight. For instance, rather than commenting on a gain in weight or saying that the student "looks good," which she will interpret as "fat," state something like "it's good to see you again" or "you seem happier." This shows that her worthiness of attention is based upon more than mere external appearance.

Reach out to the student. If she begins to withdraw from activitiities, check this out. Is she being more assertive and deciding for herself which activities are meaningful to her rather than *expected* of her — which is a sign of health and progress — or is she withdrawing, isolating herself further? If the latter is the case, an invitation to rejoin is in order. Whether or not the student does, having someone reach out to her will be affirming in and of itself, letting her know that someone notices her absence and cares.

Since excessive exercise is typical of eating-disordered students, physical education teachers or coaches may be approached by the student with requests for longer workouts, etc. At the college level, instructors are frequently asked if the student can have permission to come to other sections of the class, perhaps even missing other classes in order to do this. The instructor is well advised to refuse requests for this excessive physical activity.

I Think My Daughter/Son/Friend/Student Has Anorexia or Bulimia. How Can I Tell?

One of the most common situations that we run into is the telephone call or visit from a concerned person regarding the possibility that someone he or she knows has an eating disorder. There is concern and a feeling of responsibility for getting that individual help, as well as an uncertainty as to how to go about doing this. The first thing we do is ascertain why the caller suspects an eating disorder. In what ways does this person resemble an anorexic or bulimic? We give a brief explanation of anorexia or bulimia and discuss the attitudes, behavior, and physical state of the third party. While we certainly would not generally declare anyone to be anorexic or bulimic on the basis of hearsay or secondhand reports, we can and do indicate whether or not there seems to be cause for concern and further investigation.

It may be that an eating disorder is unlikely but that another problem exists. A case in point is that of a college student who recently came to the attention of one of the authors because she was not eating and had lost a significant amount of weight in spite of being rather thin to begin with. As it turned out, this young woman was not attempting to avoid food per se, but rather had other psychological problems. She was a bit of a recluse, depressed, and living alone. Basically she did not have any desire to cook or eat alone — aand alone she was the majority of the time. On those occasions when she was with others, she would eat with apparent enjoyment without overindulging. In this case, the friends were told that their concern was not misplaced. Clearly a problem existed which merited professional attention; however, that problem was not anorexia nervosa.

Much of the time, however, we find others' assessments or suspicions of the presence of an eating disorder to be quite accurate; that is, what they describe is very much in line with the criteria set forth earlier in this book for anorexia and/or bulimia. The questions then invariably put to the therapist are, What should I do? How can I get him/her help? These are critical questions indeed. Being a helping professional, you of course are in the position of knowing (or being able to find out) the best resources for assessment and treatment in your locale. Then again, you may *be* that resource.

The underlying concern of the above questions, though, may not be so much *who* to contact for professional help (after all, they are now in touch with you) as *how to broach the subject* with the individual suspected of having the eating disorder. This is the next question.

How Should I Approach the Person I Think Might Have Anorexia and/or Bulimia?

There certainly is not any one way of approaching a person who might have an eating disorder. The approach taken will be at least somewhat dependent upon the relationship of the parties involved. As a general guideline irrespective of relationship, however, the individual should be approached with compassion and forthrightness, with a statement of concern and the basis for that concern. We encourage the individual to avoid focusing the remarks solely on weight. "Looking too thin" is interpreted as a compliment of the highest order and signifies "success." As alternative comments, emphasize that she looks unhealthy, seems unhappy, and so on; that you care about her and are worried for her well-being; that help is available. When confronting binge-purging, be straightforward about what you know or suspect; call a spade a spade. State your observations. Making the observation or raising the question may open the door for the afflicted person, particularly the bulimic, to confide in someone, often for the first time. It can be a tremendous relief to have the "secret" out in the open, especially if it is received with compassion rather than the feared disgust. The victim may or may not be familiar with information on eating disorders, and sharing a magazine article or book on the subject might further encourage her to seek help.

It is important to go into the situation prepared with specific information regarding the prospects for help: where to go, whom to see, how to go about getting an appointment, how much it will cost, and so forth. It may even be helpful to offer to go along, set up the appointment, and/or provide the transportation.

If it is friends who are planning the intervention, they will more than likely be quite concerned about the possibility of triggering an outburst of anger. Naturally they would prefer not to become targets for the hostility that may well erupt. On the other hand, they can be reminded that a live, angry friend is better than a severely ill or dead one. Sometimes a dramatic statement such as this is necessary to help people past an overconcern for peace at all costs. They must be prepared to face the anger and not be put off by it. While there is no guarantee, it is unlikely to be the end of the friendship if they can "hang in there." You can reassure them that you will be available if problems arise and that they can count on you for support. Being on a college campus, we will at times accompany concerned friends and meet with the identified student together.

What If the Person I Suspect Has Anorexia or Bulimia Refuses Help?

It is more than likely that someone with an eating disorder will refuse help — particularly the anorexic who clings desperately to her condition, flatly denying that anything is the matter. The person with bulimia, in our experience, is more apt to be willing or even anxious to begin treatment, possibly because the binges are so distressing. If the individual does refuse to seek help, we tell people not to be discouraged or overly pushy. Give him or her time, and bring it up again later. While information about the ill effects of the disorder can be provided, scare tactics are neither appropriate nor effective.

Sometimes the reasons for refusing treatment are based on perceived barriers such as not wanting parents to know, financial considerations, not wanting to interrupt school work, not feeling and not wanting to be seen as "crazy," stating they can do it (and should do it) on their own, and so forth. These concerns should be met with understanding and reassurance, but not accepted as reason enough to refuse treatment.

If it is the parents who are encouraging treatment and meeting resistance, it can be helpful to enlist the aid of other people whom their son or daughter admires, respects, and trusts — other relatives, friends, teachers, ministers, physicians, or counselors. These others can usually have far more impact than a parent. If the person remains unconvinced, a firm decision is called for on the part of the parents (or other persons in authority) that treatment is necessary and will be initiated absolutely. One writer suggests that the individual can be told that she is obviously no longer able to make decisions which are healthy ones for her, so other people who care about her are going to assume that responsibility until she is able to do so herself.

Can a Person with an Eating Disorder Be Forced into Treatment against His/Her Will?

It is possible under certain conditions forcibly to hospitalize an anorexic or bulimic (see Chapter 8). When the threat of suicide exists or when the person's physical condition is unstable, hospitalization is a necessity. If the individual refusing treatment is not a minor, hospitalization can be more problematic, but it can be arranged. Although not always possible, it is usually best to arrange this at a hospital which has an established program for treating eating disorders.

Forcing someone into the hospital, however, is not to be equated with ensuring a "cure." For treatment to be effective in the long run, the patient must decide it is something she wants. At that point she becomes a voluntary patient, and it is then that real progress can be made. So the answer is yes, a person can be forced into treatment, but for treatment to be successful, it cannot remain forced.

Will Insurance Cover the Costs of Treatment?

Insurance coverage is not an insignificant question raised only by mercenary parents or spouses — quite the contrary. Although it can be used as a hedge or excuse to avoid facing the problem, it is also a pratical question and a critical one at that. Hospitalization costs can be astronomical.* There are differences in insurance coverage from policy to policy which must be individually checked. An organized effort is also being made by some of the national self-help organizations listed in Chapter 9 to increase insurance benefits for the treatment of eating disorders.

---

*Small monthly payments can usually be arranged if necessary though, and if a person is indigent, some hospitals will help make other arrangements for billing.

In addition to inpatient treatment, which not everyone requires, individuals with anorexia and/or bulimia *will* need outpatient therapy, perhaps for several years. Here again, insurance policies vary in their coverage. If converage is provided, most policies require that the therapy be done under the auspices of a physician, psychiatrist, or Ph.D. psychologist in order to qualify for benefits.

Not all outpatient treatment is costly, however. Community mental health centers usually assess fees based upon a sliding scale, according to the family's (or individual's) ability to pay. Many university health centers and/or counseling centers provide services to their students with no additional charge besides that assessed for tuition and student activity fees. Inexpensive student health insurance is also available. A few therapists in private practice are even willing to barter, that is, exchange their professional services for other services or commodities. Treatment costs then vary widely, depending on the severity of the disorder, the types of services required, insurance coverage, and the availability of services. A point not to be overlooked is that the cost of treatment may be much less than the cost of food for the binge-eater, not to mention the other "costs" associated with such disorders.

How Does One Go About Finding a Therapist?

Most of the organizations listed in Chapter 9 will provide therapist referral information. The local county medical society, your local mental health center, or your physician may also be able to provide information regarding the accessibility of therapists experienced in dealing with these disorders.

REFERENCES

American Anorexia Nervosa Association Newsletter 4 (1):(January, 1981).

Bruch, H. *The Golden Cage: The Enigma of Anorexia Nervosa.* Cambridge, Mass.: Harvard University Press, 1978.

Crisp, A. H. *Anorexia Nervosa: Let Me Be.* New York: Grune and Stratton, 1980.

Guidelines for Teachers and School Health Personnel. New York: Center for the Study of Anorexia and Bulimia, 1982.

Jones, D. Structural discontinuity and the development of anorexia nervosa. *Sociological Focus* 14(3):233-245 (1981).

Palmer, R. L. *Anorexia Nervosa: A Guide for Sufferers and Their Families.* New York: Pelican Books, 1980.

Conclusion

As we survey the chapters of this book and attempt to include all information we think is valuable, we get a sinking feeling. This book is meant as a guide, a help, a handbook to pull off the shelf for quick review. The sinking feeling comes when we realize that we must finish and that the book cannot be all things to all people.

We hope the book has been helpful and that you have found it a book to draw from. The hardest work is left, and that is all up to you. We hope you and your clients experience progress and recovery. Good luck and carry on.

Appendix A
Sample Interview

The following questions are listed as a guide for professionals when first visiting with clients for whom anorexia or bulimia may be a concern. These close-ended questions are designed as a general guide, not as specifically descriptive of your interview.

1. *Do you have any health concerns?*

    This question may help to discern whether other problems could have led to the anorexic's weight loss or the bulimic's physical complaints; it leads directly into the next question.

2. *Have you had a physical examination lately?*

    It is important to have a medical doctor evaluate whether other ailments may be the cause of the eating problem and whether the person's physical state is stable (electrolytes, potassium, etc.).

3. *Have you recently lost weight? How many pounds in what period of time? What is your present weight? What is your ideal weight?* (This will give an indication of the individual's goal for weight loss.) *What is your height?*

    The diagnostic criteria in the DSM–III define a 25 percent loss of original body weight as an indicator of anorexia nervosa. However, a 15 percent weight loss should be considered a significant sign if other symptoms are present. The weight loss must be viewed separately in each individual situation. If the individual was overweight previously, lost 15 percent of her weight, and is now content, the situation may not include an eating disorder. Look at the total picture when weight loss is involved. If the person has gained weight, she may have bulimia, if other signs are also present.

4. *Is your menstrual cycle regular?*

    If the menstrual cycle is not occurring, this may be an indication of a reduction in the percentage of body fat or a sign that there has been a great deal of weight fluctuation or fasting. This may also be one of the first symptoms of anorexia nervosa. With bulimia, the cycle may or may not be occurring, and if it is, the cycle may be irregular. There are various medical reasons for loss of the menstrual cycle, and a physical examination is recommended.

5. *Do you often "feel fat?" Do other people think you should lose weight?*

The first question deals with the third diagnostic criterion for anorexia. The person will "feel fat" even when she becomes emaciated. The second question allows the client to share the messages she is getting from other people regarding her weight.

6. *Are you afraid of becoming overweight? What do you consider to be overweight for you?*

A diagnostic criterion for anorexia in DSM–III is this inordinate fear of being overweight which does not diminish as weight is lost. The last question reveals how distorted the anorexic's thinking is about weight.

7. *Do you ever fear not being able to stop eating?*

The response to this question indicates the extent to which the person feels out of control. The individual may fear that if she starts eating, her eating will become a binge. This is one of the diagnostic criteria for bulimia and also occurs with anorexia.

8. *Do you ever binge-eat?* (By binge-eat, we mean eat large amounts of food in a short period of time.)

This is a behavior always found with bulimia and often found with anorexia. The behavior is a diagnostic criterion for bulimia. Of course, people define "large amounts of food" differently, so it is helpful to find out how much the client eats during a binge.

9. *Does eating behavior interfere with your life? To what extent and in what areas?*

Tremendous variation occurs both in frequency of binge-eating and in the amount consumed during a binge.

10. *Do you feel uncomfortable eating in front of other people and prefer eating alone?*

Eating is often hidden in both disorders, but inconspicuous eating is a diagnostic criterion for bulimia.

11. *Do you ever induce vomiting after you have eaten? How often?*

This self-induced vomiting is found in both anorexia and bulimia. However, it is one of the diagnostic criteria for bulimia.

12. *Do you ever fast? How often? For how long?*

Continual fasting or severely restrictive dieting can be an indication of anorexia nervosa. Repeated fasting and dieting, alternating with eating binges and frequent weight fluctuations in an attempt to lose weight, are indicative of bulimia.

13. *Do you ever use laxatives to lose weight? How much laxative is used?*

This may point toward an obsession with weight loss and can be indicative of anorexia nervosa or bulimia. Laxatives are used to counteract the binge. Such use is one of the diagnostic criteria for bulimia. If the client indicates a use of laxatives, it may be advisable to have the person tested for dehydration, electrolyte imbalance, potassium deficiency, and so forth.

14. *Do you exercise? What type of exercise plan do you have?*

If the individual is compulsively exercising because she "feels fat," this may be another signal that the individual is anorexic or bulimic. The anorexic is more likely to follow a strict form of exercise, and she may also deny that the exercise is connected to weight loss.

15. *Do you think your eating pattern is normal or abnormal?*

Very often the anorexic will indicate that her eating is normal, as is her weight loss, or she may have rationalizations as to why it is not. Such individuals exhibit a denial of any problem. They think they have found the answer. The bulimic, on the other hand, usually realizes that her eating pattern is abnormal. This awareness of abnormal eating pattern is included in the diagnostic criteria for bulimia.

16. *Do you find yourself thinking about food and calories much of the time?*

This focus on food is present in both anorexia and bulimia. In the therapist's office, this obsession shows up in some clients' willingness to discuss for hours on end what they have eaten and will be eating while other clients will be unwilling to discuss their food use in any detail.

17. *Do you feel free to discuss your real thoughts and feelings with your family and friends?*

In many instances, the eating-disordered person is a "people pleaser" who will playact the responses she believes others expect of her. She has great concern over anyone "not liking her"; this includes the therapist. She may attempt to answer most of these questions in whatever way she thinks you want to hear.

18. *Have you ever been treated for an eating disorder before?*

We have found, after working for a while with several clients with bulimia, that they had been diagnosed as anorexic several years earlier. It helps to have this information immediately.

These sample interview questions are not all-inclusive; we recommend that you add other questions of your own as the situation indicates. For example, if depression seems to be present, questions relating to this problem would be necessary (see "Depression and Suicide" in Chapter 8).

Diagnosing anorexia nervosa or bulimia is at times very easy: all the answers seem to fall into place. However, at other times the symptoms will not easily or completely fit the pattern. In these cases, further careful exploration is important, since other conditions may mimic anorexia or bulimia. If the individual answers like an anorexic but has no weight loss, or like a bulimic but has bingeing behaviors just appearing, the individual may be preanorexic or prebulimic, and professional help is critical at this stage. We find that the clients in this stage show relatively easy and complete recoveries.

Appendix B
DSM-III Diagnostic Criteria
for Anorexia Nervosa

The following material is a reprint of the diagnostic criteria for anorexia nervosa from the *Diagnostic and Statistical Manual of Mental Disorders,* Third Edition (DSM–III), published in 1980 by the American Psychiatric Association, Washington, D.C.

307.10 Anorexia Nervosa

The essential features are intense fear of becoming obese, disturbance of body image, significant weight loss, refusal to maintain a minimal normal body weight, and amenorrhea (in females). The disturbance cannot be accounted for by a known physical disorder. (The term "anorexia" is a misnomer, since loss of appetite is usually rare until late in the illness.)

Individuals with this disorder say they "feel fat" when they are of normal weight or even emaciated. They are preoccupied with their body size and often gaze at themselves in a mirror. At least 25% of their original body weight is lost, and a minimal normal weight for age and height is not maintained.

The weight loss is usually accomplished by a reduction in total food intake, with a disproportionate decrease in high carbohydrate- and fat-containing foods, self-induced vomiting, use of laxatives or diuretics, and extensive exercising.

The individual usually comes to medical attention when weight loss becomes significant. When it becomes profound, physical signs such as hypothermia, dependent edema, bradycardia, hypotension, lanugo (neonatal-like hair), and a variety of metabolic changes occur. Amenorrhea often appears before noticeable weight loss has occurred.

Associated features. Some individuals with this disorder cannot exert continuous control over their intended voluntary restriction of food intake and have bulimic episodes (eating binges), often followed by vomiting. Other peculiar behavior concerning food is common. For example, individuals with this disorder often prepare elaborate meals for others, but tend to limit themselves to a narrow selection of low-calorie foods. In addition, food may be hoarded, concealed, crumbled, or thrown away.

Most individuals with this disorder steadfastly deny the illness and are uninterested in, even resistant to, therapy. Many of the adolescents have delayed psychosexual development, and adults have a markedly decreased interest in sex. Compulsive behavior, such as hand-washing, may be present during the illness. A higher than expected frequency of urogenital abnormalities and Turner's syndrome has been found in individuals with Anorexia Nervosa.

Age at onset. Age at onset is usually early to late adolescence, although it can range from prepuberty to the early 30s (rare).

Sex ratio and prevalence. This disorder occurs predominantly in females (95%). As many as 1 in 250 females between 12 and 18 years (high-risk age group) may develop the disorder.

Course. The course may be unremitting until death by starvation, episodic, or, most commonly, a single episode with full recovery.

Impairment. The severe weight loss often necessitates hospitalization to prevent death by starvation.

Complications. Follow-up studies indicate mortality rates between 15% and 21%.

Familial pattern. The disorder is more common among sisters and mothers of individuals with the disorder than in the general population.

Predisposing factors. In some individuals the onset of illness is associated with a stressful life situation. Many of these individuals are described as having been overly perfectionist "model children." About one-third of the individuals are mildly overweight before the onset of the illness.

Differential diagnosis. In *Depressive Disorders,* and *certain physical disorders,* weight loss can occur, but there is no intense fear of obesity or disturbance of body image.

In *Schizophrenia* there may be bizarre eating patterns; however, the full syndrome of Anorexia Nervosa is rarely present; when it is, both diagnoses should be given.

In *Bulimia,* weight loss, if it does occur, is never as great as 25% of original body weight. In rare instances an episode of Anorexia Nervosa occurs in an individual with Bulimia, in which case both diagnoses are given.

Diagnostic criteria for Anorexia Nervosa
   A. Intense fear of becoming obese, which does not diminish as weight loss progresses.

B. Disturbance of body image, e.g., claiming to "feel fat" even when emaciated.
C. Weight loss of at least 25% of original body weight or, if under 18 years of age, weight loss from original body weight plus projected weight gain expected from growth charts may be combined to make the 25%.
D. Refusal to maintain body weight over a minimal normal weight for age and height.
E. No known physical illness that would account for the weight loss (pages 67-69).

Appendix C
DSM-III Diagnostic Criteria for Bulimia

The following material is a reprint of the diagnostic criteria for bulimia from the *Diagnostic and Statistical Manual of Mental Disorders,* Third Edition (DSM-III), published in 1980 by the American Psychiatric Association, Washington, D.C..

307.51 Bulimia

The essential features are episodic binge eating accompanied by an awareness that the eating pattern is abnormal, fear of not being able to stop eating voluntarily, and depressed mood and self-deprecating thoughts following the eating binges. The bulimic episodes are not due to Anorexia Nervosa or any known physical disorder.

Eating binges may be planned. The food consumed during a binge often has a high caloric content, a sweet taste, and a texture that facilitates rapid eating. The food is usually eaten as inconspicuously as possible, or secretly. The food is usually gobbled down quite rapidly, with little chewing. Once eating has begun, additional food may be sought to continue the binge, and often there is a feeling of loss of control or inability to stop eating. A binge is usually terminated by abdominal pain, sleep, social interruption, or induced vomiting. Vomiting decreases the physical pain of abdominal distention, allowing either continued eating or termination of the binge, and often reduces post-binge anguish. Although eating binges may be pleasurable, disparaging self-criticism and a depressed mood follow.

Individuals with Bulimia usually exhibit great concern about their weight and make repeated attempts to control it by dieting, vomiting, or the use of cathartics or diuretics. Frequent weight fluctuations due to alternating binges and fasts are common. Often these individuals feel that their life is dominated by conflicts about eating.

Associated features. Although most individuals with Bulimia are within a normal weight range, some may be slightly underweight and others may be overweight. Some individuals are subject to intermittent Substance Abuse, most frequently of barbiturates, amphetamines, or alcohol. Individuals may manifest undue concern with body image and appearance, often related to sexual attractiveness, with a focus on how others will see and react to them.

Age at onset. The disorder usually begins in adolescence or early adult life.

Sex ratio. The disorder occurs predominantly in females.

Course. The usual course is chronic and intermittent over a period of many years. Usually the binges alternate with periods of normal eating, or with periods of normal eating and fasts. In extreme cases, however, there may be alternate binges and fasts with no periods of normal eating.

Familial pattern. No information, although frequently obesity is present in parents or siblings.

Impairment and complications. Bulimia is seldom incapacitating except in a few individuals who spend their entire day in binge eating and self-induced vomiting. Electrolyte imbalance and dehydration can occur in those below normal weight who vomit after binges.

Prevalence and predisposing factors. No information.

Differential diagnosis. In *Anorexia Nervosa* there is severe weight loss, but in Bulimia the weight fluctuations are never so extreme as to be life-threatening. In *Schizophrenia* there may be unusual eating behavior, but the full syndrome of Bulimia is rarely present; when it is, both diagnoses should be given. In certain neurological diseases, such as epileptic equivalent seizures, CNS tumors, Kluver-Bucy-like syndromes, there are abnormal eating patterns, but the diagnosis Bulimia is rarely warranted; when it is, both diagnoses should be given.

Diagnostic criteria for Bulimia
    A.   Recurrent episodes of binge eating (rapid consumption of a large amount of food in a discrete period of time, usually less than two hours).
    B.   At least three of the following:
        (1) consumption of high-caloric, easily ingested food during a binge
        (2) inconspicuous eating during a binge
        (3) termination of such eating episodes by abdominal pain, sleep, social interruption, or self-induced vomiting
        (4) repeated attempts to lose weight by severely restrictive diets, self-induced vomiting, or use of cathartics or diuretics
        (5) frequent weight fluctuations greater than ten pounds due to alternating binges and fasts

C. Awareness that the eating pattern is abnormal and fear of not being able to stop eating voluntarily.
D. Depressed mood and self-deprecating thoughts following eating binges.
E. The bulimic episodes are not due to Anorexia Nervosa or any known physical disorder (pages 69-71).

Appendix D
Food Diary

Date:_____   Name:_____

Time	Minutes Spent Eating	Activity While Eating	Location and with Whom	Food and Quantity	Feeling

Appendix E
Intensive Treatment Program for
Individuals with Bulimia

BEHAVIORAL HEALTH CLINIC/ADULT OUTPATIENT PSYCHIATRY
University of Minnesota
Minneapolis, Minnesota

FORMAT

Our intensive program is designed for two purposes. The first is to offer an alternative to inpatient care for those people with severe bulimic behaviors. The second is to address directly the problem of binge eating and vomiting or laxative abuse. The intensive program is a two month program providing a highly structured and supportive environment designed to interrupt the bulimic behavior and sustain abstinence. Group therapy is the basic mode of treatment, however, individual consultation is provided in specific areas where the client may need more help.

The first week of the program consists of five nightly four-hour sessions and is gradually reduced over a month's time to weekly group therapy sessions in the second month. The format for each evening during the first three weeks includes a 1/2 hour of relaxation or exercise instruction; and a didactic presentation on bulimia, eating disorders in general, problems in relationships and families, diet and nutrition, stress management, or other topics pertinent to the initial stage of recovery. From 6:30 to 7:30, clients will eat a meal together which is provided through our dietary department. The dinner is served cafeteria style. Group members make their own dinner selections and are encouraged to eat a balanced diet. The dinner hour itself is unstructured and provides an opportuntiy for informal discussion among the group members. From 7:30 to 9:00 clients will participate in group therapy in groups of 10 or less, designed mainly to structure their activity until the next group.

We make extensive use of abstinent volunteers in the treatment program. Our volunteers are people who have completed the program and wish to solidify their abstinent behavior by actively working with other recovering bulimics. We believe volunteer work is beneficial to both the new clients and to the volunteers themselves. Their involvement in the program creates an open and healthy climate essential to recovery.

After abstinence is obtained and the program is completed, individuals are referred to an aftercare group. We are recommending that they continue in group
therapy on a weekly basis for a total treatment period of six months to one year
to attain stability in those areas which might otherwise lead to a return to binge
vomiting. Individuals completing the program are also encouraged to participate
in the treatment program as active volunteers with new clients. We have found
the volunteer work to promote long-term abstinence and prevent reoccurrence
of the bulimic behavior.

OPTIONS

Those people who are not abstinent after the end of the two month intensive
program will be referred on staff recommendation to a support group, individual
therapy, or repetition of the intensive program.

Those people who become abstinent during the two month program will have
the option of recontracting to go on in therapy with a group that is appropriate
to their specific needs.

University of Minnesota TREATMENT PROGRAM FOR BULIMIA

First Week   Monday–Friday (5 sessions)
                  3:30–5:30 Relaxation/exercise
                  5:30–6:30 Lecture and discussion on bulimia, honesty and
                             awareness, nutrition and meal planning, cues for
                             binge–eating and chained behavior, weight manage-
                             ment, rational thinking, and recovery
                  6:30–7:30 Dinner and informal discussion
                  7:30–9:00 Group therapy assignments
Second Week   Monday, Tuesday, Thursday, Friday (4 sessions)
                  5:00–5:30 Relaxation/exercise
                  5:30–6:30 Lecture and discussion on stress management,
                             assertiveness, relationships, and abstinence
                  6:30–7:30 Dinner and informal discussion
                  7:30–9:00 Group therapy assignments
Third Week   Monday, Wednesday, Friday (3 sessions)
                  5:00–5:30 Relaxation/exercise
                  5:30–6:30 Lecture and discussion on depression and associated
                             features of bulimia, course of the illness, and pat-
                             terns of recovery
                  6:30–7:30 Dinner and informal discussion
                  7:30–9:00 Group therapy assignments

Fourth Week   Monday, Wednesday, Friday (3 sessions)
                       7:00-8:30 Group therapy (Monday & Wednesday)
                       5:30-8:00 Volunteer Night (Friday)
                                     Talk by a recovering bulimic
Fifth-Eighth Week Monday, Friday (2 sessions per week)
                       5:30-7:00 Group therapy (Monday)
                       5:30-8:00 Volunteer Night (Friday)
                                     Talk by a recovering bulimic

NOTE: Informational meetings for family and friends will be held on the second and third Mondays of the program from 5:15 to 6:45 P.M.

Appendix F
Examples of Bulimia Therapy

The following are examples of bulimia therapy and support groups offered by the University of Minnesota in addition to the intensive treatment program.

MEN'S GROUP

For men who wish to stop binge-eating and vomiting/using laxative/fasting or who wish to maintain their abstinence. The focus of the group will be abstinence. Issues and attitudes as they relate to bulimic behavior and abstinence will be explored.

INSIGHT GROUP

For individuals who are abstinent and who wish to focus on issues related to their continued recovery. This insight-oriented group uses dynamic, experiential, behavioral, and general supportive techniques.

BEHAVIORAL GROUP

For individuals who are non-abstinent. In treatment there will be a focus on learning techniques in changing bulimic behavior. These techniques involve manipulating cues or signals that precipitate problem behaviors, and manipulating consequences of your binge-eating behavior in order to facilitate abstinence. There will also be an emphasis on learning new coping skills such as assertion, relaxation, rational and positive thinking, stress management, and ways to deal with depression. Finally, there will be sessions on relapse prevention.

RELAXATION, STRESS MANAGEMENT AND ASSERTION

For individuals who wish to learn the areas of relaxation, stress management, and assertion. The first seven sessions deal with techniques of progressive muscle relaxation and stress management. The final five sessions will deal with assertiveness. Basic principles of assertion will be discussed and implemented through role playing.

INSIGHT GROUP

For individuals who are abstinent and who wish to focus on bulimia and/or other concerns of group members. Examples of possible issues include: assertiveness, loneliness, independence, family, and women's support.

STRUCTURED SUPPORT GROUP

For individuals who are abstinent and who are concerned with avoiding relapse. This group will more thoroughly explore the lecture topics presented in the intensive program (cues and chains, meal planning, assertiveness, family systems, stress, depression, and rational thinking) and help members relate them to personal life experience and recovery.

ONGOING SUPPORT GROUP

For bulimics who are non-abstinent, struggling to recover, and desire group support to do so. Weekly attendance is optional, and new members will be added periodically.

BULIMIA SUPPORT GROUP

For individuals who are presently binging and vomiting/using laxatives/fasting and who wish to focus on getting abstinent. The primary goal of the group is to stop binge eating and purging. Honesty and awareness are emphasized as keys to achieving and maintaining abstinence.

FRIDAY NIGHT MEETING

A meeting open to all recovering bulimics. It is an ongoing group for individuals who wish to develop a support system for themselves through contact with others who are recovering. It provides an opportunity to meet and share experiences with other bulimics and has come to be called "Volunteer Night" because it also provides an opportunity to assist others in achieving and maintaining abstinence.

Appendix G
Questionaire

The eating-disorder history form suggested below is a modification of the University of Minnesota Department of Psychiatry's Social and Psychiatric History Form for Eating Disorders developed by

Elke Eckert, M.D.
Janes Mitchell, M.D.
Richard Pyle, M.D.
Department of Psychiatry
University of Minnesota

HISTORY OF EATING PROBLEMS
(Mark N.A. if item doesn't apply)

1. Present weight   _____ lbs.

2. Current height without shoes (in inches)   _____ inches

3. Have you ever had episodes of eating an enormous amount of food ("binge eating" or bulimia)?   _____ Yes _____ No

4. Lowest weight since onset of "binge eating"   _____ lbs. at age _____

5. Highest weight since onset of "binge eating"   _____ lbs. at age _____

6. Weight just prior to onset of "binge eating"   _____ lbs.

7. Have you ever vomited after eating in order to get rid of the food eaten?   _____ Yes _____ No

8. Have you ever "spit out" food after chewing it in order to prevent it from getting to your stomach?   _____ Yes _____ No

9. Age of onset of vomiting after eating   _____

10. Lowest weight since onset of vomiting   _____ lbs. at age _____

11. Highest weight since onset of vomiting   _____ lbs. at age _____

12. Weight just prior to onset of vomiting   _____ lbs.

13. What weight would you like to be?   _____ lbs.

14. What weight do you think you should be?   _____ lbs.

DID YOUR EATING PROBLEMS START WITH

15. Voluntary dieting? _____ Yes _____ No

16. Dieting after insults or encouragement from family members?

    _____ Yes _____ No

17. Dieting after teasing, insults or encouragement from peer group?

    _____ Yes _____ No

18. Were there any particular events, positive or negative, in your life which coincided or briefly preceded the onset of your eating problem?

    _____ Yes _____ No

    If "yes," describe: _____

    _____

19. During the entire last month, what is the average frequency that you have engaged in the following behaviors?
    (Check one for each behavior)

	Binge Eating	Vomiting	Laxative Use	Use of Diet Pills	Use of Water Pills	Use of Enemas	Exercise to Control Weight	Fasting (Skip Meals)
Never								
Less than once/week								
About once a week								
Several times a week								
Once a day								
More than once a day								

Explain if necessary: _____

_____

_____

20. Which of the behaviors, "binge eating" or vomiting after meals came first?
    (Check one)
    "Binge eating" came first. _____

Vomiting came first. _____

They both occurred together at the same time. _____

Neither came first. I have only "binge eating" episodes. _____

Neither came first. I have never had "binge eating" or vomiting episodes.

_____

Neither came first. I have only vomiting episodes.

_____

21. Give an example of what would constitute a "binge" for you; include all foods and amounts that you would eat and drink during a typical "binge":

_____

_____

Is there any particular food that you use to end a "binge?" (explain)

_____

22. How often are you now able to eat a "normal" meal without "binge eating" and without vomiting? (Check one)

Never _____   Several meals a week _____

Less than one meal a week _____   One meal a day _____

About one meal a week _____   More than one meal a day _____

23. After a "binge", how do you usually feel? (Check all those that apply)

Relaxed _____   Still hungry _____

Worried _____   Satisfied _____

Guilty _____   Too full _____

Other (please specify) _____

24. After eating a "normal" meal, how do you usually feel? (Check all those that apply)

                                        Too full _____

I never eat a "normal" meal _____   Relaxed _____

Worried _____   Guilty _____

Still hungry _____   Satisfied _____

Other (please specify) _____

25. Why do you "binge eat?" Because you:
(Check all those that apply)

Are so hungry _____   Can't control your appetite _____

Crave certain foods _____   Are unhappy _____

Can't sleep _____   Feel tense and anxious _____

Other (please specify) _____

26. How do you best describe your appetite?

I have no appetite _____   I have a normal appetite _____

I have a stronger than normal appetite _____

27. For what purposes do you use laxatives? (Check all those that apply)

To relieve constipation _____ To get rid of food from the body _____

To "clean out" the system _____ I don't use laxatives _____
Other (explain) _____

28. How many minutes a day do you currently exercise (include going on walks, riding bicycle, exercise at home, swimming, etc.)? _____

29. What devices do you deliberately use to control weight? (Check all those that apply)

Exercise _____   Fasting (skipping meals) _____
Vomiting _____   Water pills (diuretics) _____
Laxatives _____   Diet pills _____
Enemas _____   Saunas _____
Other (explain) _____

30. Do you feel you have ever had an alcohol or drug abuse problem? If so, when, and describe: _____ Yes _____ No
_____
_____

31. How frequently have you used drugs (such as sleeping pills, tranquilizers, anti-depressants, or "street drugs") since the onset of your eating problem?

Never _____   Less than once a week _____
Every day _____   About once a week _____
                        Several times a week _____
If you have used them, please describe: _____
_____

32. Have you ever tried physically to hurt yourself (i.e., cut yourself, hit yourself with intent to hurt, burned yourself with cigarettes)
_____ Yes _____ No
Describe: _____
_____

33. Have you ever made a suicide attempt? _____ Yes _____ No
Describe:_____
_____

34. How would you rate yourself in terms of being afraid of becoming fat? (Check one)

Not at all _____   A little _____
Moderately _____   Very much _____
Extremely _____

35. How would you rate yourself in terms of being afraid of "losing control" of food intake? (Check one)

Not at all _____   A little _____

Moderately   _____   Very much   _____

Extremely   _____

36. Since the onset of your eating problem, has there been any disruption or impairment of your life in any of the following areas?
(Check all those that apply)

Financial   _____   Intimate interpersonal   _____

Social   _____   Religion   _____

Work   _____   Recreation   _____

Family   _____   Other (specify)   _____

37. Approximate regularity of menstrual cycles since the onset of Bulimia:
(Check one)

Fairly regular (Same number days + or − 3)   _____

Somewhat irregular (Variation 4–10 days)   _____

Very irregular (Variation greater than 10 days)   _____

Never menstruated   _____

Appendix H
Referral Notice

Counseling Center — Health Service

Name of Student: _____

Referred by: _____

Date: _____

Reason:

_____

_____

Additional comments:

_____

_____

Appendix I
Starvation Effects

Studies of starvation effects can help us further our understanding of some changes which occur with the development of anorexia nervosa. Individuals who have experienced starvation for reasons beyond their control — individuals in concentration camps or third world countries for example — exhibit many symptoms similar to those of anorexics, although such individuals do not themselves develop the disorder.

Food Related:
    Eating binges
    Slow eating
    Food fads (gum, coffee drinking)
    Increased hunger after eating
    Food preoccupation and dreams
    Enjoyment in cooking
    Hoarding

Cognitive:
    Decreased concentration
    Indecisiveness

Affective:
    Irritability
    Anxiety
    Depression
    Mood swings

Other:
    Withdrawal
    Sexual disinterest
    Sleep disturbance
    Loss of menstruation
    Fatigue

Anorexics differ from other starving individuals in that they display an intense fear of fatness, frequent body image distortion, and excessive energy.

Index